ADVANCE PRAISE FOR *ON THE RECORD*

"This book needs to be in your vinyl collection. It's what every DJ needs to be in the game and every music fan needs to understand the game. I put all my producers and DJs on this 'cuz it's what's gonna take them to the next level."　　—Snoop Dogg

"*On the Record* is a blueprint for anyone who has ever thought about getting into DJing. It explores how we do it, but more importantly, why we do what we do. The old- and new-school masters break it all down here."　　　　　　　　　—Z-Trip

"Having worked with many DJs in my life and being one myself, I can tell you that this book is a must-read. If you're a battle champion, a club DJ, or just a music enthusiast, you will definitely benefit from reading this book. Every one of us is a DJ. This book just makes us better. It's about time!"

—Darryl McDaniels of Run-D.M.C.

"This book is needed to introduce the world to the hip hop DJ pioneers. We live this culture seven days a week, 365 days a year, and if anybody wants an insight into the true essence of hip hop, the DJs who started it, and how they can follow in our footsteps, they must read *On the Record*."

—Grand Wizard Theodore, inventor of the scratch

"It's time for someone to document the success of the art of DJing and where it's going. . . . We need some kind of bible that covers every aspect of DJ culture. This book is it."

—DJ AM (Adam Goldstein)

"This book is important for understanding why and how the DJ revolution helped to shape the hip hop movement. From Kool Herc to Q-Bert, the DJ is the cornerstone of hip hop, without whom this culture would have no foundation."

—Grandmaster Caz, founding member of the legendary Cold Crush Brothers

"This is a real good time for a book like this because it's going to let the mainstream world know what we're about in the DJ culture and the DJ world. We don't just sit there and play records. We work!"

—DJ Skribble

"DJs are such an important part of our culture. They define and shape it every day. This book shines light on their art form, their culture, and most importantly, it helps bring out your inner DJ. It's a must-read."

—Doug E. Fresh

ON THE RECORD

ON THE RECORD

THE SCRATCH DJ ACADEMY GUIDE

PHIL WHITE *and* **LUKE CRISELL** *with* **ROB PRINCIPE**

FOREWORD *by* **MOBY**

ST. MARTIN'S GRIFFIN
NEW YORK

www.stmartins.com

Book design by Rich Arnold

ISBN-13: 978-0-312-53124-9
ISBN-10: 0-312-53124-9

First Edition: April 2009

10 9 8 7 6 5 4 3 2 1

CONTENTS

 **FOREWORD**

It sounds like something from a twelve-step program: "Hi, I'm Moby and I'm a DJ." At which point the twenty other dissolute DJs in the room say, dissolutely, "Hi, Moby," and I tell my story . . .

Before I delve into my twelve-step DJ program backstory, I want to say a few words about this art form, this profession, and the universal connector that is music. First on music.

Music has an amazing ability to move people. Literally and figuratively. The transformative property inherent in music is powerful and universal. Music can do many things. It is an emotional currency. It comforts, inspires, and connects us. It's a part of us. There are few other forces in life that can deliver such things.

I am honored to consider myself a musician. To have changed people's lives with my music is incredibly powerful. And for that I am thankful. But in addition to just being a musician, I consider myself part of an amazing dynamic—that of the DJ.

DJs take the infinite catalog of music that exists in the world and help to translate it via their creative lens. They find music that we can't. They introduce us to music we'd never know. They take us places we'd never have otherwise gone. Professional DJs are amazingly creative people who have taken what is a hobby for most of us and turned it into a profession and, better yet, a craft.

It is through their lenses that many of us discover music. This practice has been happening for generations. My hope is that through this book, through the legacy of Scratch DJ Academy, this art form can continue to grow, enlighten, and give back for generations to come.

Here's my story . . .

I started DJing in 1984 at a tiny, tiny, tiny club/bar in Port Chester, New York, called The Beat. I had just dropped out of college (where I studied philosophy, a very practical major, assuming you never want to actually have a job). I was broke, and I was depressed. Ostensibly, I had left college to pursue music, but once I actually dropped out, I realized that I had no idea how to go about doing that. I had played in punk rock bands in high school, and I had studied classical music from the ages of nine to thirteen, but I had absolutely no idea how to pursue music as a career.

I started hanging out at The Beat, and eventually persuaded the owner, Tommy, to let me DJ on Monday nights. The Beat was pretty lively on weekends, but on Monday nights it was the bar of last resort for junkies, criminals, and random drunk university students. I DJed from nine till four in the morning in return for twenty dollars and all the ginger ale I could drink. On one hand it was intensely depressing—if you've ever played Joy Division records for five junkies at 1:00 A.M. on a cold Monday night, you'll know of what I speak—but it was also incredibly exciting because I was actually working as a DJ.

Time passed and I started DJing Wednesdays, too. More time passed and I found myself DJing Wednesdays, Fridays, and Saturdays. At this point I had actually started playing dance music, although dance music in 1985 was incredibly eclectic. I'd play James Brown and New Order, and the Peech Boys and Daf, and Cabaret Voltaire and Prince, and the Doors and Run-D.M.C., and so on and so on.

Before I started DJing I was a punk rock/New Wave kid, and I only liked dance music if it was made by white British guys from Manchester. But through DJing, I suddenly found myself playing (and loving) hip hop and protohouse, and dancehall and more obscure forms of electronic music. I found myself wanting to make dance music of my own.

Before I started DJing, I did everything in my power to sound like Morrissey meets the Cocteau Twins. But after two years, I started saving my money and buying synthesizers (Casio CZ-101), samplers (Akai S-900), drum machines (Roland TR-606 and Alesis HR-16), and trying to make dance music of my own.

DJing changed me. It turned me from a depressed twenty-year-old trying to sound like Morrissey, into a depressed twenty-two-year-old trying to sound like Cabaret Voltaire and Eric B. & Rakim.

Then house music happened. House music was the perfect synthesis of everything I liked about the dance music that preceded it. It had the 4/4 kick (making it easy to mix in and out of New Order and Dead or Alive), it had the weird electronics (making it easy to play next to Daf and Nitzer Ebb), yet it was soulful in ways that a lot of the earlier electronic music wasn't.

By 1988 I was DJing four nights a week and playing house music and hip hop almost exclusively. I got my big break by landing a DJ job at Mars, a club in New York City on the West Side Highway. (Now, alas, it's a parking lot.) Mars was the coolest club on the planet—before it became a hangout for homicidal crack dealers—and somehow I ended up as one of a handful of DJs working there, alongside Mark Kamins, Clark Kent, Stretch Armstrong, Duke of Denmark, and others.

Musically, this was an amazing time, with remarkable new records by Inner City and Todd Terry and the DJ International label and Transmat and Strictly Rhythm coming out every week. I made a hundred dollars a night DJing, which went right back into buying records. Friday was the best day to buy vinyl; I'd make my regular pilgrimage to Vinyl Mania and Dance Tracks and stand around and buy just about everything I could get my greasy little hands on.

Meanwhile, I continued working on my own dance music, desperately trying to get signed to a dance label. I would drop demo tapes off at 4th and Broadway and Strictly Rhythm and Wild Pitch and any label that had an address printed on their record sleeves. My only goal at this point was to make a 12-inch that might somehow get played in a club. That was it.

Eventually, I signed with tiny Instinct records. The second 12-inch I released was *Go*. A few months later, I went to hear Derrick May play at the Limelight and he played *Go*. I thought my life was complete. If I had died ten minutes after that I would have died a happy man/DJ.

Without DJing, I would probably never have gotten involved in dance music. Without DJing, I would probably never have made records. To put it simply, and I apologize for the cliché, but DJing saved my life.

I've been DJing now for twenty-five years—yes, I'm old—and I'm still excited by it. I still think that the newest records are the best records I've ever heard, and I still get overwhelmed by 10 or 100 or 1,000 or 10,000 or 100,000 people putting their hands in the air for a flawless breakdown.

If you're a professional DJ, you're lucky, as I am. We get to make our living playing great records and making people (including ourselves) unbelievably happy. In closing, I'd like to humbly say to the god of DJs: thank you.

—MOBY
New York City, 2008

It was a simple idea: Provide anyone with the opportunity to learn how to DJ. I saw DJs everywhere and wanted to become one, but I didn't understand how or where to get started. The equipment was expensive, and the number of potential students outweighed any supply of possible teachers. If I'd wanted to learn to play the guitar, it would have been simple to find lessons and fairly inexpensive. In fact, living in New York City, I could have explored some of the most obscure interests conveniently. And yet, learning how to DJ seemed out of reach.

The idea for Scratch came to me at a party where the legendary Kid Capri was spinning. The cavernous space offered a number of different rooms, VIP areas, and nooks, but that night, they were mostly empty. More than a thousand people were on the dance floor (or at the bar). Capri kept the place moving during his entire six-hour set. Somehow he knew what song I wanted to hear long before I knew I wanted to hear it.

I went home that night thinking, *I want to do that!* I didn't want to quit my job to become a DJ, but I did want to explore DJing as a hobby. What's more, I knew I wasn't the only one who felt this way, as most of my social network when polled showed similar interest. At that moment, I saw an opportunity. That's where the beat began—literally and figuratively. Scratch DJ Academy was born that night.

Set the needle forward three years. I told my family and friends that I had decided to pursue a new professional direction and start a company. At first, I received tremendous support and encouragement. Then I told them that the company had no historical footprint in an industry in which I had no experience: I wanted to start a DJ academy. Silence. Then the comments came: First, they asked if I had banged my head and woke up the next morning with this business idea. Nope, I answered. No falls or accidents. Then they asked if this was my misguided attempt to pursue a law degree. Huh? Nice try, I said. Then slowly coming to terms, they asked if this concept was a hobby to be pursued and not a business venture to invest time and money into. When all else failed, it finally came:

"Rob, I just read an article about people your age having a 'quarter-life crisis.' I'll send it to you."

With a confused mind but a clear vision, I plunged ahead.

While building the business plan, I quickly realized that I would need a partner to help me navigate this undertaking. My ideal associate would be a professional DJ who had:

1. Household-name recognition
2. Plenty of credibility and respect among his peers
3. A long-standing commitment to DJing

Then I started to make a list of names. While there were many people who fit my requirements, one stuck out: Jason Mizell, aka Jam Master Jay of Run-D.M.C. This man had catapulted the role of the DJ onto the international stage while creating the sound and style for a musical genre that would become one of the highest grossing in music history. A good friend of mine, Jesse Itzler, reviewed my business plan and kindly offered to introduce me to Jay, who happened to be his close friend.

I spent months preparing to meet with Jay, but his hectic international performance schedule was on par with Madonna's, and we could never manage to catch up. Finally, in the spring of 2001, I got a call from Jay's manager saying that Run-D.M.C. was going to perform on the David Letterman show and that Jay wanted to meet with me beforehand.

"That's great," I said. "When?"

"Well," his manager replied, "the taping begins in about thirty minutes. So you'll have to hurry."

I was downtown, and the Ed Sullivan Theater is north of Times Square. I made it to the studio with five minutes to spare. Jay was in the green room getting his hair cut. There we were: me and him (and his barber). I had my proverbial two minutes, the opportunity to deliver my "elevator speech." As briefly as possible, I laid out the basics of my plan and asked Jay if, together, we could build a platform from which to promote.

As the barber continued his work, we discussed how the progression of the DJ crafts was very similar to the story of jazz. Few understood jazz in its early years, and many dismissed it, but others knew it had tremendous energy and artistic value. Today, jazz is taught in every major university around the world. And the world is undoubtedly a better place because of it. We agreed that the dynamic craft of the DJ similarly deserved to be accepted, appreciated, and taught with the same level of dedication and enthusiasm. When his haircut was complete, Jay introduced me to Joseph "Rev Run" Simmons and Darryl "D.M.C." McDaniels (his bandmates) as his new business partner. After I watched their performance I sat on side-door steps to the theater for an hour afterwards, collecting my thoughts. Few moments had been as powerful for me as that one was. And so the partnership began.

From the beginning, Jay and I worked hard to build a curriculum, taking what DJs from the beginning had done instinctively and through trial and error, distilling it into something tangible. This meant making the techniques explicit and articulating them in plain English without draining them of their meaning. A clear, explicit curriculum would allow a novice to learn with confidence. We felt that no musical medium should have a barrier so high that it discourages participation and pursuit.

Once we had our curriculum designed and our class schedule organized, Jay and I ran into our first major stumbling block: We didn't have any turntables to teach on. I should mention at this point that I was funding the business with my unemployment checks, the hourly rate I earned teaching tennis from six to ten each morning, and a lucky "senior moment": My grandfather accidentally added another zero to a hundred-dollar birthday check.

Without any DJ equipment, we decided to kick things off by holding a symposium series, inviting DJs to discuss their work at a moderated forum with an open audience. We organized the series on everything from battle DJing to beat matching to the business end, all hosted and moderated by my close friend Reg E. Gaines, two-time Tony nominee for writing the hit Broadway musical *Bring in Da Noise, Bring in Da Funk*.

The lectures were a huge success because they succeeded in demonstrating the level of interest that the artists and audience alike had in a discussion of the craft by those who help create it. DJs are generally heard but not seen, and these events flipped that around. The presentations revealed an incredible hunger for education and access: People were curious about DJing.

The success of the series helped convince an equipment manufacturer to provide us with forty turntables and twenty mixers, along with speakers, needles, slipmats, and all the other required components. They realized that along with our success could come the next wave of consumers for them. Now we were in business, planning our first hands-on semester. Things were the way we wanted them to be.

The early semesters were the most exciting. We were getting our feet underneath us, still nervous before every class. Jay taught many of the sessions himself, thoroughly enjoying the process of passing on his craft to the next generation, and savoring the personal interactions with each student.

We learned early on that the heart of Scratch DJ Academy was the dynamic between the teachers and the students. It wasn't just the lessons, but rather the new community that had begun to form around the school. With each passing semester, our classes broke down socioeconomic barriers. Shattered them, actually. At Scratch, we saw doctors, artists, school principals, corrections officers, and everyone in between, working together and bonding over a common interest in music and the desire to interact with it more. Grandfathers were learning next to grandsons.

We began to realize that what we were doing was really meaningful: We were spreading the knowledge of music, communicating and sharing its value. And we were the only ones doing it at this level.

Over the years, we have taught the craft of the DJ to those who never would have had the ability, access, or means to learn it otherwise. We have also given DJs a chance to pass on their knowledge, passion, and expertise to those sincerely interested in learning from them. The plan was working. We have been validating, legitimizing, and elevating the status of DJing, and, in the process, growing a community.

And grow is what it did. Since its inception, Scratch DJ Academy has graduated more than twenty thousand students representing all fifty states and more than twenty countries. Scratch has also taught hundreds of thousands of people the DJ basics through nationwide tours and events. To date, we have been a part of more than six thousand events and fifty national tours with our corporate partners.

A door closes and a window opens. The door closing was the abrupt and shocking loss of Jam Master Jay on October 30, 2002. Jay was a musical and cultural icon, a loving family man, and a hero to many, including me. I learned many things from Jay, but most importantly he taught me that you have to give before you can expect to receive. Give of yourself, your time, your love, your friendship, your music. Sadly, Jay's life was cut far too short to receive all that he deserved.

The window opening was the commitment we made to honor his legacy by leading the Scratch DJ Academy forward. It was also the window of opportunity to continue learning, teaching, appreciating, and valuing this craft. We do this for Jay. We do this for ourselves. We do this for you.

We are all a part of a global community, and DJing helps us bring this community closer together. Jay used to say that DJs make the world go around. I agree.

I'd like to thank my family for their unending support (even if they've switched to thinking I'm having a mid-life crisis now), as well as my colleagues here at Scratch for all their dedication, hard work, and passion. A special thank you to Mike Cannady for his tireless work, savvy business sense, and for helping to make this book a reality. I'd also like to thank my fellow board members who selflessly serve the Jam Master Jay Foundation for Music charitable organization (which we created after Jay's passing).

I'd also like to thank Terri Mizell and her and Jay's wonderful children for continuing to be an inspiration to me and many others.

Lastly, I want to thank all the DJs out there for using music to help make this world and my little part of it a better place.

I hope you enjoy this book.

—ROB PRINCIPE
Founder & CEO
Scratch DJ Academy

# INTRODUCTION

Everyone is a DJ. That is the premise behind this book, and upon which the Scratch DJ Academy was founded in 2002 by Rob Principe, Reg E. Gaines, and the late Jam Master Jay of Run-D.M.C. And, just as the Academy is about lowering the entry barrier for those interested in DJing and music production, so this book you're holding in your hands is about not just learning more about DJs—their lifestyle, culture, abilities—but also about bringing them out of the shadows, from behind the glass in the dark booth in the corner of the room and out into the spotlight. It's about understanding them, and, most importantly, finding the DJ within yourself.

The majority of other books in the comparatively slim annals of DJ literature tend to add to the DJs' mystique, setting them even further apart from the crowd, but here you'll see that, actually, DJs aren't so different from everyone else after all. The professional DJ is a passionate, consumed, and—almost always—talented person, but anyone can get to that level. Precisely how to do that is one of the things we'll address later.

If you've yet to begin DJing, this book might just be the perfect catalyst. If you're already on your way, you'll find plenty to help you along in the following pages. From technical insights from some of the world's top DJs, to the history of DJing, to the best places to find, listen to, and buy music, it's all here. You'll discover how the DJ selects and performs music, learn about the influence DJs have on fashion, film, and TV, and, most importantly, find out how you, too, can release your inner DJ.

In many ways, there has never been a better time to write this book. Culturally, sociologically, and, of course, musically we are at a transition: DJs have, in many cases, overtaken rock stars in terms of fame and their ability to draw a crowd. In 1993, superstar DJ Paul Oakenfold went on tour with arguably the biggest band in the world, U2, warming up the crowd for the Irish rockers before they took the stage. It's possible to imagine, sixteen years later, the roles being reversed.

In clubs, DJ battles, magazines, movies, TV shows, and on the radio and beyond, the DJ has become an almost ubiquitous force that can transcend music. While DJs play the tracks of today, they also define what we'll be listening to tomorrow. The DJ is a trendsetter, a visionary, and a cultural barometer who can sense and react to the ebb and flow in trends, and transmit these changes to the public. If a well-known DJ takes a liking to a track and plays it on a radio show or in a club, it can help a new artist break through. Or, in the case of hip hop, house, and other genres, the music and style DJs introduce can redefine the musical and cultural landscape.

Some art forms are limited to certain countries or regions, but the music and lifestyle of the DJ is truly global. From a block party in New York to a festival in the idyllic English countryside to a **superclub (a large club that is involved in other ventures, such as music festivals, radio stations, and record labels)** in Sydney and everywhere in between, DJing is a uniting force that brings together people from all backgrounds in a celebration of music. Regardless of where you live or what language you speak, DJing is a part of the culture you inhabit. Music lovers from across the world make an annual pilgrimage to the tiny Balearic island of Ibiza, clubbers flock to Miami each March to attend the Winter Music Conference, and the World DJ Championship and its many local heats attracts a diverse, multinational crowd. The attendees' motivation is the same—checking out the best music played by the best DJs together with thousands of like-minded people. In this book, we'll explore how the DJ arrived at this position.

Throughout this book, you'll see certain words in bold. These are terms that are key to understanding the life and culture of the DJ, so we've put them in a glossary, which starts on page 299.

Look elsewhere for a definition of DJ and you'll find elaborate descriptions implying membership of a chosen elite. The most common misconception about DJing is that it's purely for professionals, mysterious individuals who inhabit distant DJ booths, who are part of an unreachable in-crowd. This perception is reinforced by VIP rooms, restrictive dress codes, and celebrity-heavy guest lists at exclusive clubs that are more about getting tabloid coverage than having a vibrant musical experience. Add to that a jargon that sounds like it has been from a *Star Trek* convention, like **cutting**, **EQing**, and **dropping** on the "one," and the average music enthusiast can't help feeling excluded. But the idea that DJing is only for a select and privileged few is just a myth. The truth is everyone is a DJ.

DANCING THE NIGHT AWAY

At their core, most DJs want to make people move, to evoke a physical and emotional reaction from the audience. Whether it's a killer vocal hook looped over and over until the dancefloor goes bananas, lightning-fast beat juggling and scratching, or laying down a mellow groove perfectly timed to bring the evening to a close, the DJ is trying to evoke a physical and emotional reaction from the audience. Producing a tangible response to the music they have chosen, and in an ever-increasing number of cases that they have actually made, is what gets the DJs out of bed in the morning, and keeps them up all night.

This book features interviews with the DJs that have perfected this art—the DJs who draw crowds so huge that club promoters sometimes have to leave their names off the flyers for fear of overcrowding. While their ability to inspire small audiences at intimate house or block parties is important, the talent of the superstar DJs to draw and hold the attention of massive crowds is a more telling demonstration of DJ power in action.

In July 2002, Fatboy Slim—his mom, Mrs. Cook, still calls him Norman—spent around two hundred thousand dollars staging his second outdoor show on a beach in Brighton, England. He expected some sixty thousand people to show up, but instead more than a quarter million made the trip to the coast, making it the biggest outdoor concert in British history.

Other notable festivals that prominently feature DJs include the Love Parade, which attracts up to a million people annually to the streets of Berlin, Germany, the Bonnaroo festival in Tennessee, which is as well-attended by lovers of hip hop and house music as it is by rock fans, Barcelona's Sonar Festival, which is fast emerging as one of the most progressive and exciting in the world, and the Winter Music Conference, which takes over South Beach, Miami once a year; what was once a meeting for professionals to swap tracks has now become the highlight of the clubbing calendar.

"The great thing about being a DJ is that you're given a platform to stand on in front of a huge crowd of people, and play the music that you're passionate about," says British wunderkind DJ and Sasha protégé James Zabiela. "That's an incredible feeling and I think everyone can relate to it because they love music and would want that time to shine."

Those DJing in smaller, more modest venues are no less important to modern music. Whether club DJs are playing new tracks or the latest Top 40 hits, they're reacting to what clubgoers want as well as suggesting future listening. The DJ is charged not just with being technically proficient, but also with finding an equilibrium between commercial appeal and underground credibility, balancing new music with old classics. The superstar DJ and the spinner at a local club with a crowd of one hundred and fifty people have more in common than you may think—most notably a passion for connecting people with the music they love and that they will, hopefully, come to appreciate.

At many of the more established venues, the crowds are familiar not just with the style and sound of the headlining DJ but also with the two or three preceding him or her. It's not just about the records the club DJs play but also how they play them—how they manipulate the mix to produce the desired reaction, and the effects and tricks they use. The DJ is constantly reading the crowd and adjusting track selection, tempo, and more, based on the reaction of the dancefloor, to make sure the crowd is not only grooving but also engaged.

The track order is often thought out in advance, but the successful DJ must be flexible—able to hold the audience's attention on instinct. If it's a warmup set, the DJ has to be intimately familiar with the style of the headliner so he can get the crowd ready by progressively building the energy of the records. If headlining, a DJ must take the musical baton from the warmup spinner and go for it, or the anticipation of the crowd will be lost. Timing and the ability to know what to play, when, at what speed, and with what effects can make or break a set and an entire evening.

At the club Cielo in New York City's Meatpacking District, long an arbiter of classy, informed electronic music, a mirror is tilted behind the DJ booth so that the crowd can see what the DJ is doing. But what's actually going on today in the DJ booth and what's going on in the mind of the DJ? What happens when it all goes horribly wrong, but more importantly, what goes into getting it all right? We'll examine the role of the club DJ in detail later.

In addition to playing in clubs, DJs host radio shows, create mixtapes, produce and remix tracks, play social events such as weddings and parties, participate in **battles (nonviolent contests between DJs, MCs [master of ceremonies, who first talked and later sang over the records DJs played] and/or break-dancers)** against other DJs and more. The latter type of DJing, which developed out of contests between hip hop pioneers such as Kool Herc, Grandmaster Flash, and Afrika Bambaataa in the mid-'70s, and brought new levels of creativity to the art of DJing, became known as **turntablism (using a turntable as an instrument by manipulating records in a way that creates percussive elements and other new sounds not present on the record)** after DJ Babu coined the phrase in the late '90s.

"We'd think about how people who play the piano are pianists, and so we thought, 'We're *turntablists* in a way, because we play the turntable like these people do the piano or any other instrument,'" Babu said in an interview with British hip hop Web site UKHH. "Beyond that, it was just me writing 'Babu the Turntablist,' because it was something I did to make my tapes stand out." For turntablists, who play, live, and participate in events such as the DMC World Mixing Championship, the challenge is all about technical innovation—inventing new methods of record manipulation and redefining techniques such as **scratching (moving the record back and forth rhythmically), beat juggling (combining the beats from two records so that they create a new rhythm), and body tricks (such as scratching with an elbow, or doing a headstand while DJing),** all in a brief time frame (between three and six minutes in the DMC event).

Radio DJs are equally influential in moving DJ culture forward, their jobs, in some cases, are even more difficult than those of the club DJ, or live turntablist, because they cannot see the reactions of their audience. Whether it's Pete Tong on BBC Radio 1's *The Essential Selection*, Funkmaster Flex on New York's HOT 97, or a less-famous local DJ with a small but loyal band of listeners, the radio DJ will only keep a show running if the track selection and mixing is continually of a high caliber and is (ahem) in tune with what the audience wants.

With many radio stations now streaming live on the Internet, listeners from all over the world can tune in simultaneously. It is a testament to the power of the DJ that many of the posts on Tong's Radio 1 Web page are from listeners in Australia, the U.S., and Asia, and that Flex's podcast has subscribers from across the globe. Their musical influence transcends national boundaries and is as potent in countries that speak different languages.

Despite different motivations and audiences, turntablists, club spinners, and the many other different types of DJ share a common passion—discovering new music and trends and sharing these with the rest of us before we're even aware that they're exactly what we're looking for.

A SPIRITUAL THING, A BODY THING, A SOUL THING

DJing is not just about playing and modifying music, it's about the creation of a vibe, a prevailing emotion that starts in the DJ booth and breaks through the venue like a wave. While it's true that some DJs, promoters, and clubbers abuse drugs, and even claim that they can only have a good night out by doing so, the music is enough. For the real DJ or music fan, nothing more than a groove is required to achieve the emotional and almost spiritual high that comes during a night behind or in front of the decks.

Those who fully embrace DJ culture are not paying for the privilege of listening to music at a trendy club or for the right to drink fifteen-dollar cocktails—they're spending their hard-earned cash to partake in a one-time ephemeral, communal experience that will never be duplicated. It's the same with a block or house party—you're there to be part of a community, forged by a common soundtrack. Music can be appreciated on your own, of course. But gathering with fifty (or fifty thousand) fellow enthusiasts to hear beloved classics blended skillfully with fresh new **joints (songs)** truly brings the music alive.

For the DJ, bringing tracks to life and giving people music that moves them is everything. The thousands of dollars spent on records, the hundreds of hours spent practicing, the day spent packing the record boxes or CD cases or prepping software like Scratch Live with the perfect set, have all led to this climactic moment. While any DJ can prepare a playlist, a good one reads the crowd's response to each track and adjusts the tempo and tune selection to take the set where they want it to go. The wrong track can clear the floor in seconds, while playing too many **stormers (hits)** without **filler (less popular songs used to bridge the gaps between crowd favorites)** tracks is anaesthetizing. Balancing what the DJ wants to play with what the listeners want to hear is the ultimate challenge.

Once the show is over, the DJ breaks down the performance— the perfect mix here, the beat clash there—and often studies the set list using Scratch Live or a similar program to make sure the mistakes aren't repeated, the good points are enhanced, and the next set is even better. The best DJs never settle into a comfortable routine, but always look for ways to innovate—whether it's piping in samples from other genres, like Grandmaster Flash in the early '80s, adding a third deck as Carl Cox did in the mid-90s, or using Ableton Live software to mix on a laptop like Sasha, post-2000. Creativity and the mastery of new technology push the DJ ever onward.

DJING: A GLOBAL PHENOMENON

For DJs, the continual internationalization of dance-music culture has created a globe-trekking lifestyle that takes them across continental and musical boundaries. The reception for top American DJ and turntablist Klever is as rapturous in Shanghai or Berlin as it is in his native Atlanta, Georgia; foreign music fans are just as knowledgeable and passionate as their American counterparts.

Similarly, European DJs such as Sasha, Tiësto, and James Zabiela play to clubs packed with rapturous crowds wherever they go. The pressure of packed schedules and sleepless nights spent in different time zones taxes the DJs as much as selecting tracks and performing, but the unparalleled thrill of connecting with a new audience at an unfamiliar club keeps them going. And when a DJ returns to his or her hometown club, there is the warm welcome of friends, the comfort of the tailor-made DJ booth, and the enthusiasm of the regulars to make them truly feel like he or she is back in their element.

With Internet and satellite radio, and online Webcasts, DJs have new ways to share their craft with music-hungry listeners and viewers from all over the globe. When they relied on vinyl, DJs had to deal with limited playlists when traveling abroad. With the advent of MP3s, this logistical restriction has been lifted, and DJs are now able to carry twenty-thousand tracks on a laptop or hard drive for sampling, mashing up, and plugging straight into the mixer in a booth anywhere.

MOVING OUTSIDE THE MUSIC

The DJ is positioned to know the big tracks before they're big, to sense musical trends before anyone else, and to know what's going to be here for a while and what will be a passing fad. Top DJs are on so many record company mailing lists that some even employ assistants to help them wade through the deluge of new tunes. Some spinners actually have the latest acetate vinyl or CD test pressings hand-delivered to them. Their musical acumen is so finely tuned that they can listen to several sections of a record for just a few seconds and know immediately if it's a hit or a dud, something to be passed over, or dropped in the box. Their frenetic travel schedule lets them sample the latest music from around the world, sometimes before anyone in their homeland has even heard it. They are uniquely qualified to be arbiters of cool. Fans of every type of music listen to and read their favorite DJs' buzz charts on radio shows, read their latest Web posts, and subscribe to publications such as *The Source, DJ Times,* and *BPM* to stay up on what's new. The public trusts the DJ to clue them in to what's worth listening to at the time, which gives the DJ an enormous amount of cultural sway.

The impact of DJ culture on the global scene extends far beyond music, including fashion. In the '80s, you could find as many kids wearing laceless Adidas Superstars (aka the shell top or shell toe), gold chains, and black Kangol hats (imitating Jam Master Jay and his Run-D.M.C. co-members) in Paris as is New York or Chicago. The trend of music crossing over into couture continues today; sneaker aficionados the world over look at the kicks their favorite DJs are wearing, and many special editions, such as the recent Run-D.M.C. 35th anniversary Superstars and Nike's collaborations with hip hop graffiti artists Futura 2000 and Stash. DJ AM's Air Force 1s sell for hundreds of dollars on eBay.

DJ culture has also spawned uber-successful clothing lines such as Jay-Z and Damon Dash's Rocawear, FUBU, and Ecko, and more recently UNKLE front man James Lavelle's Surrender brand. If the DJ wears something new, the item is immediately hot property—proof that they are forward-thinking and influential outside of the club.

Film and television are other mediums profoundly impacted by the DJ ever since DJ Jazzy Jeff appeared in the now-synonymous show *The Fresh Prince of Bel-Air* in 1990. From Dr. Dre and 2 Live Crew's cuts on *Friday* to the partnership of DJ/producer BT and The Roots on the *Stealth* soundtrack to every track on Moby's *Play* album being used on national TV commercials, DJ productions are the new backdrop for the big and small screens. Movies such as *8 Mile, Hustle & Flow,* and *Juice* achieved box office success, critical acclaim, and awards, and there are even internationally distributed movies about DJ culture, such as *It's All Gone Pete Tong, God is my DJ,* and *Rhyme & Reason.* The fact that these films even exist is a testament to the desire of a certain element of the public to learn as much as they can about DJing and the culture that surrounds it, in an effort to give context and meaning to the music they're buying in stores and online.

DJs are also crossing over into the world of sports. DJ Irie is employed by the Miami Heat NBA team and has played at half-time during several Orange Bowl games, DJ Bedz works for the Denver Nuggets, and Q-Storm supplies the music for the Atlanta Hawks. Ron Artest of the Houston Rockets has his own record label—Tru Warier—and Shaq has teamed with Irie to put out hip hop records. DJs also provide create the aural backdrop to the X

Games and Winter X Games. Sports entertainment organizations such as WWE use DJ-produced introductions, and even the Olympics has gotten in on the act, featuring Dutch DJ Tiësto in the opening ceremony of the 2004 Athens Games. Tiësto also appeared in The Coca-Cola Company's worldwide "Live Olympic on the Coke Side of Life" campaign for the 2008 Beijing Games (along with fellow house DJs Benny Benassi and Kaskade).

Soundtracks for video games are another avenue for DJs: BT supplied the beats for *Tiger Woods Golf, Wipeout* featured the Chemical Brothers and Run-D.M.C., and Afrika Bambaataa appeared on the *Grand Theft Auto* games. Video games can provide DJs with large paychecks and enable them to reach hundreds of thousands of people who may not typically go to clubs or buy DJ albums and mix compilations.

While theater was once the sole domain of those who wouldn't know their hip from their hop, the phenomenal rise to prominence of Broadway shows such as Will Power's *The Seven, Russell Simmons' Def Poetry Jam on Broadway,* and *Bring in Da Noise, Bring in Da Funk* (which beat *Rent* for Best Choreography, Best Direction of a Musical, and Best Featured Actress at the Tony Awards in 1996) demonstrates that DJ culture is impacting theaters the world over. By embracing DJ and rap-inspired productions, Broadway and London's West End have opened their doors to a whole new demographic, which is just as passionate about urban poetry as the elder statesmen are about the Queen's English. So significant is the entry of hip hop onto the stage that it led Jeremy McCarter to claim in his *New York* magazine article "Straight Outta Broadway," "Hip hop can save theater."

If you're going to see one of these plays in New York, London, or elsewhere, you may well stay at a boutique hotel, in which case you'll find something that you may not expect in the lobby when you return from the show—a DJ. Since the Hotel Costes in Paris first employed Stéphane Pompougnac to spin in 1997, and launched a series of mix CDs two years later, hotels such as The Standard (New York City, Los Angeles, and Miami), Soho and Tribeca Grand hotels (New York), and the Lydmar Hotel in Stockholm have employed world-class DJs, and others have in-house clubs, including The Ivy in San Diego and LAX at The Luxor (Las Vegas).

Many forward-thinking clothing stores such as We Are Superlative Conspiracy (WESC) in Los Angeles, and Trends in New York, have in-house DJs to enhance consumers' shopping experiences, and many upscale coffeehouses and lounges hire DJs instead of bands to attract new clientele. A few retailers, such as Diesel, have chosen to include permanent DJ booths within the layout of their stores. So if you're in a major city anywhere you'll never be far from DJ culture.

REPEAT AFTER US: I AM A DJ

Those who make a living from DJing are some of the most fortunate people alive, as they've turned their love of music into a profitable enterprise. Pro DJs play in clubs and at parties, in battles, on mixtapes, on the radio. Regardless of their chosen format, the level of proficiency reached and the respect earned among his or her peers is directly linked to the number of hours that a DJ has dedicated to the art form. While the mission of the Scratch DJ Academy is to make DJing available to all comers, many enrollees start erroneously thinking that what professional DJs do is easy, not least because the pros make it look so simple—which is, of course, why they're the pros.

When new students come into the studio and can't figure out how to start a turntable or plug in their headphones—let alone mix two records—they quickly realize that DJing well is about much more than playing one record after another. The basics can be learned during the Academy's six-week program, but mastery of the decks is honed and developed much longer. In some cases, a lifetime.

DJ Craze, the only DJ to win the DMC World Mixing Championship three times, says:

> "The best advice I can give aspiring DJs is to put a lot of time and work into it. If you really want to be like the DJs you admire, you can do it! It's just gonna take time and a lot of practice."

Part of any good DJ's preparation is the hours spent listening to and buying music, and then choosing which tracks to fit into a set. We all share the ability to filter music. Good DJs often listen to thousands of tracks before deciding which ones to include and with what modifications, such as scratching and adding samples. Sure, you may not know all the technical tricks or terminology, but when you introduce a friend to your new favorite song, you're basically doing the same thing DJs do when they're paid to play to an audience—connecting people with music. When you change a CD in your car, download music online, or create an iTunes playlist, you're essentially DJing, because at the most basic and purest level, a DJ is someone who simply controls the music.

A key step in awakening your inner DJ and unleashing your potential is learning to appreciate many styles of music. Even if a DJ plays primarily house music, he or she will usually be familiar with funk, soul, rock, blues, and everything in between; a broad musical base enhances the ability of the DJ to cater to a diverse audience and truly appreciate his or her chosen genre.

Many pioneering DJs from older generations of DJs learned how to beat mix tracks by playing a record on one turntable while blasting a tune from a randomly selected radio station through their speakers. Once they'd synched up these tracks, the DJ would rotate the dial, going through a range of styles until comfortable with mixing each one with the vinyl on the deck. DJ Nu-Mark explains the importance of a balanced musical diet: "I could just listen to hip hop, but you've got to know a lot of different genres to be a well-rounded musician, and it helps you bring something new to the type of music you really love. I bring some samba to hip hop, it adds a new flip to it. If I bring some Latin style to hip hop, it'll bring something new, and people love it when you play that stuff live. If you play one genre of music all night it gets boring."

Another way in which the Scratch DJ Academy and this book can help you discover your inner DJ is by teaching you how to listen to music in a new way. Learning how to evaluate **tempo (the speed at which a passage of music is played)**; **pitch (sound frequency, often simplified as highs and lows)**; and **rhythm (a sequence of sounds, usually drums, organized to create a certain beat)**; and to tell musical elements such as **melodies (rhythmically organized sequences of sounds)** and **harmonies (combination of two or more melodies)** apart, can give the music you love a deeper significance. We're not going to tell you what to buy, play, or listen to, but we will try to open your eyes and ears to a new range of audio possibilities.

We will also show you how to use the tools of the DJ trade—primarily turntables and mixers. You'll learn that you *can* DJ, and you can do it in a way that nobody else will be able to duplicate.

"The DJ market is saturated, so it's important to develop a unique sound and an original touch that can be recognized as yours," says DJ A-Trak, who won the DMC World Mixing Championship at age fifteen in 1997. "The more you can be creative with your selection and the way you assemble your songs the better you'll be—originality is the most important factor." The purpose of this book is to equip you with an appreciation of musical history plus the knowledge and skills you will need to DJ more effectively. You don't need celebrity endorsements, a background in music production, or a degree to be a DJ. All you need is your tracks, your creative flair, and, above all, a love of music.

PART ONE

HISTORY OF THE DJ

ONE

THE EARLY DAYS *of the* DJ

Today's superstar DJs are household names who command a hundred thousand dollars or more per gig, crisscross the globe to play, and exert as much influence in fashion, film, and television as they do on the dancefloor. But the DJing profession has not always been as glamorous—just seventy-five years ago the term "disc jockey" didn't even exist.

A thorough understanding of the history of the DJ will not only provide you with a better appreciation of music in general, it will also give you perspective on the role of the DJ as it moves into the future. From the inaugural radio broadcast to the first discothèque to the birth of hip hop and house, this chapter will give you a comprehensive understanding of where DJs came from and, just as importantly, where they're going.

IN THE BEGINNING . . .

If we're going to define DJing at its most fundamental level as the art of controlling music, then the most important DJ-related technological advance occurred in 1877 when Thomas Edison invented the phonograph—the first device capable of recording sound and then playing it back by making indentations in a cylindrical sheet of tinfoil. Ten years later, German-American Emile Berliner patented the Gramophone, the great-grandfather of the modern turntable, along with the discs to play on it.

We're tempted to delve into geeky technical details here, but rather than bore you and embarrass ourselves by revealing the extent of our nerdy knowledge, let's fast forward to 1906, when the wonderfully bearded Canadian Reginald Fessenden broadcast the first ever spoken AM radio program from Brant Rock, Massachusetts, earning him the title "The Father of Radio Broadcasting." This was the advent of radio, and soon enough people would be able to hear music—mostly swing, jazz, and classical—from the comfort of their homes instead of attending live performances.

While Fessenden's brief debut was only picked up by a few U.S. Navy vessels puttering around the New England coast, it marked the dawn of a new age in entertainment, one in which radio DJs would eventually become kings.

In 1921, electronics company Westinghouse established the first commercially supported radio stations in Pittsburgh, Boston, Chicago, and New York, and many other media companies soon entered the market. In just a few short years, the radio business was to become as cutthroat as piracy in the waters around the West Indies, but with fewer rules of engagement. A year after Westinghouse's first stations went on air, the British Broadcasting Corporation, or BBC, made its first broadcast from its London studios, marking the start of commercial radio in the U.K. Five years after that, in 1927, Christopher Stone, dressed in a dinner jacket and tie, became Britains's first disc jockey when he started his BBC radio show, playing jazz records to a fairly small audience that quickly grew to encompass much of the radio-owning British public.

But while radio technology was advancing apace, the audio equipment itself quickly was becoming outmoded. Gramophones and early turntables were unwieldy, using huge, noisy motors that delivered power inconsistently and, thanks to their thick steel needles, quickly wore out records. Most of the early discs played on the pioneering radio stations were equally hard for the radio DJ to handle—made of hard rubber, shellac, or other dense materials that were not easily manipulated and produced a lot of distortion.

These early records could hold only a few minutes of music at 78 **rpm (revolutions per minute)**, and were worn out after a hundred or so plays, meaning that many radio shows were forced to rely on live performers. But things began to change in 1930 when RCA Victor introduced the first long-playing (LP) records.

The prototypes weren't commercially viable at first, but record label executives quickly realized that the new discs were cheaper to produce, lighter, and more durable. And, as vinyl records rotated at 33rpm, there was less friction against the needle and therefore less hissing. Vinyl LPs were to the earlier records what CDs were to cassettes (and what MP3s are to CDs).

Record companies were quick to adopt the new format. Columbia Company took several years to build up a catalog of its most popular artists' recordings and, in the process, further refined the vinyl that RCA Victor had introduced and the duplication process required to effectively distribute records nationwide. Columbia also partnered with stereo system manufacturer Philco to produce a turntable for playing 33 rpm records which was priced at just thirty dollars. For the first time, the turntable became a viable home entertainment option for American families.

When Columbia released the first selection of LPs—primarily recordings of classical music—in 1948, both the records and the Philco stereos sold fairly well. Not to be outdone, RCA came back with the introduction of 45 rpm records and a thirteen-dollar turntable. These also sold fairly well, but because consumers were confused by the different speeds (think Blu-ray versus HD-DVD), neither format became dominant until 1954, when record companies settled on the 45 rpm option for sending music to radio DJs and selling it to consumers.

Television was still several decades away at this point, so people in the U.S., the U.K., and elsewhere still relied on the radio for entertainment. At first, radio show hosts were referred to as announcers. Then, in 1935, American newspaper and radio commentator Walt Winchell coined the term "disc jockey" in reference to Martin Block, whose ABC radio show *Make Believe Ballroom* was receiving twelve thousand letters a month. The moniker seemed to suggest that the announcers passively "rode" the discs, implying that they were cursory figures. But the term stuck.

Frank Singiser was another popular radio DJ of the '30s and '40s, hosting *Your Hit Parade* on NBC's Red Network. Singiser played the week's most popular songs and promoted brands for commercial sponsors such as Lucky Strike, which paid big bucks to have its name associated with nationally syndicated broadcasts. To take advantage of the growing popularity of the radio DJ in the so-called Golden Age of American broadcasting, record producers began to send and even hand-deliver their latest hits to radio studios.

These early promotional copies ensured maximum exposure with minimal cost, and taking the DJs out for a few drinks certainly didn't hurt the record promoters' cause either (before the days when the big labels would allegedly bribe DJs to play their latest releases). With the release of an affordable transistor radio in 1948, radio audiences reached an all-time high, and DJs became more influential than ever before, evolving from mere announcers to cultural tastemakers. Without the support of the radio DJ, musicians such as Frank Sinatra, Elvis Presley, and Tony Bennett would arguably never have achieved commercial success.

OUT OF THE STUDIO, INTO THE CLUB

Most DJs in the '40s were content to stay in the radio studios, but a few of the more enterprising ones opted for the less profitable, but often more emotionally rewarding, route of playing records for live audiences. This was a daunting task, as crowds in the U.S. and U.K. were accustomed to live bands and orchestras, not some guy standing behind equipment, head bent over in concentration—which, come to think of it, is often the case today. Indeed, the crowd's only familiarity with recorded music was what they played on their primitive home turntables, or heard on the radio or on the jukeboxes that had become popular at bars and restaurants. British DJ Jimmy Savile decided he was bored with radio and held his first dance party in 1943 using a makeshift stereo system built by a friend from spare parts. The few people who came to the function room of the Loyal Order of Ancient Shepherds (perhaps the best name for a club, ever) in Otley, England, probably didn't know what to think. After a few more performances, however, Savile developed a loyal following, and soon worked out a deal with nationwide dance hall proprietor Mecca Ballrooms to hold similar gatherings elsewhere in England.

Four years later, Savile decided that the single turntable he was using was too restrictive, and hired a local metalworker to weld two decks together—making him, for all intents and purposes, the godfather of the modern DJ. The wonderfully eccentric Savile (who owns a mountain, was friends with Elvis Presley and John Lennon, and had over a hundred fights as a pro wrestler) went on to DJ for powerhouse Radio Luxembourg and to host *Top of the Pops,* the British TV institution that, until 2006, counted down the Top 40 singles chart and featured several live acts each week. Savile's example was followed by Jamaican DJs such as Count Suckle in London, who used powerful sound systems to blast out the sounds of early ska to crowds at outdoor and indoor venues. Wild jazz parties held by DJs and attended by foppish teenagers known as "ravers" were also held throughout the city.

While Savile, Suckle, and the jazz ravers were laying the foundations for the modern club DJ in England, an equally significant development was unfolding across the English Channel in Paris. It was here that entrepreneur Paul Pracine opened Whisky a Go Go, the world's first discothèque (the word is a portmanteau of *disc* and *bibliothèque*), in 1947. The Chez Castel and Chez Régine clubs soon opened nearby, giving Parisian music aficionados a triumvirate of quality venues from which to choose.

DJs in the U.S. quickly followed the Europeans' lead, and started to host dance parties known as *sock hops* in school gymnasiums, so called because you weren't allowed to wear dancing shoes in the gyms in case they damaged the floor. While distinctly unglamorous, and despite having a silly name, sock hops helped young music fans connect with the radio DJs they'd grown up listening to, in addition to spurring several technical advances.

The most notable innovation was the introduction of the double turntable by Bob Casey in 1955. Although Savile had used two individual decks, Casey's was the first custom-built–double-player system that featured an independent volume control that gave him more control over sound output.

To provide clubbers with an alternative to the jazz clubs that were popular in many areas of New York City and the wildly successful rock 'n' roll record parties at the Brooklyn Paramount,

French promoter Oliver Coquelin imitated his homeland's Whisky a Go Go format with the opening of Le Club discothèque in 1960. In the decade that followed, technology continued to improve, and the increasing popularity of dance clubs gave DJs a viable career alternative to radio broadcasting.

In 1965, Terry Noel, resident DJ at New York's Arthur club, became the first well-known spinner to build what we now refer to as a **set (series of records seamlessly mixed together)** although these sets were technically imperfect by today's standards due to the dearth of dedicated DJ equipment. **Mixing (combining the sound of two records that have matching rhythm and tempo)** became a lot easier later that year when Alex Rosner, who installed sound systems in many of New York's best venues, put together "Rosie," a new kind of stereo mixer that allowed DJs to listen to how two records went together before playing the result through the speakers.

Although Rosie was built for Rosner's personal use, it inspired manufacturer Bozak to create the CMA series of mixers in the late 1960s, the first commercially available models designed specifically for DJs. Similar technology from now-defunct stereo supplier Reco-Cut enabled DJ Francis Grasso, a regular at the Sanctuary club in New York's Hell's Kitchen, to improve on Terry Noel's example by **beat matching (matching the beats of two records before mixing them together)** in 1969, setting a precedent for all the DJs who followed him.

Within twenty years of Savile's first dance party, clubs in New York, London, Paris, and other major cities that played jazz, soul, rock 'n' roll, and funk records became *the* place to go out. Young people realized that their favorite tracks and exciting new music creatively blended together by a skilled DJ was better than anything a jukebox could offer, and sometimes even better than watching a live band. While the radio DJ continued to be a prominent trendsetter within youth culture, the momentum shifted to club DJs such as Noel, Grasso, and John "Jellybean" Benitez, who became the new hit makers. The times were a-changin' and, with the advent of disco and hip hop in the '70s and house music in the '80s, the profile and influence of the DJ would soon climb to even greater heights.

TWO

THE HISTORY *of the* HIP HOP DJ

People gravitated towards hip hop because it offered a positive vibe and lessened the severity of the poverty, the drugs, and the gangs. It created a community of like-minded people with a different outlook.
— Grandmaster Caz, DJ/MC with the Cold Crush Brothers

THE FOUNDING FATHERS

New York City is a cultural melting pot. In the 1940s and 1950s, large numbers of Jamaicans relocated to the U.K. for job opportunities. The 1962 Commonwealth Immigration Act put an end to this, but new U.S. legislation enabled them to obtain American citizenship. They settled predominantly in Queens and Brooklyn, but also throughout the city's five boroughs. One of these families was the Campbells, who moved from Kingston, Jamaica, to the Bronx in 1967. When twelve-year-old Clive Campbell started at Alfred E. Smith High School, he began lifting weights regularly. Soon he was taller and more muscular than the other kids; they called him Hercules—or Herc for short.

Besides working out, Herc's other passion was music. He had grown up around Jamaica's vibrant ska scene, attending outdoor parties where "selectas" played records over powerful sound systems. Calling himself DJ Kool Herc, he began hosting music parties with his sister, Cindy, in the recreation room of their apartment building at 1520 Sedgwick Avenue, charging his classmates a quarter for admission.

While he was using vinyl like every other DJ at the time, Herc was doing it in a way nobody had before. He realized that the crowd danced most excitedly when the instruments climaxed and the vocals faded out (known musically as the **break**), so he focused on extending this. He would get two copies of the same record, and as the break of a song ended on the first copy, he'd **cue (get the record on turntable two to the appropriate place in the track to mix it into the record on turntable one)** up the start of the same break on the second. Then he'd fade the volume on the first turntable as he brought up the levels on the second deck—repeating the break.

This was the first time anyone had **looped (repeated a small segment of a track)** a break, and the young partygoers were transfixed by the skill, which not only revolutionized DJing but also led to a new style of dancing—break dancing, which soon became known as "b-boying." Darryl "D.M.C." McDaniels explains how he, Herc, and other fellow DJs used breaks to get block parties rocking:

> "To get people's attention, we'd put on our beats and play them loud. Then, the MC would say something like, 'Clap your hands, stomp your feet, everybody get down to the beat' and people would start dancing. We looked for a better place to go in our music. Hip hop was visionary."

The revelers who attended Herc's parties were also impressed with his stereo system, which was capable of delivering more volume than usual without distorting the music, and his graffiti, which was to become an integral part of hip hop culture. Word of Herc's parties spread and they quickly became too large for the recreation room, so he began playing outdoor block parties in Cedar Park and at other locations. Grand Wizard Theodore says:

> "The DJs set the tone for the whole block party scene. We brought our crates, our equipment, found a power source in someone's house or brought a light pole, did everything. Before the party, the DJs would go to the graffiti artists to get flyers made. The **MCs** would rhyme for a little while and then go and talk to girls in the crowd. The b-boys and b-girls were doing their thing on and off, but the DJs played the entire night. There was no party without the DJs."

GRAND WIZARD THEODORE'S TOP 10 RECORDS OF ALL TIME

1. James Brown—"Give it Up, Turn it Loose"
2. The Incredible Bongo Band—"Bongo Rock"
3. John Davis—"I Can't Stop"
4. Earth, Wind and Fire—"Brazilian Rhyme"
5. James Brown—"Sex Machine"
6. Herman Kelly—"Lets Dance to the Drummer's Beat"
7. Bob James—"Nautilus"
8. Discotech—"Scratching"
9. The Incredible Bongo Band—"Apache"
10. James Brown—"Funky President"

For McDaniels, the events held by Herc and the DJs that followed his lead were far more than just musical gatherings for young people: "The block parties were very important," he says. "Once the DJ had set out his equipment and put down the first beats the whole neighborhood came. People dropped what they were doing and went to the party in the park, street, or house. Old people, kids, teenagers—everyone came. It gave us a chance to forget our problems for a while."

Another reason that these parties were important is that they brought peace, if only for a few hours, to some of the neighborhoods of New York. Despite the ever-present threat of violence from gangs such as the Savage Skulls, Black Spades, and Reapers, Herc managed to keep his parties peaceful. Just like the selectas he'd grown up watching in the rough neighborhoods of Kingston, this young maestro was somehow keeping the peace between gangs who, elsewhere, were killing each other. There was something hypnotic about the beats Herc played, and dancing was a cathartic process by which members of a divided community could purge their frustrations by dancing. "If a fight broke out, the DJ would often get on the mic and threaten to pack up his gear and leave if it didn't stop," explains Grand Wizard Theodore. "[Whoever was fighting] would quit right away, because they knew that if the DJ left, the party was over."

McDaniels agrees that the parties on street corners and in school yards, parks, and apartments had a good influence that could calm the tensions between the gangs and different ethnic and socioeconomic groups. "At the block parties, for those few hours, there were no differences between white, black, Hispanic, or rich and poor," he says. "There was no violence. You would have enemies looking across the block or the park at each other and knowing they couldn't do anything, because at the party it was accepted that there was none of that. Everyone was just there to have a good time."

Herc's innovation with breaks and his ability to throw a party that brought entire neighborhoods together set him apart from other DJs, who soon began to imitate him. Legendary hip hop DJ and MC Grandmaster Caz, who was a member of the Cold Crush Brothers, one of the first crews, explains Herc's influence on his career and how other DJs followed his lead:

> "I saw Kool Herc DJing when I was thirteen and I was so inspired that from that point onward I was on a mission. I wanted to obtain the same records, get the same sound system, set up parties for myself—the whole thing. Me and my friends wanted to be connected to the DJ scene, because it was the coolest thing. I lived on the West Side of the Bronx, close to Herc. He played basketball with my brother in Clemente State Park, and in the summer everyone would meet up there to swim, play, and just hang out. That's where Herc would set up his block parties. He was a quiet guy, even though he was huge and kind of intimidating. I wanted to be accepted as part of the hip hop and DJ culture he'd created. I was like his disciple. There were different levels of DJs at that time—nobody was going up to Kool Herc and asking him where to find new records because you just didn't do that. You had to earn the right. But there was a group of younger DJs like me who shared information about tracks, equipment, parties—everything."

Herc assembled a crew—including MCs Klark Kent, Coke La Rock, and Timmy Tim, together known as the Herculords—

who competed against other New York crews in musical battles staged throughout the city. According to McDaniels:

> "The battle culture was all about evolution. If another crew was doing something, your crew would take it and do it better, do it differently. We had this term called '*biting*.' If you were a DJ and you played my records, dressed like me, and DJed like me you were a 'biter,' and this was unacceptable. To be recognized, you had to innovate. If a guy could rock a party for four hours with one MC, the next crew would come back with two MCs, another would bring three, and so on until you got Flash with his five MCs. The scene was about growth and creativity. If you didn't create, you might as well give up."

THE NEW BREED

Hip hop was unplanned. It was an alternate way of showing joy. Disco was one way, but we didn't want to get into that. We wanted our own sound.

— Grandmaster Flash

In 1975, aspiring DJ Theodore Livingston, who later became known as Grand Wizard Theodore, was practicing with his brother's turntables when his mother shouted something to him from another part of the house—probably something along the lines of "Turn that music down!"

The thirteen-year-old put his hand down to stop the record, so he could hear what she was saying, and accidentally moved the vinyl back and forth slightly against the needle, making a scratching sound. He liked what he heard. Theodore had invented

scratching, which was to prove as important as Herc's use of break beats in the development of the burgeoning hip hop style. Theodore says:

> "I was always practicing and messing around with new techniques because I wanted to be different from the other DJs and to be the best so, although I came across the scratch by accident, it was the product of that experimentation. Thirty years later, the scratch is still one of the main techniques for DJs. I'm thankful to be involved with the scene in that way."

Theodore is also credited with pioneering the **needle drop (whereby he dropped the needle onto the starting point of the record instead of cueing it up).** "I also lifted up the needle and dropped it back on the record so it sounded like I was looping it," he says. Theodore's development of the needle drop and scratching through hours of practice and experimentation each day demonstrate the value of hard work and innovation for aspiring DJs.

"A DJ should always be original," he says. "You have to do your own thing because otherwise you'll be lost in the crowd and just be written off as a copycat."

Joseph Saddler, who came to be known as Grandmaster Flash, began adding other technical innovations that would add a new dimension to the genre. Flash's technical courses at a vocational high school gave him the know-how to create a new kind of **mixer (a device that allows the DJ to combine, filter, and alter input from audio equipment such as turntables and microphones that is outputted to speakers)** that he called the "peek-a-boo system" from a combination of a microphone mixer, some preamps, and a studio mixer. This new setup enabled him to preview the combined sound of two records through headphones before it went through the speakers. "I could not only control the mix, but also take a peek into it without other people hearing," Flash says.

The new mixer also enabled Flash to put his **Quick Mix Theory (moving rapidly between certain parts of records while keeping them synchronized)** into practice. By combining accurate cueing, **cutting (quickly switching the crossfader on the mixer from left to right to "cut" from the sound of one record to another)**, and **backspinning (spinning a record backwards to repeat part of a track)**, Flash was performing by hand what modern samplers and producers do automatically—extending the break of a song indefinitely so that the crowd could keep dancing to it. To complement his sound, Flash put together the Furious Five, comprised of MCs Melle Mel (whose real name was Melvin Glover), Cowboy (Keith Wiggins), Kid Creole (Nathaniel Glover), Rahiem (Guy Todd Williams), and Scorpio (Eddie Morris), and from 1976 onward they played at clubs, block parties, and in battles across the five boroughs of the New York area. The group's 1981 album *The Adventures of Grandmaster Flash on the Wheels of Steel* combined advanced scratching variations, sampling, and MCing to great effect, and it is widely regarded as the seminal hip hop album of the '80s.

"It was the first time a DJ was cutting, backspinning, and extending breaks on an album," Theodore says. "It showed that DJing was the driving force of hip hop, and opened the door for all the DJs that followed to experiment on records." A year after the release of his *Adventures*, Flash released "The Message," one of the first socially conscious hip hop tracks (tackling the full gamut of inner-city issues, from inadequate education to crumbling housing projects to violent crime)—that would inspire the lyrics of rappers such as KRS-One, Tupac Shakur, and Biggie Smalls.

"Up-and-coming DJs need to learn about Herc, Flash, Bam and the other pioneering hip hop DJs so they can understand the scene and better appreciate the music," says Theodore.

"There's a different lesson to be learned from each of the early hip hop DJs: Herc had the loudest system and messed with the breaks; I scratched; Bam [Afrika Bambaataa] was the King of Records because he had the rarest tracks; Flash had his Clock Theory and Quick Mix Theory; Hollywood, Luv Bug Starski, and Caz rhymed while they DJed. If you learn about each of these elements and put them together, you'll have all you need to be a successful DJ."

The fourth of the hip hop DJ pioneers was Kevin Donovan, aka Afrika Bambaataa. He was a member of a Bronx gang, the Black Spades, but his attention soon turned from his gang to music. He got his start as a DJ at Bronx River Community Center, where he was known for playing any and every style of music that would get people to dance (including the rock 'n' roll tunes his hip hop peers wouldn't dream of dropping). Bambaataa dedicated scouring for rare vinyl gems all over New York and neighboring cities earned him the nickname "Master of Records," in addition to his other alias, Afrika Bambaataa, a nod to his appreciation for African culture.

Bambaataa formed the Zulu Nation, a collective of DJs, MCs, b-boys, and graffiti artists whose aim was to spread hope and the message of reconciliation through unity. Theodore explains:

> "So many people were dying, and that's why Bam formed
> the Zulu Nation. He was tired of seeing the impact of
> drugs and violence. He started teaching people about
> their shared history and brought them together
> through music."

Grandmaster Caz was also profoundly influenced by Bambaataa's philosophy: "Everyone used to be out for themselves, but Bam was inclusive and wanted everyone to come together for good. Most of the people I knew in the scene bought into that idea of brotherhood," he says.

In addition to battling and playing at clubs and block parties, Bambaataa soon got into music production, using the skills he'd honed as a DJ and his eclectic musical taste to breathe new life into hip hop by adding new artistic and cultural elements. First, he assembled the Jazzy 5 crew, with whom he released the single "Jazzy Nation" in 1980. Two years later, Bambaataa sampled Kraftwerk's "TransEurope Express" and used new drum machine programming methods on his hit genre-bending Soulsonic Force LP *Planet Rock*, which defined the new electro-funk sound. The other members of Soulsonic Force included several individuals who can be considered hip hop greats in their own right: Jazzy Jay, Kool DJ Red Alert, and Busy Bee.

THE EIGHTIES—IT'S LIKE THAT, AND THAT'S THE WAY IT IS

It was the sound of the parks, the blocks, and the house parties, and the DJ was central to that.

—Darryl "D.M.C." McDaniels

The spirit, innovation, and passion for music possessed by Bambaataa, Herc, and Flash was the spark for a cultural fire that was fanned by the frustrations coming from high unemployment, poverty, and the violence prevalent in inner-city New York in the early to mid-'70s. The new brand of DJing artistry they were practicing not only introduced hip hop, but also provided a creative and social outlet for a struggling community. Grandmaster Caz says:

"New York was broke and corrupt in the '70s. There were no community centers, no after-school programs, so kids had nothing to do. Landlords were so desperate for money that they were torching buildings to claim the insurance payments. There weren't a lot of uplifting things in that environment. People gravitated towards hip hop because it offered a positive vibe and lessened the severity of the poverty, the drugs, and the gangs. It created a community of like-minded people with a different outlook."

In the late 1970s, significant breakthroughs in the record industry helped to force hip hop out of the New York underground and into the mainstream. It first spread to other major metro areas such as Chicago and Philadelphia and, later, across the globe. In 1979, the Sugarhill Gang's "Rapper's Delight" became the first hip hop single to crack the Top 40, and a year later Kurtis Blow—managed by Russell Simmons, brother of Joseph "Run" from Run-D.M.C.—signed a recording deal with Mercury, making him the only rapper on a major label. His single "The Breaks" climbed into the Top 5 and went on to achieve gold status.

In 1981 and 1982, Bambaataa and Flash's studio work put the genre in the spotlight again and stretched the boundaries of early turntablism, by adding new sounds and techniques such as backspinning and sampling. Indie labels such as Sugar Hill Records, Paul Winley Records, and Enjoy Records backed the early recording efforts of the scene's Bronx pioneers, but after the first few hit singles, major labels such as Tommy Boy, Priority, and Jive used their financial clout to pry away the best talent, realizing that people from all ethnic groups were now buying hip hop records and recognizing the potential for mainstream success: Hip hop was being commercialized.

One of the biggest markers of the growing influence of hip hop DJing was the commercial and critical success of the 1983 Herbie Hancock single "Rockit," which prominently featured Grandmixer D.ST, aka Grandmaster DXT, scratching. In addition to gaining a Grammy, the video won all five categories it had been nominated in at the inaugural MTV Video Music Awards in 1984. While radio was still a popular medium for DJs to reach local audiences, the advent of the music video exposed a nationwide audience to hip hop, including the middle-class suburban teenagers who have since become the largest consumers of hip hop.

The unexpected success of "Rockit" inspired DJs and proved that their passion could be translated into a commercially viable enterprise. One of those aspiring DJs was Jam Master Jay, of Queens. In 1983, he founded Run-D.M.C. with friends Jason "Run" Simmons and Darryl "D.M.C." McDaniels. The band was promptly signed to Profile Records. The first Run-D.M.C. single, "It's Like That," sold 250,000 copies, making Profile's two-thousand-dollar deal one of the bargains of recent music history.

McDaniels explains how Run-D.M.C. was the first group to prove that a DJ doesn't have to settle for complementing a band— he or she can *be* the band:

> "The DJ is the foundation of hip hop. At our shows, people didn't pay much attention to me and Run, they wanted to watch Jay DJing because he brought the good stuff every night."

Run-D.M.C.'s self-titled 1984 debut LP featured two tracks—"Jam Master Jay" and "Jay's Game"—that showcased Jay's energetic turntablism and drum programming and acknowledged him in their titles. In the mid-80s, many rappers had moved away from using DJs, preferring the cheaper alternative of having studio-produced beats to back up their rhymes. Simmons and McDaniels made sure their DJing comrade remained a key member of the group and got the credit he deserved, according to Grandmaster Caz:

> "Run and D.M.C. kept the idea of DJs being the band and supplying the music behind the MCs. Jam Master Jay resuscitated the role of the DJ in hip hop, showing that the DJ is what makes this music true."

Jay proved that the turntable could be more than just a machine that played sounds. Rather, it could be a tool for practicing new forms of musical expression: "Jam Master Jay reminded people that the turntable is an instrument," says Grand Wizard Theodore. "Instead of Run and D.M.C. touring with a band or using preprogrammed beats like a lot of MCs were, they had Jay. This showed other MCs and the music industry that the DJ was necessary. Jay brought the craft of DJing back into the limelight as it had been when hip hop was in its early stages." The first Run-D.M.C. album went gold and set a new benchmark for hip hop, receiving rave reviews, getting major air time on radio stations across the country, and video exposure via the rapidly emerging MTV network (the single "Rock Box" was the first rap video played on the station). McDaniels explains:

> "In 'My Adidas' there's the line, 'We took the beat from the street and put it on TV,' and that was true. The scene and the music weren't ours, they belonged to the streets. It was the sound of the parks, the blocks, and the house parties, and the DJ was central to that. That's why every new generation connects to our sound—because it was authentic."

McDaniels and the other members of the group wanted to capitalize on their newfound fame, and wasted no time in producing a sophomore release. *King of Rock* dropped in 1985, and featured driving guitar riffs and other elements of rock music alongside Jay's beats and Simmons's and McDaniel's sharp-tongued rhymes. According to McDaniels:

> "Our vibe was a rock sound that set us apart from the pack. Everyone knew they couldn't do a rock thing because it was ours. Back in the day all the early hip hop DJs had rock records because the hard drums and aggressive guitars were perfect for MCs to rhyme over. We rapped over tracks like 'Miss You' by the Rolling Stones. A lot of people thought we did 'Walk this Way' and the *King of Rock* album to appeal to a white crowd, but that isn't true. We were just mirroring the eclecticism of the hip hop DJs we'd grown up listening to. There's no blueprint to hip hop. It's always been spontaneous and unlimited in where it can go. If you can flow over a track, create with it, and it sounds good, it doesn't matter what genre it's from—it's hip hop."

King of Rock, which came out in 1985, outsold its predecessor, becoming the first hip hop LP to go platinum. Run-D.M.C. and their DJ Jam Master Jay were now at the apotheosis of their popularity. The following year, on their third album, *Raising Hell,* the group delved further into rock music, collaborating with Aerosmith on a remake of "Walk This Way" that is to this day referred to as one of the greatest **mash-up (combination of tracks from different genres)** singles in history. It introduced a whole new audience to the Run-D.M.C. sound and earned them the #4 spot on the *Billboard* chart.

The single "My Adidas" reached #5 that same year, and this

ode to the Adidas Superstar, aka the shell toe, which the trio famously wore untied or laceless, reinforced Run-D.M.C.'s influence on the fashion world. They won a sponsorship deal from the
German sportswear brand, another first for a hip hop act. Since
its debut, the album has sold more than three million copies.

For McDaniels, the impact of the record was even greater
when performed live: "Our best tour was when we promoted
Raising Hell, because every track on the album was dope," he
says. "We didn't care how good your band was, how many
dancers you had, or what guest MCs were with you, we had a
quality DJ playing live and he was better than your whole show.
It wasn't just Run-D.M.C.—it was Run, D.M.C., *and* Jay."

While Simmons and McDaniels were at the center of the
stage when the band performed, they always remembered to
give props to Jay, both in their rhymes and naming conventions
for the band's songs. "At live shows Run and I insisted that we
wouldn't play unless Jay was included," McDaniel says. "Shows
like *American Bandstand, Soul Train,* and *Top of the Pops* had to
rewire their sound systems to include Jay, as they were only set
up to play taped beats. Jay was also huge for us in the studio:
Those famous beats on 'Peter Piper' came directly from his
turntables."

At live performances, Jay would go out first, warming up the
crowd until the noise was almost deafening, before introducing
Simmons and McDaniels as they bounded onto the stage.
Grandmaster Caz says:

> "Jay's energy and willingness to follow the example of
> the hip hop pioneers set him apart. He believed that
> Run-D.M.C. had to keep to the high standard of the
> original DJs in everything the band did, so he was chan-
> neling the energy of the original scene. He had a unique
> sound and a swagger that was all hip hop. The DJ is the

cornerstone of hip hop. DJs create the vibe and the environment that the other elements — MCing, b-boying, and graffiti — feed from. Everything happened based on what the DJ did."

In 1984, inspired by the meteoric rise to stardom of his younger brother's band, Russell Simmons joined long-time production partner Rick Rubin at his newly formed Def Jam Records. After inking a six-figure distribution deal with Columbia Records, Rubin and Simmons quickly demonstrated their aptitude for talent spotting, signing seventeen-year-old rap prodigy LL Cool J and the Beastie Boys (whose first DJ, Hurricane, was introduced to the band by label-mate Jay).

Rubin and Simmons's newest acts accompanied Run-D.M.C. on a national tour in 1985 and soon released hit albums that allowed them to claim top billing in their own right. The Beastie Boys's *License to Ill* was the first hip hop album to top the *Billboard* album chart and to date has sold more than five million copies. The group continued Run-D.M.C.'s tradition of relying on a DJ instead of a band, with Hurricane and later Mix Master Mike (who co-founded pioneering battle DJ collective the Invisibl Skratch Piklz), supplying the beats.

The fact that the Beastie Boys were three middle-class white Jewish kids challenged the public's conception of hip hop as a solely black art form and paved the way for artists such as Eminem: "The Beastie Boys were white but they were using all the elements of hip hop, so their color didn't matter," McDaniels says. "We told the Beastie Boys to check out Jay's friend DJ Hurricane and they started using him. The fact that they had a black hip hop DJ was one of the reasons they didn't talk about killing people or how many diamonds they could afford. A big reason for their success was always having a DJ perform. A lot of people thought those guys were just trying to sound black, but they were for real, because, like Run-D.M.C., they were representing the streets."

Other groups followed the example set by Run-D.M.C. and the Beasties by using a DJ instead of a band. One example is California outfit Jurassic 5, which included DJ Nu-Mark and Cut Chemist from Unity Committee. Nu-Mark explains how the band's live shows differed from those of their peers:

> "When we played live, we would just dictate roles to each other like 'Hey you should probably play this instrument or throw a sound effect in'—like passing a baton. We had drum machines and four turntables. We wouldn't do sampling live on stage but we would have beats ready to go."

Jurassic 5's first two albums, *The Jurassic 5 LP* (1997) and its follow-up *Quality Control* (2000) defined the emerging "alternative hip hop" sound, which incorporated jazz, funk, soul, and other genres, and showed that including a DJ (or in this case two) can breathe new life into a band's sound. McDaniels says:

> "If you go to see a rapper and he doesn't have a real DJ playing with him, you need to ask for your money back because that's not hip hop. For live hip hop shows, there can't be a guy at the back of the room pushing buttons on a machine," he says. "There needs to be a DJ performing and manipulating records."

IN DA CLUB

Alongside the business acumen of media moguls such as Rubin and Simmons, and the raw musical talents of acts such as the

Beastie Boys, Run-D.M.C., KRS-One, LL Cool J, and Public Enemy, the good old-fashioned nightclub also played an integral
part in the evolution of hip hop.

The club was, and always will be, a place where new musical
styles are nurtured, explored, and enjoyed. The dancefloor is, after all, the acid test for any track. In New York in particular, hip
hop clubs provided a forum for people to get together with their
friends and dance to the latest joints being played by the city's
most talented DJs.

One of the most influential venues in early hip hop was Disco
Fever in the Bronx. As the name suggests, the club started out
playing disco when it opened in 1976, but when owner Sal Ab-
batiello (who went on to found Fever Records in 1982) caught
wind of the DJing abilities of Flash, Herc, and Bambaataa, he invited Flash to play a set in 1977. From then on, "The Fever" became a hip hop hub, with Sweet Gee, Luv Bug Starski, DJ
Hollywood, and a then fourteen-year-old Jam Master Jay man-
ning the decks in front of rapturous crowds. In 1985, Warner
Bros. immortalized the club by featuring it in the movie *Krush
Groove.*

Tunnel was another influential New York club, founded in
1987 by Peter Gatien, who also ran the Limelight, Palladium, and
Club USA. Afrika Bambaataa, DJ Enuff, and other famous DJs
played regularly at this 40,000-square-foot mecca for house music, which incorporated an abandoned train tunnel. Funkmaster
Flex, whose radio show on New York's HOT 97 has more than
two million weekly listeners, had a long-running residency there
and released a live mix CD, *The Tunnel,* in 1999.

Tunnel was legendary because its ear-splitting sound system
and trendsetting décor, but DJs such as Flex, and the unusual
mix of ordinary New Yorkers and hip hop celebrities who turned
out to listen, were the real story. In a 2001 article in the *Village
Voice,* Frank Owen wrote:

"It was at the Tunnel where such rap superstars as the Notorious B.I.G., DMX, and Jay-Z got their first big breaks. Eve, Busta Rhymes, Jah Rule, Missy Elliot, Foxy Brown, and Lil' Kim are all regulars—not cloistered away in a VIP room, but mixing with their followers out on the floor."

In addition to playing clubs across New York City and releasing landmark albums, Bambaataa, Flash, and their peers spread hip hop using a new medium in the early '80s—the mixtape. While their DJ sets were usually recorded on less-than-stellar tape decks, making the audio less clear than a radio broadcast, mix tapes of individual DJ performances and battles quickly became highly sought after, Grandmaster Caz reveals:

"Hip hop was powerful. People from other areas of New York and beyond had heard of it and wanted to check it out for themselves. To satisfy this demand we recorded parties, battles, and even practices, and sold the tapes for five bucks each. The cassettes were great because people could not just hear the music but also get the energy of the parties."

Desperately looking for a more adventurous and reputable identity than the predictable and safe suburbs could provide, middle- and upper-class white kids turned to this mysterious new music that was coming out of the Bronx and other inner-city boroughs. The release of the Sony Walkman in July of 1979 allowed people to take their mixtapes with them wherever they went.

"The mixtape was a very important way for us DJs to advertise ourselves," says Theodore. "Once the tapes circulated, people would start to recognize how good you are on the decks.

Why would someone come to see you play at a club or party if they hadn't heard you DJ and didn't know what you were about? Some people couldn't come to the parties because it was too far, so they'd get a tape. The cassettes got copied and sent to friends and family around the country. We'd do as many block parties as we could in the summer and then focus on making tapes and flyers when it got cold."

In addition to being played on Walkmans, mixtapes found their way into boom boxes across the country. DJ Z-Trip recalls his favorite boom-box memory:

> "I got turned on to Run-D.M.C. at a swap meet. I heard 'It's Not Funny' blasting from a guy's boom box and was blown away. I went to the guy selling the hip hop cassettes and told him I wanted every Run-D.M.C. tape he had, and anything else like it. He also gave me Fat Boys and Kurtis Blow tapes. I went home and played them for hours. It was the boom box that enabled me to hear that. You're not going to get that from someone who's wearing closed headphones. We live in a music culture where everything is personalized—iPods, playlists, etc.—but music loses its power if it's just about the individual. You develop a true appreciation of music by learning about, sharing, and playing it in a community with other DJs and people who love music like you do."

ALL THE RIGHT MOVES

As hip hop DJing grew, break dancing helped bring DJ culture to the masses. The term was first used by Kool Herc to describe those who danced to the break beats he played. As the popularity of the DJs increased, break dancing (also known as breaking and b-boying) became an essential part of the hip hop scene, along with graffiti (which actually preceded hip hop DJing), and later, MCing.

At first, breaking was just a free-form response to whatever the DJ was playing, but this dance style soon developed named groups of moves such as the backspin (self-explanatory), top rocking (part of the dance when the dancer is on his or her feet) and floor rocking (moving on the ground) and various types of freeze (suddenly halting movement while in the middle of a move).

In addition to breakers being included in the DJs collectives, the b-boys and b-girls formed their own crews, such as the Rock Steady Crew, the Dynamic Rockers, Zulu Kings, Starchild La Rock, and the Bronx Boys, and these came to include DJs to supply the soundtrack for breaking. The first crews were primarily black and Puerto Rican, but soon the craze spread beyond New York City and people of all ethnicities began breaking.

Break-dancers competed as fiercely as the DJs, for territorial dominance and respect. "B-boying is an art form, a way of connecting to the DJ and the audience creatively," says Theodore. "It caught on in so many places because it was something new and rugged, and it represented the hip hop scene visually. It looked good in music videos and when kids were breaking on *American Bandstand* and *Soul Train*. It was a new flavor of dance."

In the early '80s, newspapers, magazines, and TV crews were covering breaking battles (such as the legendary 1981 Lincoln Center Outdoors Program contest between the Rock Steady Crew and the Dynamic Rockers), and suburban kids were coming to downtown dance studios to learn from the masters, most of whom were poorly paid by the proprietors, who pocketed most of the profits.

Some of the breakers used pre-recorded beats, but the most notable collectives retained the DJ as a source of musical and style guidance. In 1982, Bambaataa invited the Rock Steady

Crew to join the Zulu Nation, and they accepted. The next year, promoter and manager Kool Lady Blue took Crazy Legs's collective on the Europe-wide Roxy Tour with Bambaataa, Fab Five Freddie, and other DJs. Not only was this the first hip hop tour, it also brought breaking and DJing into the consciousness of European youths, and soon they were as popular abroad as in the U.S.

Eighties movies such as *Wild Style, Breakin', Beat Street,* and *Style Wars* gave mainstream American audience an insight into hip hop culture, and they embraced the nylon tracksuits and fat-laced PUMA, Adidas, and Fila sneakers that b-boys and b-girls wore as they tried to imitate the athletically and rhythmically gifted breakers.

These movies also bolstered the reputation of the DJ as an arbiter of cool. The cast of *Beat Street* reads like a *Who's Who* of early hip hop spinners, with Herc, Bambaataa, and Jazzy Jay among those featured. And in *Wild Style,* you can see Flash's hands flying between three turntables in his kitchen and listen to a soundtrack that features the likes of Grand Wizard Theodore, Grand Mixer D.ST, and the Cold Crush Brothers.

DJs chose the tracks that breakers spun, froze, and body rocked to in these movies and at the neighborhood parties, and, now, the world was listening. Grandmaster Caz says:

> "The music that DJs played enabled the b-boys and b-girls to dance, which then inspired the DJs to find better songs. That kept things interesting and drove hip hop forward."

The outbreak of b-boy fever paved the way for The New York City Breakers to perform at the 1984 Los Angeles Olympics. "The Dynamic Breakers commanded fees that started at $10,000 and lent their name to a line of 'Breakdance Fever' toys . . . Thom McAnn ordered 17,000 shell-toed Wild Style brand shoes . . .

McDonald's finally did a hip-hop themed commercial," writes Jeff Chang in *Can't Stop Won't Stop*. (St Martin's Press, 2005)

Breaking drifted out of the limelight in the late '80s and early '90s, but made a resurgence in the mid-'90s, which Nelson George explains in his book *Hip Hop America* (Penguin, 2005): "In 1997, the GhettOriginals, an all-star–break-dancing crew that included the seminal b-boys K-Swift (Kenny Gabbert) and Crazy Legs (Richie Colon), did an international tour sponsored by Calvin Klein." These godfathers of breaking, who had pioneered the art form that originally went hand-in-hand with DJing at block parties and is now taught in dance studios and colleges around the globe, were finally getting the acclaim and financial rewards they'd deserved.

Break dancing has been transformed from a regional, underground art form into a worldwide phenomenon that's featured in top-rated TV shows such as FOX's *So You Think You Can Dance,* Bravo's *Step It Up and Dance,* and MTV's *America's Best Dance Crew,* movies like *You Got Served,* and even award-winning Broadway hits like *Bring in Da Noise, Bring in Da Funk*.

By pioneering the use of break beats in a DJ set, Herc was really the founding father of breaking as well as hip hop music, and as break dancing spread out from the Bronx, across New York, and across the globe, DJs continued to create the beats that made breaking possible, even creating remixes and producing tracks tailored to the dancers' routines.

BROADCASTING ON ALL FREQUENCIES

While the great hip hop clubs rose and fell, radio DJs have been a consistent and central source of new life for the hip hop scene. Since the early '80s, getting playtime on a respected station has given rising stars credibility that can later translate into CD and

MP3 sales in the suburbs, the residents of which often look to urban radio stations to decide what's cool.

"On New York radio in the '80s you had guys from our neighborhoods who were real DJs rather than just radio personalities," McDaniels says. "They knew what records to play and it gave exposure to the DJs because now they were playing their records to a huge audience."

In 1983, New York's KISS FM hired DJ Jazzy Jay (a member of Afrika Bambaataa's Zulu Nation) to present a hip hop show. When Jay left the station, his cousin Kool DJ Red Alert (Fred Krute) took the reins. While in high school Krute had attended Kool Herc's block parties, and he had been blown away by the records and technical innovation on display. Krute bought his own decks and mixer and became an apprentice of his older cousin Jay.

In Krute's first year at KISS FM, he founded the now-legendary *Dance Mix Party* show, which he ran for eleven years. After a brief but successful stint at HOT 97, he went back to his old position at KISS FM in 2007, and his program is again one of the most listened to shows on New York radio. In addition to his radio and club DJing endeavors, Krute is an active producer whose credits include the intro and outro on the Fugees's seminal album *The Score*.

"Red Alert is another guy who knew what was real on the streets," McDaniels says. "He took that and recreated the vibe over the airwaves to the whole of the city. That's why radio at the time was so powerful and diverse. Chuck, Red Alert, Marley Marl, and those guys were recreating their battles on the radio, doing the same things in the studio that they did at the block parties."

Another pioneering force in hip hop radio who established his reputation in the '80s is Chuck Chillout (Charles Turner). He built up credibility in the scene by releasing the single "Rock the House" as one third of the Bronx-based crew the B-Boyz in

1983. From there Turner went to work for KISS FM in 1987, where he became one of the nation's foremost hip hop radio DJs.

With Turner and Krute on the roster, KISS FM fought a battle for the New York airwaves against archrivals WBLS, whose *Rap Attack* show (hosted by Mr. Magic, real name Tony Pearson) was the first major hip hop program on the air. Turner, Krute, Pearson, and fellow WBLS host Marley Marl (Marlon Williams) played all the big tracks that no other radio DJs could even get their hands on. Today, KISS FM (which not only re-hired Krute but also recently lured back Turner) still competes with WBLS and against HOT 97—which features programs with Funkmaster Flex, DJ Mister Cee, and Cipha Soundz—and with Power 105.1. McDaniels says:

> "Chuck Chillout had every record ever made, I swear. He was an extension of Grandmaster Flash, the original Master of Records. Chuck took DJing seriously and never had a day off. If he heard a good song he didn't care about playlists, copyright, or anything, he was going to play it on his show. And they were tracks from every genre."

It's not just citywide and national radio that have impacted the hip hop scene—DJs at independent and college stations have long been an important bridge between the genre's underground and commercial success. While a student at Columbia University in the early '90s, Stretch Armstrong (Adrian Bartos) co-hosted *The Stretch Armstrong and Bobbito Show* with Bobbito Garcia (formerly a member of the New York break dancing and DJing collective the Rock Steady Crew) on the university's WKCR FM radio station. Bartos explains how the show came about:

"In 1990, an older classmate at Columbia told me I should do a radio show, so I went to the guys at the station and told them I wanted to do a hip hop show. Someone took my idea and I made a big stink about it, so they allowed me to alternate with the guys they'd given the show to. I asked my friend Bobbito Garcia to host the first show, on October 31, 1990, because I didn't want to talk on the mic. Eventually we got so popular that the other guys quit."

In addition to playing the latest hits, the duo spun tracks from newcomers. The list of new hip hop acts first featured on the show: Biggie Smalls (later the Notorious B.I.G.), the Wu-Tang Clan, Nas, Mobb Deep, Jay-Z, and DMX, to name just a few. The program ran from 1990 to 1998, with *The Source* magazine naming it the best radio show of all time in the magazine's 100th issue.

Bartos went on to play on HOT 97 and now produces records for the label Planet Music. Garcia founded streetball magazine *Bounce NYC*, became a broadcaster for the New York Knicks, and wrote *Where'd You Get Those?* (Testify Books, 2003), a book about New York City's sneaker culture.

TURNTABLISTS AND SUPERSTAR DJS

There is no hip hop without the DJ.

—Darryl "D.M.C." McDaniels

While DJs such as Grand Mixer D.ST and Jam Master Jay were introducing hip hop to the mainstream American music scene, many DJs were building on the formative record-manipulation techniques of Kool Herc, Grand Wizard Theodore, and Grandmaster Flash. The hip hop duo World's Famous Supreme Team (comprised of the modestly named Just Allah the Superstar and C Divine the Mastermind) first gained exposure on Malcolm McLaren's single "Buffalo Gals," which cracked the U.K. Top 10 in 1982. The Supreme Team's furious scratching gave this single its soul, and the twosome continued to expand the possibilities of turntablism on New York's WHBI radio station.

DJ Jazzy Jeff was the next DJ to move the art of scratching forward. He took DJ Spinbad's **transform scratch (moving the crossfader back and forth four times on each beat)** technique to a whole new level in the mid-'80s, and mirrored the eclecticism of the early hip hop DJs by playing and enhancing tracks from other musical styles, including soul, funk and, as his name implies, jazz. Jeff was joined on the scene by DJ Cash Money, and together they elevated the profile of the Philadelphia scene and pushed the art of DJing forward.

"Cash Money and I came from the same area but growing up we didn't know each other," Jazzy Jeff explains. "I came up through the scene before him, so I helped him out by making introductions to promoters and having him play with me at parties. I was technically sound and he was the best showman—he'd spin on his head during a set and scratch behind his back and with his elbows. He was incredible. We played together a lot as the Kings of Spin, but we never battled against each other. When Will [Smith] and I got our record deal, people across the world knew who I was, and it kind of killed the rivalry with Cash, which was always friendly anyway. Then Cash and Marvelous got their own deal and it became more about the records than the DJ circuit."

While Jeff was soon to achieve worldwide acclaim as one half of DJ Jazzy Jeff and the Fresh Prince, the Philadelphia native's roots were firmly planted in the underground music scene. He has returned to playing at clubs and house parties and is revered by other pioneering DJs.

The rise of Jazzy Jeff and Cash Money coincided with the

creation of a new battling competition in which turntablists would have six-minute slots to show off their beat juggling, scratching, and body-trick skills—the DMC World Mixing Championships. Since British spinner Roger Johnson won the inaugural event in 1985, the contest has become one of the most imporant DJ events in the world. It has spawned a popular DVD and CD series and launched the careers of many young turntablists, including the 1995 winner Roc Raida (of renowned New York turntablist outfit the X-Ecutioners), A-Trak (who was just fifteen when he won in 1997 and was recently Kanye West's tour DJ), and Craze, who is the only person to have won three consecutive titles (from 1998 to 2000).

In the 1990s, many hip hop stars moved away from using DJs, opting instead for pre-programmed beats and effects, but the emergence of turntablism not only kept the art of the hip hop DJ alive but also took it to new heights. And with superstar hip hop DJs/producers Funkmaster Flex, DJ AM, and Mark Ronson dominating award shows, hosting their own TV and radio shows, and being an integral and well-publicized part of the Hollywood scene, DJing has re-emerged as the most vibrant and influential part of the hip hop genre.

THREE

THE HISTORY *of* HOUSE MUSIC

Electronic music will continue to evolve and move forward. People are not going to stop going out and dancing on a Saturday night, and electronic music is the soundtrack to that.

— Sasha

Created in Chicago in the early '80s, house music has spread around the world, permeating every musical genre. That four-on-the-floor beat, the hypnotic groove, the driving rhythm that keeps dancefloors moving all night long, has evolved from sparse, simple tracks to fully fledged songs with intricate layers and sounds covering subgenres from techno to deep house. DJs like Sasha, John Digweed, and Paul Oakenfold pack clubs in Shanghai, Cape Town, and Buenos Aires as readily as they fill dancefloors in house music centers such as New York, London, and Ibiza. They do this because there is something universal and timeless about the tracks they are playing, and something compelling about the musical tapestries they create.

THE HOUSE THE DJS BUILT

Just as the instrumentation contained in house is more complicated than in hip hop, so too is its recent history. While the early days of hip hop is essentially the tale of five boroughs, the development of house spans two continents and numerous countries. To tell the full story would take an entire book, but as several have already been written, we'll keep it simple.

Before Herc, Bambaataa, and Flash created hip hop, the New York DJ scene was dominated by disco. Clubs such as the Gallery in SoHo, the Loft, and most famously the decadent Studio 54 were the places where disco hits were made and tested. Long before John Travolta brought disco to a new level of international fame in the 1977 film *Saturday Night Fever,* the music was the soundtrack for clubbers and partygoers everywhere.

While it undeniably defined music and fashion in the early and mid-'70s, disco didn't last, as the excitement surrounding new genres (such as hip hop) overtook it, first in terms of musical innovation and, later, in cultural significance. But, as evanescent as it may have been, disco left a lasting legacy: the influence of DJs. They became the foundation for house music. Hip hop began with DJing, but the other elements—MCing, b-boying, graffiti, and knowledge—were arguably equally important to the scene. Not so for house, which was, is, and always will be all about the music and, therefore, all about the DJ.

Larry Levan (real name, Lawrence Philpot) and Frankie Knuckles (Frances Nicholls) became friends on the disco club circuit and soon took their first DJing gigs at the Continental Baths club in 1973. While Knuckles relocated to Chicago soon afterward, Levan remained in his native New York, and after brief stints at clubs around the city he moved onto the club that was to secure his place in the annals of DJ history—the Paradise Garage.

Levan's larger-than-life personality quickly drew crowds. While the owners of the Paradise Garage wanted to create something akin to Studio 54, attracting the same rich, white clientele, having Levan behind the turntables ensured that blacks, Latinos, and punks filed through the doors of the Greenwich Village club. To create the most electrifying dancefloor experience possible, Levan designed a powerful system that emphasized the bass in the tracks he played; a setup so sensitive that he would change his needles throughout the night, using progressively more high-quality ones as the peak hours approached. The famous sound system at the Tunnel was modeled on the Paradise Garage's setup, and Levan was hired by London house superclub Ministry of Sound to design its system in the '90s.

More important than the frequency response or volume output of his speakers was the music Levan played—a seamless blend of soul, funk, disco and even rock that gave new meaning to the word "eclectic." Garage, the modern sibling of house music characterized by soulful vocals, is so called because of the music Levan played at the Paradise Garage.

In addition to his engaging DJ style and ahead-of-its-time sound system, Levan was one of the first notable DJs to venture into remixing, infusing tracks with new basslines and beats. Levan's remixing was not confined to the studio. It also made its way into the DJ booth at the Garage, as he introduced components of the track on the second turntable to the song playing on the first, effectively reconstructing it live. The combination of a diverse musical taste, sublime DJing, remixing and production skills, groundbreaking sound and lighting systems, and a personality too big for any DJ booth to contain, enabled Levan to create an atmosphere and mystique at the Garage that has often been imitated but never replicated.

Levan's old friend and DJ partner Frankie Knuckles was just as influential in the development of house music When he moved to Chicago after the Continental Baths closed for good in 1976, Knuckles wasn't sure what he was in for, having lived in New York all his life and growing up in the disco era. He quickly fell on his feet, however, landing a residency at the Warehouse, which was where the term "house music" comes from.

Knuckles took the vast and diverse record collection he'd acquired over many years in the Big Apple with him when he moved, and began using a reel-to-reel tape player to edit, loop, and sample parts of a wide range of tracks, incorporating the remix into his sets at the Warehouse. He used a drum machine to augment the reworking of classic soul, funk, and disco music, in the process creating an early blueprint for the house music of today.

One of the revolutionary things about the Warehouse was that, unlike the hedonistic clubs in New York (not least the Paradise Garage), it boasted a juice bar in lieu of alcohol. In this sense, the club was truly just for dancing; its patrons were there for no other reason than to move to the music Knuckles was playing.

In 1982, Knuckles left the Warehouse and started his own club, the Power Plant, where he continued to advance the house sound. Knuckles later went on to found house label Def Mix and in 1997 won a Grammy for Remixer of the Year. In 2005, then-Senator Barack Obama oversaw the renaming of the street where the Warehouse once stood to Frankie Knuckles Way.

When Knuckles, the "Godfather of House," departed from the Warehouse in 1982, the club's owners renamed it the Music Box, and hired Ron Hardy to fill Knuckles's place. Hardy's upfront, raw style stood in stark contrast to Knuckles's sets, and in many ways was more similar to the rough, unpolished vein of early New York hip hop DJs than that of the man he'd replaced.

Hardy was one of the first house DJs to work with the frequency control knobs on the mixer—punching up the bass one minute, and cutting the mid-range the next, and often played two copies of the same track or two versions to extend vocal hooks, beats, and breakdowns. Hardy also increased the volume of the Music Box sound system so that it rivaled even Levan's legendary Paradise Garage setup for sheer musical force. Like Knuckles and Levan, Hardy played a lot of vocal-heavy, gospel-inspired house tracks that he had reworked with bigger basslines, more cut-up rhythms, and less schmaltz. In the heyday of the Chicago scene, the DJing of Hardy and Knuckles was creating the same level of buzz as the prowess of Herc, Flash, and Bambaataa did for hip hop, in New York.

HOUSE TAKES TO THE AIRWAVES

The sound comes from a pure place and it started the most important musical movement of its era.

—DJ Oscar G

Much as with the hip hop, the development of house was spurred by innovative radio programming. In 1981, Chicago's WBMX was inspired by the growing reputation of Knuckles and Hardy to start playing house tracks, and turned to a group of DJs known as the Hot Mix 5.

Their *Saturday Live Ain't No Jive* show played a combination of U.S.-produced tracks and European imports, and the show's high ratings led to the creation of other programs for the Hot Mix 5: *Friday Night Jam* and *Hot Lunch Mix*. These shows had five

hundred thousand regular listeners in the early '80s. In addition
to their stellar work on the radio, the collective became sought-
after regulars on the Chicago club scene. They ruled the airwaves until 1985, when the collective went their separate ways.
The size and devotion of Hot Mix 5's audience at WBMX
demonstrated that there was a significant proportion of
Chicago residents from all walks of life who were hungry for
house music, and that radio DJs could be just as influential in the
development of the genre as those in the club.

The rise of house through the Paradise Garage, the Warehouse, Power Plant, and other clubs in New York and Chicago
and the increasing popularity of Chicago's WBMX and WGCI
radio stations encouraged talented DJs and producers to start
making house records. In 1984, Jesse Sherman started Trax Records, the first house label. Two years later, another house label, DJ
International, put out the Farley "Jackmaster" Funk and Jesse
Saunders collaboration "Love Can't Turn Around," which got into
the U.K. Top 10. The next year, fellow Chicago house DJ Steve
"Silk" Hurley did even better, going to number one in the U.K.
Singles Chart with "Jack Your Body." This success indicated the
possibility for house to blow up in Britain.

HOUSE LIVES ON

> *Every Friday, there'd be lines outside record stores in Manhattan, and
> we'd be selling* [records] *out of the box, unheard.*
>
> —Mark Finklestein, CEO, Strictly Rhythm

1987 and 1988 marked the end of two eras—with WBMX and
then the Paradise Garage and Power Plant closed—but house
proved to be more resilient than many had predicted, and New
York took back the mantle of the premier city of the genre.

Labels such as Nervous and Strictly Rhythm took the burgeoning success of Chicago's Trax Records and DJ International and
put out a string of hits that were even more popular in Europe
than in the U.S. New York radio stations WBLS and KISS,
known for bringing hip hop out of the underground and into the
mainstream, also became important in the proliferation of
house. Tony Humphries had started playing on KISS back in
1981. By the late '80s he'd reached his peak on the station, playing a show seven nights a week that was repeated the following
day. He continued playing on KISS to a huge audience until
1994. He explains:

> "My goal with the KISS shows was to play as much ma-
> terial as I could every time I was on air. I'd sometimes
> play forty songs in a show, and each one was high qual-
> ity because between my residency at Zanzibar and be-
> ing on air every day I had nowhere to hide. I had to
> bring it every time I walked in the studio."

LONDON CALLING

> *House in the U.K. became something that redefined youth culture and de-*
> *constructed the old guard of the British industry—it created a whole new*
> *movement of dance music.*
>
> —Danny Rampling

As important as the emergence of U.S. labels and radio shows
were, the impetus and excitement that drove house forward
soon shifted to Britain. Oscar G, who is based in Miami, recalls:

> "I went over to play in Sheffield when house was just start-
> ing to be heard in England. I had no idea what to expect,

but it was amazing. There were about three hundred people, it was pitch black, and there was this booming sound system that just shook the whole place. There was no booze because people didn't need it. I played for six hours and people danced hard the entire time. From then on I knew house was going to take off there."

The chart-climbing of tracks such as "Jack Your Body," "Love Can't Turn Around," and other Chicago house singles, inspired U.K. DJs to follow in the footsteps of Larry Levan, Frankie Knuckles, and Ron Hardy. Britain has always been well situated to adopt the best music from America and Europe, and it was no different with house: "Like a lot of things, in Britain we take something that's created somewhere else and take our own spin on it to create a new scene," says Danny Rampling, one of the founding fathers of house music in the U.K. "Just like the punk, hippy, and mod movements before it, house in the U.K. became something that redefined youth culture and deconstructed the old guard of the British industry—it created a whole new movement of dance music."

Early British house DJs were influenced both by European bands such as Kraftwerk and the Chicago house sound. Graeme Park (who played at Garage in Nottingham) and Mike Pickering (resident at the Hacienda in Manchester) were among the first to introduce house to the U.K. club scene.

Arguably more influential than any of the previous events in the history of the British house scene was a 1987 visit to the tiny Balearic island of Ibiza by DJs Danny Rampling, Paul Oakenfold (who was already making a name for himself with promotional work for Def Jam subsidiary Champion), Johnny Walker, and Nicky Holloway.

Danny Rampling recalls:

"The four of us who went there were so greatly influenced by what we saw and heard in Ibiza that we came back and changed the face of the British music industry. That trip paved the way for a whole new generation of musical experience. There was magic in the air and we brought that back with us."

Upon returning to London in 1987, Rampling opened the club Shoom, regarded by many in the house scene as the birthplace of dance music culture in the U.K. "Shoom was built on idealism, freedom, and a mindset of success," Rampling explains. "The crowd was attracted by the energy that was projected by the DJs, and that became a collective consciousness that snowballed, just like it did at Future and [Oakenfold's club] Spectrum."

Oakenfold introduced a combination of the Ibiza and U.S. house sounds to the crowd at London's Sanctuary and later Spectrum, defining the distinctive sound of U.K. house music. Together the friends went from playing to a few vaguely interested and slightly confused clubbers to packing their clubs and having to turn people away.

TALKING ABOUT A REVOLUTION

With house music, the DJs didn't worry about fancy bars or music licenses, they'd just go to a warehouse and play. It was so energetic because it was spontaneous and young people were doing what they wanted.

—Annie Nightingale

While the early house clubs were gaining momentum, promoters at rival events companies Labyrinth and Genesis were hosting warehouse parties across London, which were illegal because the promoters didn't obtain event licenses. The combination of highly skilled DJs, an influx of new tracks from Europe, and the thrill of going against the staid conservatism of the country at the time gave these events a special atmosphere.

The longest-running BBC Radio 1 DJ, Annie Nightingale, recalls the impact the house scene had on her:

> "It was a social revolution. In the '80s, the clubs were all about money and flash and the promoters made you do what they wanted. With house music, the DJs didn't worry about fancy bars or music licenses, they'd just go to a warehouse and play. It was so energetic because it was spontaneous and young people were doing what they wanted."

Soon, the parties morphed into open-air raves held in fields across the country. Steve Lawler, one of the pioneering U.K. house DJs recalls:

> "It was really exciting to be part of the rave movement because it was brand new and it brought people together. There was one record shop in each major city and it would be packed with people fighting over the last copies of the hot tracks they'd heard the night before. It wasn't a big scene at the beginning, but the people who were into it were so passionate about the music and the vibe that it grew rapidly. It was a pure labor of love for everyone involved because nobody—not the promoters, DJs, nor record labels—made any money."

As the rave scene grew—only to come crashing down in 1994 with the passage of the Criminal Justice Act, which imposed strict penalties for organizers of unlicensed raves and warehouse parties—some British radio DJs remained loyal to the original house music coming out of Chicago. One of these was Jazzy M, whose *Jacking Zone* show on pirate radio station LWR in London was the first British radio program dedicated to house music.

TUNE IN, DROP OUT

We could break acts, we could help people get to number one.

—Pete Tong

The most influential radio DJ of the era was Pete Tong, who, like Rampling, Oakenfold, and company, was profoundly influenced by the music he heard while traveling. "I was doing trips to New York before I went to Ibiza," he says. "It's hard to describe how different it was. DJs didn't travel, didn't have international reputations—we were just kids really and we got thrown out of a couple of clubs. I'd done one trip to Cannes, then to Ibiza and Corfu. So we thought we could take music there, but really it was more about going on holiday with friends rather than internationalizing DJing and house music. We could never have imagined the scene becoming as big as it is today."

While his trips to New York and Corfu obviously had an impact on his musical tastes, it was Ibiza that had the most special significance for Tong, and subsequently the development of house music in the U.K. He explains:

> "The clubs in Ibiza had a history. Pacha started as a getaway for Spanish royalty looking to go somewhere the paparazzi couldn't follow, so it was pretty decadent. The clubs on the island had great facilities, and they'd be-

come very serious about clubbing. Pacha was successful and it created envy amongst promoters, so Amnesia and Space came along. Suddenly, by the early '80s, they had major venues and managers and owners dedicated to putting on parties, and lax regulations that allowed them to do daytime events and sunrise parties. Tourism increased, rave and then acid house culture exploded in the U.K. and was looking for somewhere overseas to expand to, and Ibiza was the logical place to go."

In addition to championing the Balearic sound of Ibiza, Tong also developed an appreciation for the sound of the U.S. house pioneers while working as an A&R man at London Records in the mid-'80s. In 1986 he released *The House Sound of Chicago, Vol. 1,* the first U.K. compilation of its kind. He began DJing on London's Capital FM in 1988, just as house began to really take off in England, and the following year founded record label FFRR.

Landmark releases such as Lil' Louis's "French Kiss," Orbital's "Chime," and Goldie's "Inner City Life" made FFRR one of the most influential house labels of the '90s. In 1991, Tong took over a Friday night slot on BBC Radio 1, and quickly named his new show *The Essential Selection.*

Getting Tong to name a record "The Essential New Tune" became an invaluable endorsement for DJs and house producers, as was the privilege of appearing as the guest DJ on his weekly, thirty-minute Hot Mix. "If Pete Tong played your record it could give you a hit," Lawler says. "Every DJ and producer I knew wanted his phone number because they wanted to send him new tracks as exclusives, hoping he'd play them on *The Essential Selection.* Pete has kept it interesting, valuable, and up-to-date over the years. He's the leader of dance music on the radio."

In 1993, Tong became the host of a new program, *The Essential Mix,* which features a different DJ or producer each week for a two- or three-hour mix, and has hosted such luminaries as Oakenfold (whose 1994 Goa mix is considered by many to be one of the finest DJ mixes ever), Frankie Knuckles, and Sasha, as well as up-and-coming DJs of the moment. Tong explains the significance of his Radio 1 shows:

> "*The Essential Mix* and *The Essential Selection* began to be syndicated more and helped spread the reputation of DJs. We started the Radio 1 shows at a time when the music was even more powerful than it is now, in its first global wave. We could break acts, we could help people get to number one. I did Ministry of Sound's the *Annual* and it sold over a million copies. The tricky part was 2001 to 2005, when people said house was over. We had to reinvent ourselves to get through that time when it seemed everything was against us, and now is a very exciting time again, a buoyant time with a lot of exciting music coming out and a lot of DJ innovation."

HOT OFF THE PRESS

Renaissance set the standard for DJ albums.

—John Digweed

To publicize themselves, house DJs recorded their mixes (both live gigs and bedroom productions, known as mixtapes), and distributed them to club promoters in the hope of booking gigs, and to record shops to sell to their customers. This was a low-cost, high-reward marketing tool that allowed DJs to showcase their talents to consumers, club owners, and radio stations alike.

Because of the limited number of copies available, these tapes became hot items amongst diehard house fans. Record labels eventually caught on, signing DJs to record mixes for tapes, and later CDs, in professional studios. Lawler describes how a mixtape got him a big break:

> "A friend of mine in Ibiza played one of my mixtapes for a group of people and one of them was the promoter at [legendary sunset venue] Café Mambo. He hired me and I DJed there for six hours, seven nights a week, for the whole summer in 1995. I got paid fifty pounds a week and lived on a sponge mattress in an apartment above the club, but I loved every minute of my time there. My second summer there I got a lot of gigs at other clubs and the third summer I met Darren Hughes [co-founder of Liverpool superclub Cream], who invited me to play on New Year's Eve 1996 at Cream. I rocked it so he hired me as a resident DJ. Things started happening really fast. My single 'Rise In' got into the chart, I did a compilation for Global Underground and I was DJing all over Europe. If you just keep plugging away good things will fall into place for you."

Magazines also offered valuable exposure for house DJs. While *DJ* and *Muzik* in the U.K. and *BPM, Remix*, and *Revolver* in the U.S. were to become influential and widely read, it was *Mixmag* that set the standard for dance music publications. Dave Seaman, now a superstar DJ himself, was the editor that transformed it from a glorified pamphlet into a high-quality, glossy publication. Under Seaman's direction, *Mixmag* popularized the inclusion of DJs' buzz charts, which ranked the hottest new tunes, and also started the trend of putting a free mix CD on the cover of most issues.

In late 1991, the same year that it released *Mixmag Live Vol. 1: Mixed by Carl Cox* (sold separately from the magazine), *Mixmag* put a picture of Sasha, then an up-and-coming DJ, on its cover, making him the first DJ to grace the cover of a U.K.-wide periodical. Born Alexander Coe in Wales, Sasha was first introduced to house music at Hacienda in the mid-'80s. After moving to Manchester and DJing in pubs around the city and being mentored by Hacienda's resident DJ Jon DaSilva, Sasha became the resident DJ at Shelley's in Stoke, in the north of England. He soon moved on to Renaissance, where he became famous for an epic, melodic style that often included elaborate ten- or twelve-minute-long intros. Steve Lawler recounted seeing Sasha in action. "A group of friends would go with me every week to see Sasha play at Shelley's," he says. "We'd have house music on in the car both ways. Sasha stood out because he was into the Italian house sound, a niche nobody else had found, and was technically brilliant. On the way back we'd go to a gas station and there would be a thousand people who'd just come from Shelley's and were just hanging out to wind down. Shelley's, Hacienda, and Spectrum took house music to another level, where everyone in the crowd had their hands in the air and danced all night."

Together with fellow resident John Digweed, Sasha released the three-CD *Renaissance: The Mix Collection* in 1994. It became the first mix CD to go gold, opening the floodgates for other record labels eager to capitalize on this new commercial phenomenon. The packaging of Sasha and Digweed's release was almost as groundbreaking as the music discs—the case featured classic Renaissance-era prints that echoed the lavish décor of the landmark Mansfield club, which opened its doors in 1992.

"Renaissance set the standard for DJ albums," Digweed says. "Sasha and I were lucky that we got to pick our favorite records for *The Mix Collection*. We then made a more ambient, breakbeat album for [seminal 1996 mix] Northern Exposure, which shocked a lot of people, because everyone was doing banging trance at the time. We wanted to make CDs that had longevity. Renaissance realized that you must have a quality product—nice looking packaging, good track selection, and quality mixing." Sasha and Digweed went on to release another volume of the Northern Exposure CD series, and soon found themselves playing once a month at Twilo (in New York), in Ibiza, and around the world. Nick Warren, a global superstar DJ himself, remembers Sasha's power to draw huge crowds:

> "For Sasha at Twilo there'd be two thousand people in the queue at three in the morning waiting to get in. You know, in the late '90s the house scene was just at its peak at that time. It was just so huge."

THE FAME GAME

> *Cream, at its peak, was just an amazing club. At 8 P.M. there'd be a thousand people outside.*
>
> —Nick Warren

The release of *Renaissance: The Mix Collection* and subsequent bestselling mix CDs were supported by an innovative marketing and branding campaign that included full-page ads in national magazines and newspapers. The club's promoters were soon hosting club nights on every continent, making Renaissance the first true superclub. As the profile of resident DJs Sasha and John Digweed grew in England, Renaissance made a splash in Ibiza, first at Ku and then at Pacha. The club's record label also flourished, selling more than a million copies of its releases.

Another superclub that dramatically impacted the house scene was the Ministry of Sound, which first held small, secret gatherings in 1991 and officially opened in London's Southwark district the following year. Clubs such as Ministry were also an alternative to the rave scene, which was under constant threat by the police and government and was losing attendees fed up with dancing alongside Ecstasy- and LSD-fueled, glowstick-waving teenagers in muddy fields.

Pioneering New Jersey–based house DJ Tony Humphries mixed the first of Ministry's many CDs in 1993, and four years later Ministry became one of the first clubs to set up a radio station, which continues today online. It took the Renaissance branding model even further, creating the most recognizable club logo in the world, which now appears on DJ equipment, merchandise, and even a cell phone. There are Ministry outposts in Egypt, Singapore, India, Australia, and Taipei, with more set to open. Humphries recalls the magic of the club:

"Larry Levan had come over and given them the specs of the setup at the Paradise Garage, and it was not just powerful but also very high quality. During breaks in the instrumentation people were yelling and blowing whistles—it was an amazing response to my set. Everyone stayed till the end of the night, bugging me for encore after encore until security made everyone leave. It was the closest thing to the atmosphere of the Paradise Garage."

Cream was the third of the original U.K. superclubs (not counting the Hacienda, which was hugely influential but was limited to just clubbing). The first weekly Cream night was staged at Liverpool's Nation club in 1992, but it was when Paul Oakenfold became the resident DJ in 1997 (after a worldwide tour with U2) that Cream truly became a force on the international clubbing scene.

"Cream, at its peak, was just an amazing club," says Nick Warren, who along with Lawler and Oakenfold was the other resident at Cream during its heyday. "The energy in that place was just phenomenal. At 8 P.M. there'd be a thousand people outside."

Cream was the first club to break into large-scale festivals, holding the inaugural Creamfields outside Winchester in the south of England in 1998. While several other big house festivals, such as Homelands and Tribal Gathering have since ceased, Creamfields has kept going strong, celebrating its ten-year anniversary in August 2008.

The enduring appeal of Creamfields is a combination of stellar DJs and the biggest electronica live acts in the world, who lure the forty-thousand-plus partiers out to brave the unpredictable British weather. In addition to holding Creamfields events in the U.K., the club has staged festivals in fifteen other countries, including Portugal, Ireland, and Chile. The annual Creamfields Argentina event attracts more than sixty thousand people, making it the biggest dance music festival in South America. Lawler gives a first-hand account of the festival scene:

> "Creamfields, Homelands, and Tribal Gathering were great because they gave us the opportunity to reach massive audiences. People could come for fifteen or twenty hours and choose from the best live acts and DJs in the world. I've always played the biggest tents and the atmosphere in those larger arenas can't be matched by any club—it's an incredible rush to have thousands of people just focused on what you're doing with the music you love."

Cream, Ministry of Sound, and Renaissance paved the way for the next generation of U.K. superclubs. Gatecrasher began as a series of outdoor and indoor dance parties in 1993, and four years later the company opened its own nights at the Republic in Sheffield (the venue was later renamed Gatecrasher One).

The unprecedented amount of publicity, meanwhile started an era of collaboration between the superclubs (for both their club nights and festivals) and national radio stations, which introduced DJs to a larger audience.

"In the '90s, Radio 1 piggybacked off the scene that we'd created," says Danny Rampling. "It gave us the chance to have national shows and at that time was very important to the club culture. My *Love Groove Dance Party* program was broadcast in a golden period. The show was a platform for independent labels and the artists on them that were driving the club scene. Me and Pete Tong were flying the flag of British club culture at home on Radio 1, while Sasha, Digweed, and some other guys were focusing on America."

With Radio 1, KISS FM, Galaxy 101, and other stations broadcasting recorded and live DJ sets, a clubber could go to a festival, set his tape or CD deck at home to record the accompanying radio show, and have the music to keep for good. In the case of Gatecrasher, the club soon had a powerful connection at Radio 1—resident DJ Judge Jules, whose show pulled in over a million listeners each week.

Fabric, a 25,000-square-foot venue with a floor that has speakers underneath it to—literally—get East London clubbers moving, is another of the new superclubs; it has three separate sound systems for its three rooms. Fabric is renowned for its diverse, genre-bridging lineups both at the club and on the Fabric and *FabricLive* mix series.

Fans who don't want to go to record stores or online to get their hands on the latest installment can sign up for a yearly membership and have the monthly CDs delivered right to their door, just like a magazine subscription. Another innovative mix

CD series is Global Underground, which became the first to include DJs on the cover. Each release is based on a DJ's experience in a world city and putting the DJs' pictures on covers promotes the global influence of the DJ. Nick Warren, who has recorded several volumes of the Global Underground series, explains why the brand is important in the house music scene and to his own career:

> "I've sold almost 750,000 albums now and it's really made my name around the world. Everywhere I go, there's always somebody in a club that comes up with a pen and an album for me to sign. Global Underground has always stuck to their guns of not telling us what to put on there. My job is to find young unknown producers and really push them, because they're the future."

As DJs such as Sasha, Digweed, Oakenfold, and Warren captured the imagination of the music-listening public, Britain's electronica acts reached the apex of their creativity and commercial success. DJ duo Tom Rowlands and Ed Simons, collectively known as the Chemical Brothers, got their start DJing at celebrity favorite the Heavenly Social club in 1994, and the following year released their debut album *Exit Planet Dust*. Two years later, they collaborated with Oasis's Noel Gallagher on the house/rock hybrid track "Setting Sun," which went straight to number one in the U.K. Top 40. Their next single, "Block Rockin' Beats," also grabbed the top spot and later won a Grammy for Best Rock Instrumental Performance, and the 1997 LP *Dig Your Own Hole* sold over two million copies. The Chemical Brothers' third album, 1999's *Surrender,* summitted the album chart, a feat its 2001 follow-up, *Come with Us,* also achieved, as Rowlands and Simons continued to DJ at clubs worldwide. The duo's 2006 LP *Push the Button* won a Grammy, as did its number one single "Galvanize." They were really the "Superstar DJs" their 1999 song "Hey Girl, Hey Boy" described.

In 1992 DJ Neil Barnes, who got started behind the decks at revered venue the Wag Club joined forces with Paul Daley (formerly of the bands Brand New Heavies and A Man Called Adam) to form Leftfield. After the group released *Leftism* in 1995, a new subgenre was named after the band; the record is considered by many to be the greatest dance album of all time. The follow up, 1999's *Rhythm and Stealth,* featured many notable collaborations, including "Afrika Shox," featuring Afrika Bambaataa. Many people were first introduced to that album when the song "Phat Planet" was featured on a Guinness TV ad, which was later voted as the best commercial of all time in Channel 4's Top 100 Adverts list in 2000. The ability of Leftfield to infiltrate both the advertising industry and the festival scene demonstrated that DJing innovation can cross boundaries and permeate all aspects of popular culture.

The groundbreaking chart successes of DJ/producers Fatboy Slim, the Chemical Brothers, Leftfield, and the groundbreaking U.K. electronica acts of the mid to late '90s and the rise of Sasha, Oakenfold, Digweed, and the other big name house DJs indicated the British public's fervent desire for a share in DJ culture. Previously, pop and rock music had dominated the charts, airwaves, and music press in the U.K., but just as punk had done two decades earlier, house music spurred new creativity and awareness not only among DJs but also throughout youth culture. Suddenly, kids weren't looking to the latest big rock band for musical direction but to the house DJs, who became rock stars in their own right.

The arrival of the superstar DJ on the U.K. music scene inspired countless kids (us included) to take their love of house music one step further and to begin DJing, shown by the fact that in
the late '90s turntables outsold guitars in the U.K. (and they continue to do so). Record shops such as London's Blackmarket Records and Birmingham's Hard to Find Records, which are still two
of the best in the business, became more than just stores—but
also a place where DJs could congregate and talk business. During
the week, thousands listened to Pete Tong, Danny Rampling, and
Judge Jules on BBC Radio 1, bought DJs' mix compilations, and
shopped for club-friendly attire at stores that sometimes had DJs
playing in them. On the weekends, the entire social calendar re-
volved around getting ready for, travelling to, and dancing for
hours at clubs and DJ parties. And it wasn't only the superclubs
that did a roaring trade. Clubs became the focal point of local
communities at night, for both people spilling out of the pubs and
bars at closing time (pubs in England closed at the grandfatherly
time of 11:00 P.M. until recently) and the dedicated clubbers that
would dance as enthusiastically to the warm-up DJs as to the
headliners that followed. Each summer, tens of thousands of the
country's young people traveled to festivals such as Creamfields,
Homelands, and Tribal Gathering (later Global Gathering) and
made the annual pilgrimage to the club Mecca of Ibiza. The rich
rock heritage of the '80s had been replaced by a dance nation.
Danny Rampling says:

> "It was a time of great social change. We were in an op-
> pressive political climate and there was very little oppor-
> tunity for certain parts of society. There were massive
> changes in the air—apartheid ending, the Berlin Wall
> coming down. If you look at the early gospel house rec-
> ords, like 'Promised Land' and 'Sunday,' they brought a
> sense of optimism and hope to a country that had been

depressed and downtrodden for so long. That's part of why the emergence of house music in the U.K. was so powerful."

The tastemakers that set this trend in motion—with club nights like Shoom and Phuture and the raves and warehouse parties between 1988 and 1991—advanced it with the residencies, album releases, and merchandise of the superclubs in the mid-'90s, and still break new ground today, are and will always be the house DJs. As some of the legends of the scene retired, new DJ pioneers such as Nic Fanciulli and James Zabiela, Danny Howells, and collective Above & Beyond have stepped up to take the house sound to the next generation of clubbers. The energy and universality of the music they play and produce, and the cool factor of DJing, has transcended British shores and proved to be a global phenomenon. "Electronic music will continue to evolve and move forward," Sasha says. "People are not going to stop going out and dancing on a Saturday night, and electronic music is the soundtrack to that. You might go through a patch of a couple of months where you think there's nothing fresh coming out and then a new record will come along that blows you away."

In the years that followed, the DJing, remixing, and production work of Fatboy Slim, Paul Oakenfold, Tiësto, and others enabled the European house DJ to reach a level of public adoration, critical acclaim, and wealth that good old Jimmy Savile could never have imagined when he played his dance party in the tiny upstairs room of a social club in 1943. And with the club scenes in cities such as Miami, New York, San Francisco, and other major U.S. cities, house is going strong in its home country. It is and will continue to be the sound of club nights and parties across the globe, with the superstar DJs ruling like the kings of a musical feudal system. Oscar G chimes in:

"House has touched every corner of the globe and will continue to grow. There are more people DJing, more fans packing clubs, and more people making tracks than ever before. I can remember when there were just a few DJs who'd travel, but now there are guys flying out every day. House is the world's music."

OSCAR G'S TOP TEN EARLY HOUSE LABELS

1. Traxx
2. Strictly Rhythm
3. Nu Groove
4. DJ International
5. Nervous
6. Tribal America
7. Freeze
8. Irma
9. Junior Boys Own
10. FFRR

FOUR

EVOLUTION OF THE DJ

Timeline of DJ History

We've tried our best to distill the landmark events in DJ history into this handy timeline. Some of you might argue with us about what we left out or put in, but hey, nobody's perfect, right?

1877—Nerdy inventors' hero and teacher's pet Thomas Edison invents the phonograph, which played recorded sounds on a rotating cylinder.

1886—Emile Berliner invents the Gramophone.

1906—Reginald Aubrey Fessenden makes the first spoken AM radio broadcast from Brant Rock, Massachusetts.

1921—Westinghouse sets up major radio stations in Pittsburgh, Boston, Chicago, and New York City, bringing radio programming into the homes of millions.

1922—The BBC (British Broadcasting Corporation) broadcasts its inaugural radio program.

1930—RCA Victor introduces the first vinyl LPs.

1935—The show *Your Hit Parade* is first broadcast on NBC radio, playing the top-selling songs in the U.S.

1943—British DJ Jimmy Savile hosts the first true DJ dance party, playing old jazz records to a crowd in Otley, England.

1947—Savile welds two turntables together to become the godfather of dual deck turntablism.

1947—Paris is the location of the original discotheque, Whisky a Go Go.

1958—American radio DJ Bob Casey introduces a two-deck system with individual volume controls and an early version of the crossfader at a dance in Yonkers, New York. He later invents cueing.

1965—Terry Noel pioneers mixing two records at Arthur in New York.

1965—Sound technician Alex Rosner invents "Rosie," the first DJ-specific mixer. The Bozak ZMA-10-2DL, the first commercially available DJ mixer, was based on Rosner's prototype.

1967—John Peel goes to work for landmark pirate radio station Radio London, and joins the BBC when it shuts down. Orbital and The Orb were among the many electronica acts Peel made famous.

1969—Sanctuary nightclub resident DJ Francis Grasso masters beat matching.

1972—Technics releases the SL 1200, the first turntable to boast a direct drive motor (see DJing 101 for a definition), quartz timing, and a host of other industry-defining features.

1973—Hip hop is born at 1520 Sedgwick Avenue, New York, as DJ Kool Herc hosts the first parties to feature break beats.

1974—Kraftwerk releases the *Autobahn* album, the most influential electronic music LP to date.

1975—Grand Wizard Theodore accidentally invents scratching, and DJing is never the same again.

1976—Antonio Escohotado opens the doors of landmark Ibiza club Amnesia.

1976—The Paradise Garage club opens in New York, and the style DJ Larry Levan makes his own there names a genre—garage. The name of this venue has an unglamorous origin—the building was first used as a parking garage.

1979—The Sugarhill Gang's single "Rapper's Delight" is the first hip hop single to crack the Top 40.

1980—Kurtis Blow's single "The Breaks" jumps into the Top 5 and becomes the first gold-certified hip hop record. Blow was also the first rapper to land a deal with a major record label (Mercury).

1981—Grandmaster Flash's *The Adventures of Grandmaster Flash on the Wheels of Steel* album is the first hip hop LP to feature extensive use of backspins, scratching, and sampling.

1982—Afrika Bambaataa releases *King of Rock,* a genre-bending epic that sold more than 600,000 copies.

1982—*Wild Style* becomes the first Hollywood production to feature DJs, including Grand Wizard Theodore, Grandmaster Flash, and Grand Mixer D.ST.

1983—Run-D.M.C. release their first single, *It's Like That.*

1983—Double Dee and Steinski release *Lesson One: The Payoff,* one of the most influential hip hop mixes that influenced Q-Bert, Mix Master Mike, and the other top turntablists of the '90s.

1984—Rick Rubin and Russell Simmons (brother of Run-D.M.C.'s Joseph "Rev Run" Simmons) co-found Def Jam Recordings and go on to sign LL Cool J, Public Enemy, and Jay-Z.

1984—Melle Mel, part of the Grandmaster Flash and the Furious Five collective, is the first rapper to win a Grammy,
for his part on Chaka Khan's *I Feel for You.*

1984—Jazzy Jay and T La Rock's track "It's Yours" is the debut
release on Def Jam.

1985—British DJ Roger Johnson wins the inaugural DMC
World DJ Mixing Championships title.

1985—Run-D.M.C.'s *King of Rock* becomes the first hip hop
album to go platinum.

1987—Paul Oakenfold, Danny Rampling, Nicky Holloway,
and Johnny Walker bring back the Balearic sound of
Ibiza to Britain, fusing it with U.S. house to create a
new genre and a cultural phenomenon.

1988—Public Enemy releases the *It Takes a Nation of Millions to
Hold Us Back* album. Cops, politicians, and stuffy con-
servatives everywhere are outraged by the album's content, while hip hop fans and music critics celebrate it.

1989—Danny Rampling opens Shoom, one of the most influential early house clubs in the U.K.

1990—Stretch Armstrong launches *The Stretch Armstrong
Show with Bobbito The Barber* on Columbia University's
WKCR FM.

1992—Ministry of Sound opens in London.

1993—Pete Tong broadcasts the first *Essential Mix* on BBC
Radio 1.

1993—Ministry of Sound release the first mixed compilation,
mixed by Tony Humphries.

1994—Sasha and John Digweed release the three-disc *Renaissance: The Mix Collection.*

1994—The Prodigy drops *Music for the Jilted Generation,* the
seminal album of the post-rave scene that protested
the year's passage of the Criminal Justice Act, which
outlawed raves.

1995—Leftfield releases *Leftism,* the LP that defined the progressive house sound.

1998—The first Creamfields festival is held outside Winchester, England.

2000—DJ Craze wins his third consecutive DMC World DJ Mixing Championships crown, setting him apart as the most successful spinner in the history of the event.

2001—Pioneer launches the CDJ 1000, the first CD deck that can effectively mimic a turntable. It becomes the CD equivalent of the Technics 1200—the industry's gold standard.

2002—Fatboy Slim plays to 250,000 people on Brighton Beach, England. Remarkably, the weather is actually good that day.

2004—Tiësto DJs at the opening ceremony of the Athens Olympics.

2006—The Chemical Brothers (DJs Tom Rowlands and Ed Simons) win two Grammy awards (Best Dance Recording for "Galvanize" and Best Electronic/Dance Album for *Push the Button*).

2007—Grandmaster Flash and the Furious Five become the first hip hop act to be inducted into the Rock and Roll Hall of Fame.

2008—Mark Ronson wins a Grammy for Best Producer and Brit Award for Best British Solo Artist.

PART TWO

THE LIFE AND TIMES OF THE DJ

FIVE

THE LIFE *of the* DJ

I would do this for free because it's so much fun.

—DJ Craze

Oakenfold, Sasha, AM, Flex—their monikers are as recognizable as Tiger, LeBron, and the other one-name luminaries. But for each of the DJs who now earn superstar money, the history is more or less the same: years of playing small clubs, thousands upon thousands of dollars spent on records with little to show for it, long stretches when promoters and managers would ignore their calls. And though the top DJs aren't working two jobs to pay for records anymore, they're still hustling to maintain their status and advance their craft.

There is no landed aristocracy in the DJ world, no inherited titles or automatic fast track to commercial success. Whether they hail from England, the United States, or anywhere else, every one of today's big-name DJs began their careers with two turntables (or a laptop) and some records. In this chapter, we're going to explore the life of the DJ from the humble beginnings, when it's tough to book a slot at a local club, to the breakthrough gig, to flying to a different city each week.

Here, you'll find advice from the world's top spinners on how to get that first gig, earn and keep a residency, and much more. We've included the stories of the world's most talented and renowned DJs, from how they got started to how life is at the top of their game. Throughout it all you'll notice a recurring theme: It's all within your reach.

GETTING GOING

If you just ask other DJs, they'll be more than happy to help you out however they can. Just form those relationships and you'll become a better DJ.
— Z-Trip

The urge to DJ comes from loving music. When someone decides that listening to music isn't enough — that he or she wants to share their favorite music with others — a DJ is born. Whether it's listening to a particular track for the first time, seeing a DJ play a memorable set, or befriending a DJ, something will inspire a music lover to step off the dancefloor and behind the turntables.

But before you rush out to buy a pair of Technics 1200s and a top-of-the-line mixer, it's worth examining your motivations and figuring out where you'd like to go with DJing. Grand Wizard Theodore says:

> "Everyone should ask themselves why they want to start DJing. If it's because of wanting money or hot chicks, your success will be temporary, because you don't have the passion to be in the game for tomorrow — you're just looking at today. Then you should figure out what you

want to do with DJing. Do you want to be a club DJ, a
radio DJ, a battle DJ, or something else? How do you
plan to get there? If you can answer these questions up
front, you'll find your niche, and then you just need to go
out and start DJing, and everything will come together."

Many new DJs learn their craft on their own, practicing in a
bedroom or basement, contending with parents and siblings
yelling about turning the music down—sound familiar?—while
they stumble through the basics in trial-and-error fashion. However, some of the best early hip hop DJs, such as Jazzy Jay, were
lucky enough to be tutored by the pros—he joined Afrika Bambaataa's Zulu Nation. James Zabiela was mentored by legendary
house DJ Sasha, and Q-Bert (Richard Quitevis) learned how to
DJ by watching Mix Master Mike.

You may not have access to the upper echelon of DJs, but
simply talking to other DJs will help. "I hung out with Jazzy Jay
for three weeks, and my appreciation of music and DJing knowledge went off the charts just from listening to this hip hop
elder," says Z-Trip. It might seem intimidating to shoot an e-mail
to Jazzy Jay or go up to a big-name DJ in a club, but building relationships is critical to developing as a DJ. In the end, the DJing
community is a big, worldwide family. If you want to absorb the
key aspects of the music scene you're into, you can't do so in isolation.

To learn more about the process of becoming a professional
DJ, we sat down with one of the most influential—Pete Tong:

"I was a DJ when I was in school, it was always the thing
I did. When I left school at age eighteen, I didn't get a
proper job—I was DJing at weddings and bar mitzvahs.
I had a van with a sound system that I went around in
doing parties. I was putting myself out there in an en-

trepreneurial way. There weren't superstar club DJs then, so everyone who DJed wanted to be on the radio, including me. I got a few spots on pirate radio and BBC Radio Kent and then I got on to Radio 1, talking about hot new tunes on Peter Powell's show. So I was on that station when I was nineteen. Off the back of getting established on the radio, I got asked to join a record company in 1983—London Records. I was doing everything for them: running acts to gigs, doing club promotions, and I was allowed to sign acts right away. I signed Run-D.M.C. and they blew up in the U.K. with 'Raising Hell.' Then I started my label, FFRR, and within a year house music was born. "

Many DJs start at a young age, but few find success as rapidly as DJ A-Trak (Alain Macklovitch), who was part of the now-defunct Allies collective (along with DJ Craze, Klever, and others), tours with Kanye West, won the title of DMC World DJ Champion in 1997 at the age of fifteen, and now runs the successful Fool's Gold record label. "I was influenced by local guys in Montreal like Kid Koala and by my friend DJ Devious who started teaching me some tricks," he says. "The Invisibl Skratch Piklz and X-Ecutioners were inspirational, because they made turntablism into an art form."

A-TRAK'S TOP 10 TIPS FOR WINNING THE DMC WORLD MIXING CHAMPIONSHIPS

1.   Bring something new to the table.
2.   Practice, practice, practice. Anticipate *every* possible way that something could go wrong.
3.   Study your competition.

4.   Have something catchy in your set that people
      will be talking about.
5.   Start with a bang.
6.   End with your most creative segment. That's
      what the judges will remember.
7.   Cover every base and be well rounded.
8.   Use records that sound good over a big sound system.
9.   Avoid monotone sets. Build strong dynamics in
      your set's structure.
10. Film yourself practicing. Be aware of how you
      look when you perform.

A-Trak's fellow turntablist DJ Q-Bert has won three DMC titles
(as part of the Rocksteady DJs and the Dream Team), starred in
an Apple commercial, and is widely regarded as the finest
scratcher of them all. He paid his dues as a DJ learning in San
Francisco's Excelsior District:

> "Mix Master Mike, who lived near me, started a month
> before I did, so he had the 'Rockit' scratches down. I
> went to every show he played at. He did weddings, high
> school dances, and local parties. I studied everything he
> did—he was my mentor. Me and Mix Master Mike had
> a DJ battle against each other and he whupped my ass.
> DJ Apollo was in the audience, and he hooked up with
> Mike. I started working with them four years later [to
> form the FM20 collective, which was later renamed the
> Rocksteady DJs]. The best advice Mike gave me was 'Be
> original, be yourself.'"

Q-Bert did not rely on Mix Master Mike and Apollo to do
the work for him. He is a self-confessed record junkie who

spends every spare moment honing his skills, to stay ahead of the game in a turntablist scene that is increasingly crowded:

> "I try to at least get two hours in of pure scratching each day. If I miss a day, I feel it. It's important to make varieties of beats all the time because it makes your sound better. I'm also hunting for sounds to scratch. I'm a musician on the turntables. I love it because it's an instrument, just like playing a trumpet or guitar. I am still a student, still learning."

New York native Junior Sanchez quickly progressed from being a novice to playing at the biggest clubs and festivals around the world:

> "I started DJing when I was fourteen, playing records I loved in my bedroom. A year later, I released my first track. Soon I had a residency at Club USA, and then I was traveling to the U.K. to play the Tribal Gathering festival. Anyone can DJ but you've got to be creative. I'm addicted to the gambling of being creative. Don't make music for your peers, for DJs to play, or because it's in style—make it because you believe in it. Punk is not a musical style to me, it's an attitude. Put an attitude into your music and it will be fresh."

Matt Black, who with Jonathan More is the pioneering electronic act Coldcut, has been DJing for more than twenty-five years. He tells about his life-long fascination with music:

> "I started a disco at school with my friends. From an early age, I was interested in speakers, music, and lights. I was always messing around with buzzers and bulbs, motors

and tape recorders, when I was a kid. In the old days, there were no DJ books, DVDs, or YouTube videos. Films like *Breakdance* and *Wild Style* had nuggets of information, like Jazzy Jay cutting up two copies of 'Disco Tune,' and it was like 'Aha, that's how he does it.' We borrowed from people as well. Hip hop brought that forward. It was an immediate strong attraction to the hip hop idea, set, and culture. It was like, 'Yeah, I want to do that for a living.' We were lucky to be around at a time when you were forced to work hard and come up with your own solutions. My teachers were people like [half of the Double Dee and Steinski DJ-production duo] Steinski and [American writer] Tim Leary, but I'd learned from them before I'd ever met them. Teaching yourself is about being an autodidact. The strength of autodidacts is coming up with their own solutions to problems, and the solutions you come up with sometimes have an interesting curve or texture to them, which give them character. And really, in art, character is what it's all about. It's about fusing the techniques that you learn by copying with your own identity and experience that moves things on."

The keys to getting off on the right foot, then, are identifying your goals, defining a unique sound, and practicing until your hands hurt. Having a mentor is a great way to progress, but you ultimately must find your own direction and stick with it. Mark Brown, head of U.K. house label CR2 Records sums it up perfectly: "Try to stay focused. If you believe in something, then keep going. Not everyone will succeed and break through but if you're happy with where your DJing is then don't worry about it. As long as you can stay passionate and keep reinventing yourself to stay original you'll have longevity as a DJ."

THE HUSTLE

*There's a universal lie, which is 'What I am is not enough.' People want
the job, the car, the girl, the career that makes them enough in the world's
eyes and in God's eyes. They need to work on things internally first, because everyone is enough.*

—DJ AM

For a burgeoning DJ, hustling or the grind is a stage they go
through to move up in the DJ pecking order before they make it
big. Just as we search for jobs that will strengthen our resumes,
DJs try to gain practical experience that will convince club
owners, promoters, radio stations, and the rest of the music industry of their abilities. Tong's and A-Trak's careers are atypical
in that they both went from obscurity to superstar status in a
few years.

It takes most DJs longer to climb the ladder. Too many budding DJs have the misconception that they will master the art in
a few weeks, and magically end up on magazine covers with a superclub residency and legions of adoring fans. Of course, it
doesn't work like that. In the early '90s, Steve Lawler, part of the
vanguard of British house music, considered quitting because of
the relentless grind:

"From 1990 to 1995, I was putting everything I had into
DJing but making no money and living in a horrible flat.
But I had music so I was OK. A couple of times I
thought about selling my records and doing something
drastic, like moving to India to live in a tent, but I kept
going. The first five years of my career were really hard.
Making it as a professional DJ took confidence and a belief that I could do it. As a DJ who's new on the scene,

you must keep going until someone in the industry who has clout notices you. I did a lot of gigs for free at the beginning in the hope that I'd play in front of promoters."

Like many of his peers, DJ AM, the king of the mash-up genre, experienced humbler times. "I worked at Denny's as a dishwasher, I drilled holes in bowling balls, I strung tennis rackets. I had a lot of crappy jobs, but I always DJed."

When you shell out a couple of grand for decks and a mixer, and you're always spending money on new music, whether on Web sites such as iTunes, Beatport, or in your local record store, it's understandable to want a return on your investment. Never say no to a gig, AM advises: "If it's a chance to practice in front of people, you have to do it. It took years until I could pick and choose where I played." For AM, any gig is a good gig.

But this advice should be practiced within caution. John Digweed, who with his fellow Englishman Sasha, was one half of house music's first superstar DJ duo, suggests that young DJs should make the difficult decision *not* to take a gig if they're not really prepared or at the right skill level, as it will be counterproductive: "If a guy plays to two thousand people before he's ready, he could be screwing up his career because he wasn't patient enough to learn how to read a crowd and build a set for that opening hour."

So, be honest with yourself. If you think you're genuinely ready for a gig, grab the opportunity and don't let it go. But if it's obviously more than you can handle, politely decline and go back to honing your skills so that next time someone offers you a show, you'll be up to the task.

Another way to promote yourself as a DJ is to take advantage of the Web. You can get a basic Web site designed for a few hundred dollars, or just set up a page on MySpace, which most DJs do. Nic Fanciulli, one of the fastest rising stars on the U.K. house circuit and frequent collaborator with James Zabiela, explains how to make the most of Internet marketing:

> "The Internet is the number one way to promote yourself as a DJ. Music is so changeable and disposable now that you've got to keep your online presence fresh with new podcasts, tracks, and updates to your Web site. Posting on a blog and interacting with fans in forums or on message boards is a great way to connect with people. You can record mixes and allow people to download them from your site, or give away a free track occasionally. When I do this, I make sure people provide their e-mail addresses first—that way we're connected and I can send them tour updates and news about EPs and albums."

THE FIRST GIG

When I warmed up for Jon Da Silva at Hacienda I was young and stupid, so I played lot of big tracks back-to-back.

—Sasha

Trying to build a reputation as a DJ can be tiring and frustrating. The hours put into getting a mixtape just so, finding rare gems and hot new tracks at the record stores, and buying turntables you can't really afford can seem like more effort than they're worth. But one day you get that phone call or e-mail from a promoter who wants you to play at their club, and all those doubts go away. Game on!

Beyond the intrinsic rewards, you should expect that first DJing job to be poorly paid—if you don't have to pay for your beer, you'll be lucky—because no club promoter, understandably, is going to pay top dollar for an unknown entity who can't get people in the door. But it's not about the money. A lot of the world's top DJs played for free for a long time, just to get experience and name recognition. Once you've done that first gig successfully, it's going to be a lot easier to get more.

Something else to remember regarding your first gig is not to exploit the guest list. You can ask a promoter to put the name of a friend or two down, but don't think they're going to let your whole crew in for free. That being said, you should get as many people you know to come as possible, even if they have to pay, because you'll be more relaxed if you see friendly faces on the dancefloor, and you'll make a good impression on the promoter and club owner if there are at least a few people dancing wildly.

When picking out the tracks for that first gig, remember that you have one shot to prove that you can do the same thing in a DJ booth that you do in private, so structure your set accordingly. This means balancing the types of music familiar at the venue with your own creativity. What do you want to see when dancing to a DJ you've never seen before? Let the answer to that question influence your song selection and planning. Rather than letting the pressure scare you, let it energize you—this is a chance to show off the skills you've worked so hard to perfect.

Sasha, arguably the first superstar house DJ, went from playing in his bedroom to DJing at the influential Manchester club the Hacienda under the tutelage of resident DJ Jon Da Silva:

> "When I warmed up for Jon Da Silva at Hacienda I was young and stupid, so I played a lot of big tracks back-to-back. I was scared stiff the first time. One time he couldn't make it, so I played a lot of his records. [At home] I had one belt-drive deck and an early Technics deck, and then I saved up the money to get two [Technics] 1200s."

Sasha's experience proves that you can't just play hits back to back, particularly at the start of the night. It's the job of the warmup DJ to get the crowd going, before leaving it to the head-lining act to get the glory. Nic Fanciulli explains how it's done:

> "For a warmup set, you quickly realize that you can't just go out and play all the big tracks, or imitate what you think the headlining DJ will play, or he's going to come on and be pissed off with you, and you'll have lost the chance of making a connection. Everything you do in a warmup set should be done to set up the headlining DJ. If you work hard at it, someone will return the favor for you one day."

Tim Westwood, whose long-running rap show on BBC Radio 1 in the U.K. attracts more than a million listeners each week, got started as a DJ in an unexpected way:

> "I got the opportunity to blast off at this club I worked at. I was a glass collector and it was during the era in the U.K. when this was the first black-owned club in the West End. There were pictures of Muhammad Ali and Diana Ross on the wall—it was definitely a ghetto-fabulous thing. It was one of those after-hours spots, and used to shut at seven or eight in the morning. They used to have a reggae guy by the name of David Brodigan there and working in that environment was just magical. One time David didn't turn up so I got an opportunity to DJ, and when I got on the decks I just loved it."

Miami native DJ Craze considers your attitude behind the decks to be as important as the tracks you play, whether it's your first gig or your thousandth:

"Some of the DJs who are great technically can't rock a crowd because they don't know how to vibe with them. For me, the most important thing about crowd control and keeping the crowd entertained is confidence and projecting a good vibe. You can't be up there looking like you're shook up. You can't be up there seeming timid, because people will know it. Even if you're playing the most amazing song, people aren't going to feel it if you're not feeling it. I have days when I'm just feeling bummed out and I try to fake it but people can see right through me because I'm projecting a bad vibe. Just look confident and have a good time up there."

DJing in front of a crowd for the first few times can be daunting, but, as Craze says, you can't show your nerves or it will adversely affect your performance. If you've put in the regular practice, planned your set (see chapter 5), and shown up early to get comfortable with the venue's equipment, you'll be fine. One technique frequently used by DJs at the Scratch DJ Academy when preparing for a set is to focus your set on an imaginary person in the crowd. What will get them from the bar to the dancefloor and keep them moving when they get there?

THE RESIDENCY

A residency is the most important thing for anyone.

—Steve Lawler

Getting the first gig is great, but your real goal should be to get a callback from a promoter or owner who wants you to become a regular fixture at a venue. For DJs across all genres, that first residency is often the standard by which they'll be judged.

John Digweed was promoting and DJing at parties and raves on the south coast of England in the late '80s and early '90s, and then began to break into clubs. Those early club gigs led to a dream residency at Renaissance in Nottingham that launched his career and catalyzed his long-running partnership with Sasha:

> "In 1992, I was doing Bedrock nights on the south coast and at Heaven in London, but nothing up north. I used to send my mixes to the guys at *Mixmag* because I knew the owner's son. They told me I should send a mix to Renaissance, but when I looked at their flyer I saw Frankie Knuckles, David Morales, and Sasha on the bill. I thought there was no way I'd get a booking there. I sent a mixtape to them anyway, on a Thursday I think, and got a call from Geoff Oakes, the owner, the following Monday, asking me when I could come and play. At the time, the big DJs in the north were Sasha, Graeme Park, and Mike Pickering. A lot of up-and-coming DJs tried to emulate them—same style, same records. Where I lived there weren't massive clubs, and I'd buy the records I liked and mix them in the way I liked, without paying attention to what other people were doing."

Digweed's big break at Renaissance proves that you can't just identify your favorite DJs and imitate them. Even if you demonstrate technical proficiency and a good ear for music, a lack of originality will condemn your mixtape to promoters' trash cans. You should do all you can to learn from the top DJs, but if your sound isn't your own, you could be stuck playing birthday parties for the rest of your life.

After his residencies at Cream and Home, two of the U.K.'s foremost superclubs, Steve Lawler moved on to hosting a weekly event, Harlem Nights, at the End in East London:

"A residency is the most important thing for any DJ. For my residency at Harlem Nights, I'll go in there and play for five or six hours, and those sets I create feed my creativity when I'm on tour. I have a regular crowd; 70 percent of the people there come every week. They all know each other, and they know me so it's a really warm and friendly vibe. When you have a loyal fan base like that, you can experiment musically and take them anywhere you want to go. There's nothing like the feeling of playing to your home audience. A residency teaches you about set-building, record selection, and how to read a crowd, which are three of the main lessons every DJ needs to learn."

Another U.K. DJ who built his career on a residency (in the Red Room of Passion in Coalville, England) is Mark Brown. He explains the unique situation of the club:

"Passion wasn't in a city center, so we didn't have anyone just walking up to it randomly. Everyone who was there wanted to be and made a special effort to come out each week. They backed me as a resident and made me feel welcome every time I played. José Nunez, Roger Sanchez, and Erick Morillo came to DJ at the club and had no idea what I'd play, but I did some different things and got twenty-five hundred people packed into a club in a small English town, so I think they were impressed."

Digweed, who came to prominence around the same time as Brown in the mid-'90s, reveals how he turned a one-off night into a long-running residency that spawned the seminal *Renaissance: The Mix Collection* album and bookings worldwide, and helped to build the reputation of Renaissance as *the* club of its generation:

"Even though I'd been DJing for eight years and putting on big parties, when I played at clubs I was the last DJ on the bill. I knew when I got the call from Renaissance it was my chance to shine, to become a headliner, and that I had to do well. Those opportunities don't come along often, and when they do you have to grab them with both hands. When I'd been playing there for a while there was buzz, and club owners from all over the country started calling asking me to play for them. Geoff [Oakes, Renaissance owner/promoter] told me I could go and play those venues, but that it would dilute my music. He advised me to play only at Renaissance for at least a year, and he was right. If people wanted to hear me play they had to go to Renaissance, and there was something special about that. If you're playing at an amazing club, with an amazing sound system and crowd, you'll shine. Whereas if you play somewhere that doesn't have those things, you'll sound worse and can damage how people perceive you. I was willing to sacrifice a quick buck. I hadn't DJed for that long just to throw it away for the wrong reasons. All I ever wanted to do was be a DJ, so I wasn't in a rush."

Getting a residency is hard enough, but giving the crowd a special experience each time you play so you continue to build your reputation with fans and promoters alike will take you to the next level.

Digweed's DJing partner Sasha went from playing at one seminal club, Shelley's, to another, Renaissance:

"I developed a good relationship with Geoff [Oakes, Renaissance owner/promoter] through Shelley's, which was my first big residency. I hadn't done a residency since I left there, and I told him I missed it. He found a venue in Mansfield and he asked me what I thought. I said 'It's perfect, but it's in the middle of nowhere.' That was why he liked it, because he realized that because of where it was the people that came would be there just for the music. I don't know how they got a license, but we didn't finish till 7:00 A.M. All the other clubs closed at 2:00 or 3:00 A.M., so people came from Leeds, from Manchester, from all over to go to Renaissance for my late-night sessions. It was unique at the time."

On what sets a residency apart, Sasha says:

"Having a great promoter with a vision and a high-quality venue and sound system is important. Most of the best residencies coincide with a musical movement of the time. At Renaissance the sound was just coming out and it fit the room perfectly. It was the same at Twilo—the dark, driving, progressive tracks we played were the right fit for that venue, but when Twilo ended that music didn't sound the same anywhere else."

The next chapter will address the issue of how location affects set-building in more detail.

While a successful residency can help a DJ's career take off, it's not always fun to play at the same venue week after week, particularly if you have a long journey to get there. Nick Warren says:

"Being a resident at Cream was something that I didn't always really enjoy to be frank with you. It was great for me, but then I found playing in the same booth every week slightly tedious, especially with a three-hour drive up from Bristol every week and then a three-hour drive back again. My wife and I had just had a baby at the time, and it was tough going. But it was about building up the sound that you believed in, and even at that stage there was a definite split between DJs like myself and Sasha and the more commercial ones, the people who would play Michael Jackson beats and stuff like that, as opposed to us who were much more serious about our electronic music. We were really pioneering a sound, and that was a very British sound at the time."

As an up-and-coming DJ, you should always be seeking a residency. If you play well that first time, it may be enough to get asked back, or it may take more mixtapes and regular practice to get to a weekly or monthly gig. As with your debut show, you shouldn't be picky about residencies. Whether it's a local bar or lounge or the biggest superclub, we can't overstate the value to a DJ's career of having a regular place to play. A residency anywhere will allow you to hone your skills, overcome anxiety, and learn to read and react to a crowd. And you never know who might be on the dancefloor; it could be the person who will give you your big break.

THE BREAKTHROUGH GIG

Sasha listened to my tape in his car on the way to gigs and asked me to come for a meeting with his agency. I started warming up for him and occasionally playing back-to-back and that's how I built my reputation internationally.

—James Zabiela

Once you've got the residency, you're looking for the breakthrough that will take you to the next level. It could be the residency itself, your first private party, or maybe your own radio show. You have to mix with the right company and aim high to achieve your DJing goals, and there's no limit to how far talent and hard work will take you.

James Zabiela's endeavors on the decks and in mixtape production paid off in 2000, when he won Bedroom Bedlam, an annual mixtape competition run by *Muzik* magazine. The prizes included a set on the BBC Radio 1's *Essential Mix* show, a platform Zabiela used to show off his mastery of using CD decks, samplers, and other technology alongside regular turntables. Another of Zabiela's mixtapes made it into the hands of house club favorite Lee Burridge, who passed it along to his friend, Sasha.

"Sasha listened to my tape in his car on the way to gigs and asked me to come in for a meeting with his agency," Zabiela says. "I started warming up for him in clubs and occasionally playing back-to-back, and that's how I built my reputation internationally. Then I'd go back and play at those clubs on my own, having proved myself, and with Sasha's stamp of approval. He's someone I grew up listening to and he's still on the cutting edge today, so when he says, 'Listen to this guy,' people do. I attribute an enormous amount of my success to him."

Sasha is equally complimentary of his protégé:

> "James is amazing. Making that transition from the bedroom to the club can be very hard, but you have to throw yourself into the deep end like he did. I got James to start warming up for me at these huge clubs, and he handled it brilliantly. A lot of people helped James make the right decisions. His story is a fairytale—he went from being a bedroom DJ to international superstar status. I loved helping someone so young and talented develop his career. His passion for

the music cuts through anything, and he plays the right
sets in the right venues."

Like Zabiela, A-Trak can also credit someone else with giving
him a big break. In 2004, he went from being a turntablism
prodigy to trekking the globe with megastars Kanye West and
Usher: He explains how his big break was coincidental:

> "Kanye's album *The College Drop Out* had just come out
> and he was with John Legend at an in-store promo
> event in London that I was also at. He just came up to
> me and asked me if I'd like to play on his tour. That was
> a huge moment in my career."

Once he signed the deal with West's tour promoter, A-Trak
could have simply gone through the motions, as even his most
basic sets would wow crowds that knew little about turntablism.
Instead, he used the opportunity to learn more about live
performance and to become more controlled as an artist.
"Working with Kanye really taught me also to use my craft and
my skills in just the right doses, and to know how to hold back,"
he says. "To know when it's not time to scratch like crazy when
you're in front of the crowd. There's a time to do a solo and
there's a time to just do things well in a way that's musical."

A-Trak's friend and former Allies co-member DJ Craze explains how he made the transition from being solely a battle DJ to
developing into a versatile performer who can play at any venue,
to any crowd:

> "When I was battling, I sometimes thought, 'This could
> really be my future, this could really pay my bills and
> be the job I've always wanted.' But I was mainly doing it
> for the fun, and for the art, of DJing. It was all about tak-

ing these two records and making them something completely different. And when I started winning all these competitions, I thought, 'Wait, this is still fun, but I could make a career out of it,' and that's when I started to kick in the extra skills and practice and began winning all the world competitions. And then, boom! It happened."

For Los Angeles-based DJ Vice, who often plays with DJ AM and is a regular on the Hollywood celebrity party circuit, it was a radio job that brought him out of obscurity and into the rolodexes of L.A.'s most important club promoters and radio station managers. "When I turned eighteen I got hired by the station that I basically grew up listening to, Hot 106, and that was one of my biggest dreams come true," he says. "At the time I was a bedroom DJ playing in my house, and then I'm suddenly playing on an L.A.-wide radio station that has 1.6 million listeners."

From the time he first started DJing at age eleven to achieving his current status as one of America's most respected club DJs, Vice's passion for DJing has remained strong. It's this enthusiasm that helped him get a radio show and stay relevant and ahead of the game in the ever-expanding DJ scene. But there's no point in devoting your time, energy, and money to DJing if you're not having fun.

LIVING TO DJ, DJING TO LIVE

I was holding down a day job, DJing in Manchester on a Thursday night, and showing up for work the next morning in London, and it got to be too much. So I quit my day job and got an agent. That's when I made the leap to treating it like a profession.

—DJ Yoda

Once you've got a few gigs under your belt, you'll find it more difficult to balance DJing with your main occupation. A lot of people don't quit their day job while moving up the DJ ladder, but eventually you'll have to make a choice about whether to pursue your passion for music full-time—or settle for something else. DJ Yoda says:

> "I got started playing at friends' parties, and then DJed for three years at a hip hop and funk night while at Warwick University. That helped me learn how to read a crowd and how to discover what works and what doesn't. The tapes took off and people knew about me, and I started getting calls from all over to come and play. I started my own night, Spread Love, in London when I got back from university. It became the place all the hip hop heads went to. It was a serious grind, with the promotion as well. I stopped the night because the promoting was too much. You can put twenty-four hours a day into a night and nobody will show up and then do nothing the next week and it'll be full—it was so random. I was networking, getting in touch with DJs I liked, and booking them. I was holding down a day job, but I'd be DJing in Manchester on a Thursday night and showing up for work the next morning in London and it got too much, so I quit my day job and got an agent. That's when I made the leap to treating it like a profession. It was scary, because if I failed I would've wasted a decent day job."

Quitting your job to concentrate on DJing is not a decision to be taken lightly. But if you start getting so many gigs that they're interfering with your current occupation, it is certainly time to consider jumping whatever ship you're on to become a pro DJ.

Like Yoda, Matt Black also started out promoting his own nights:

> "Jon [More, his partner in Coldcut] and I came together in London in the mid-'80s when the London warehouse scene was in effect. That was a really crucial period because it was a new thing for people of all backgrounds and races to party together and listen to different types of music together. We couldn't get into conventional clubs in the West End because they were about selling expensive drinks to rich people. We started doing our own parties where we'd take over a space or a warehouse or an empty building and do parties there.

If you're considering making the move to becoming a full-time DJ, saving up enough money to cover slow periods in the DJing calendar is a good idea: you can expect the winter holiday season and the summer to be the busiest times. Most DJs pack as many gigs into their peak-season schedules as they can, and then focus on practicing, mixing albums, production, and updating their Web sites during the slower months. In addition to booking gigs, agents can advise you how to best promote yourself throughout the year. Getting an established agent, or at least one that comes with good recommendations from people you trust, is a must for anyone wanting to DJ full-time.

THE BUSINESS OF DJING

There's only so much you can do on your own. Finding a manager is like finding a wife. They have to listen to you, be honest, be frank, and make the impossible possible.

—Harry "Choo Choo" Romero

There comes a time in the career of a DJ when the music begins to take a backseat to the necessities of booking gigs, negotiating record deals, and setting up travel agendas. That's when you need a hired gun.

Harry "Choo Choo" Romero, sees the agent or manager as a necessary part of a successful DJ's career:

> "It's a decision that's brought to your attention, a simple catch-22. No one wants to be your manager or agent until you're successful. But how do you get successful without a manager or an agent? It just gets to the stage where you need to be left to be creative in the studio and let somebody else take care of all the business side of it, decide on where you're going and how much you get paid. Hiring a manager is a big deal. My head hit the ceiling in terms of growth, and I went with X Mix Productions; they manage Felix Da Housecat, Armand Van Helden, and DJ Sneak. They enabled me to develop as an artist."

Romero believes that agents and managers can be of particular value when DJs start dealing with record companies, and he's been on both sides of that particular fence. "The label is going to try and take half the money right off the bat, try to take too much of the pie," he says. "As a young, upcoming artist you might think they won't back your project unless you let them do that, but that's not the case. I gave up a lot of my publishing rights through the years, and it taught me something. Do I make that mistake now? Hell no. You've got to get the paperwork in order and learn the business side. It's 60 [percent] business, 40 [percent] music."

Talk to the other DJs you know, as well as club owners and promoters, to get recommendations for agents who will do their best on your behalf. Or, find out who represents your favorite DJs. An agent's commission is typically between 10 and 20 percent, so avoid anyone who charges more than that. The best agents will gladly show you their DJ roster, and will also be able to talk in detail about their relationships with club promoters and record labels. To learn more about the DJ-agent relationship, we talked to Nic Fanciulli, who with James Zabiela released the landmark house compilation One+One in 2006:

> "Getting a good agent who knows the business and has connections with club promoters and the record labels is essential. While there is that community aspect, it's a competitive market with hundreds of DJs fighting to get into clubs like Womb [in Tokyo] and Zouk [Singapore], and you need the agent to be that missing piece for you—your connection with the clubs. To stay ahead you need to focus on your craft, not spend five hours a day on the phone with promoters. *That's* why the agent is so important."

Just as you shouldn't play at a big club before you're ready, Fanciulli believes you shouldn't rush into hiring representation:

> "You shouldn't force trying to get an agent—they're not going to sign you if you're not ready or are just begging for it. If you've got four or five regular gigs a month, it might be the right time to get an agent and think about DJing full-time."

Once your agent starts coming through with enough gigs to give you financial security, the next step is to employ people to handle other aspects of your career. The more successful a DJ is, the more his or her time is compressed. To enable you to remain solely focused on honing your craft, you will need someone else to handle travel arrangements, negotiate with record labels, and deal with the other day-to-day minutiae of life as a professional. "I employ eight people, including a PR rep, manager, two agents, and an engineer/co-producer," says Steve Lawler, who has come a long way from earning a hundred bucks for a week's worth of gigs. "They earn money from my DJing, and I'm happy to be both supporting them and doing something that will keep this music relevant when I'm finished with it."

PERKS OF THE JOB

I get free records and I don't pay for equipment anymore.
— Grand Wizard Theodore

Finding success as a DJ usually takes years of hard work, but for those select few spinners who have achieved it, the grind was well worth it. The DJs we've interviewed cite unlimited promotional tracks, worldwide travel, and free equipment as some of the main material rewards (to say nothing of the fees — in some cases these are in excess of ten thousand dollars a night).

"I try to travel business class because my schedule is so hectic during the week that I need to fly in comfort," says Mark Brown. "I stay in nice hotels so that I can relax for a little while between gigs."

Some DJs create movie soundtracks, while others are fortunate enough to be featured on screen. Old school hip hop legends like Herc, Caz, Bambaataa, and Flash had spots in '80s releases like *Wild Style* and *Style Wars,* and DJs are still in demand for documentaries and feature films today. The acclaimed documentary *Scratch* gave some other deserving DJs their time in the limelight. Z-Trip explains:

"Being part of *Scratch* was one of the most gratifying experiences in my career. When I first saw the movie my career was solidified and validated. All the years of hard work culminated in that moment. It was about having the respect of Flash, Bambaataa, and the other elders from the hip hop scene who were also in the movie. The fact that they acknowledged me means everything."

There are also more tangible rewards to be had for the top DJs. "It's great to be in magazines, to do interviews, and to get free stuff," says Grand Wizard Theodore. "I get free records and I don't pay for equipment anymore because I get sent turntables, needles, CD players, everything I need."

But whatever equipment, music, and other material rewards DJs receive, the intrinsic rewards have even greater worth. Theodore continues:

"I get to see things that most people don't. There are people from all backgrounds, ethnicities, and circumstances together under one roof, grooving to one sound with the aim of having a good time. Seeing that gives me the best feeling."

DJ Craze is equally satisfied with the external and internal rewards of being a world-renowned DJ:

"DJing is the greatest job because you get paid to spin music. I would do this for free because it's so much fun. You get paid to go all over the world to play the music you like. Being able to make a living through music is the best thing in the world."

For Steve Lawler, an emotional and musical connection with his fans is the ultimate reward:

> "The best part of being a professional DJ is knowing I have an audience. There's something unique and special about playing to a crowd that meets you at your musical level and responds to you emotionally. When a club is packed with people who've come to hear me DJ I feel honored."

MAKE THE CONNECTION

I travel my ass off and am always in different cities. There's a misconception that it's all fun and partying and being around cool people.

—DJ Vice

The lives of big-name DJs are completely oriented around music. Pro DJs have "made it" in the sense that they are paid large sums of money to DJ, have loyal fans, and are respected by their peers, but they also retain the same desire and hunger they had when they were playing to a dozen people in a tiny local bar, knowing that there are thousands of other DJs willing to replace them if they put a foot wrong. While there are many perks for the top DJs, most of them don't see what they do as glamorous, but rather as a vocation that they're happy to devote their lives to, despite its ups and downs.

We asked DJ Craze to take us through a typical day in his life:

> "An average day at my house in Miami goes like this: I wake up around 7:00 A.M. I take my daughter to school, come back. Then I check out my MySpace page, read e-mails, check out what's new, what music is there on

the blogs, download it if I like it, see how I can fit it into my sets. The old digging at record shops is now looking for MP3s online, and that's what I do. I spend an hour or two arranging my playlists, just going through music, reviewing what I've been playing on Serato. Then, after an hour or two of that I go to my studio, practice for a little bit. I've got two [Technics] 1200s, a Rane 57 mixer, and a MacBook Pro. I go in there and just mess around with mixes, and then I just start making my beats. That's my day. I just try to cre-ate. If I get bored of working on dope mixes, I'll just work on a beat. If I get bored I work on other music projects."

Like Craze, Mark Brown is also an early riser. "I get up at seven-thirty and go into my office studio," he says. "I do some production, maybe some remixes, and then I talk to agents about gig requests and press commitments. I might work with one of the guys on our label for a while. Then on the weekend I'm out and about DJing. I've done Australia for two weeks, America for two weeks, and then back to England."

Another key part of most DJs' daily routines is communicat-ing with their peers. "Even though the record store fraternity has all but disappeared, there's still a community aspect to DJing," says Pete Tong. "I bumped into Dave Seaman in an air-port in Australia and me, him, and [Australian DJ] Anthony Pappa went to a restaurant and were just buzzing MP3s back and forth between one anothers' laptops. I can hardly remember what we did before computers."

Busy schedules and the decline of the record store culture means less face-to-face interaction between DJs. Most still maintain the friendships they forged early on, whether it's meet-ing up when they're in one another's hometowns, or staying connected online. Like Tong, and most of the DJs we've spoken to, British house maestro Tom Middleton also uses a laptop as a means of sharing tracks and tips with fellow DJs, both in person and online.

"[Superstar DJ] Danny Howells and I have a great virtual rapport—we're online together a lot," Middleton says. "He has great taste in music, and we're always swapping remixes and productions we've done. My iChat is a primary source for great new music. It comes from DJs—tastemakers who have good sets of musical ears. There's so much music now that DJing is about filtering, so you need contacts you trust to recommend good tracks. Certain DJs will tell me about a track and I'll go to the Beatport site and buy it without even listening to it. I take a laptop and hard drive with me when I travel, and when I meet up with other DJs we swap USB sticks full of tracks."

THE GRAFT BEHIND THE GLAMOUR

"Before the Internet the only way to stay in touch would be to bump into somebody at the airport en route to a gig, or in a record shop," says Lars Sandberg (aka Funk D'Void).

> "The Internet is now the only way I interact with my DJ friends. All the DJs are much more closely connected than before. It's healthy for the growth and expanding nature of dance music and it's constantly morphing and re-designing itself because of it."

"There are ten or eleven DJs whom I'm in touch with by instant messaging and e-mail several times a week," says Fanciulli. "Because our lifestyles are so hectic we can go months without seeing each other, but when we meet up in Ibiza or wherever for a few hours between gigs it's just like old times."

"I stay in touch with my DJ friends in other cities and countries through instant messenger, Skype, or in online DJ communities," says Z-Trip. "The majority of music comes to me via e-mail with a download link or with people catching me on iChat at the right time. I send a lot of music on to other DJs."

DJing for a living sure beats being chained to a desk, but it's not all glitz and glamour. Even the richest, most respected, most recognizable DJs have days when they consider packing it in and getting the "normal" job that doubters told them they needed before they made it big. "I have a wife and kid and spending time away from them sucks," says DJ Craze. "When I was younger it was different. It was like, 'Let's go party!' But now it's like, 'Right, let's party and then I want to go home.' So the traveling sucks, but when I'm home and I'm going to clubs with my girl, it's all good."

Some DJs have changed their schedules to minimize traveling, despite the hit their bank balances take. "There is a whole other side to it that people don't see," says DJ Vice. "I travel my ass off and am always in different cities. There's a misconception that it's all fun and partying and being around cool people. A lot of people don't see the hustle that all of us put into it. In just the next few days, I'm across the whole country, you know? So I think that is one of the biggest misconceptions. I always hear like, 'Oh man, you know, you have it great,' and I'm like, 'Yeah, of course I do, 'cause I do what I love,' but I also go nonstop with what I do. There's no downtime. I live out of my suitcase."

Philadelphia-based DJ/producer Josh Wink had one of the biggest hits in house music history with the 1995 acid-house dancefloor filler "Higher State of Consciousness." "I get countless people coming up to me saying how much the track means to them," Wink says. "It's nice to have made a piece of music that helped define the sound of an era—it opened a lot of doors for me. Fatboy Slim told me that the track made it easier for people like him to break house music into the mainstream. But I didn't like the press, being recognized, or all the trappings of success. So now, with Ovum [his record label], I just do my own thing. I can still have the musical integrity of not having to make all my stuff sound like 'Higher State.'"

Wink is the epitome of the pro DJs we talked to for this book—someone who cares more about the creativity and artistic merit of music than about the material gain that success brings.

The top tier of DJs do make a lot of money, but they have a lifelong dedication to their art and are driven by the intrinsic reward of continuous improvement, of being part of a musical fraternity, and of advancing an art form. "There's no easy way to become a great DJ," Z-Trip says. "Some people may be able to get to the big residency or record deal early, but just because you're holding a prize doesn't mean you've truly won. The guys who are respected within the scene and whose careers have stood the test of time took the long road and paid their dues. They've given up sleep, money, girlfriends, jobs—whatever it took. The best DJs have made music their entire lives."

STAYING AHEAD OF THE GAME

I'll be all over the U.K. and I'll go places where acts don't go and other DJs don't go. I want to be out there deep, to stay relevant and stay connected, and to stay humble.

—Tim Westwood

It's a common misconception that when a person becomes famous, the work ceases and the checks just roll in. This isn't true for movie stars or athletes, and it isn't true for the world's best-known DJs. According to Westwood, the hustle never stops.

> "You've got to be hitting people on every level to get their attention and to create some momentum, and being a club and radio DJ just isn't enough. You gotta be on YouTube, you gotta be on Facebook, you gotta be puttin' out mix-tapes, you gotta be trying to get a TV jump-off. It's not enough just to be out there doing your thing. Those days are gone. It's not enough just to be hot on the radio, those days are over. . . . You gotta be in the club winning. You've got to be on the radio ripping it down and then on all these other platforms with a presence, so each of these things feeds into the rest."

Putting in long hours is as important as talent, whether you're earning a six-figure income or just starting out. Two to three hours of practice a day may sound like a lot, but if you're serious about DJing, it's a must; whether that's scratching or beat matching. If you're getting a mix CD ready for a club promoter or agent, it should not leave your hands until you feel it's perfect. If it takes three weeks instead of the three hours you'd originally planned, so be it. The results will be worth it. If your skills are improving, you're on the right track. "It's just that work ethic, to be honest," Westwood says. "You're in clubs in the evening and during the day you've got to focus on other things that will promote you. My biggest influence was Funkmaster Flex, who has elevated the whole DJ game. Guys get very competitive, especially in this country, but at the end of the day we're all in the same situation: We don't own radio stations so we can lose our jobs at any time. We don't own the clubs so any minute you can get sacked from them."

Playing at other people's gigs is all well and good, but being en-trepreneurial can take your career as a DJ to new heights if you're willing to take a few risks. Westwood says:

> "My advice is to really empower yourself as much as possible with what you do so you can put your own nights on. We don't make any money out of ours but we'll have five thousand people turn up at Ministry of Sound and it will be a legendary night, and we're really having an impact on young people. People are so busy and there are so many distractions that you've got to be out there trying to survive in this game. In those early days, just being on the radio playing hip hop was enough—it was extreme, there were only a few other guys doing it. But now, in this competitive age, you've gotta be out there strong."

Whether you're being paid in Heineken or making ten grand a night, you can't rest easy in the DJ business. DJs are part of a fraternity, but they are also competing against each other. Most DJs are willing to offer advice, but they also have to pay the bills. There is always someone ready and eager to outwork you, outthink you, and outplay you so they can slide into your spot. Once you've got success you've got to fight to keep it. That doesn't mean isolating yourself from other DJs, but rather realizing that you need to hone your DJ and business skills to stay ahead.

THE GIGS—SPECIAL EVENTS

Special events are a great way to tap into corporate money, hang out with peers, and most importantly be part of genre- and culture-shaping events. We've chosen a few from the past and the present that any self-respecting DJ or music enthusiast should know about.

DMC World Mixing Championships (www.dmcdjchamps.com)

The same company that publishes seminal British house magazine *Mixmag* founded the DMC World Mixing Championships in 1985 to give battle DJs an event that would bring them more acclaim. A-Trak, Craze, Cash Money, and other winners of the event have gone on to tour the world and to work with top-selling artists in multiple genres. There is now a team mixing championship, which has been won by the likes of the Scratch Perverts, the Allies, and C2C, the four-time winners from France. DMC inspired the creation of several similar contests that attract turntablists from across the globe, including Skratchcon and tournaments held by the International Turntablist Federation (ITF). Turntablists still make up the core of the audience, but with the growing profile of former winners like A-Trak and Craze, there's an increasingly diverse crowd.

The Love Parade (www.loveparade.com)

The first Love Parade was held in Berlin four months before the Berlin Wall came down in 1989 as a political demonstration calling for worldwide peace to be achieved through music. Only one hundred and fifty people showed up, but soon the organizers' emphasis shifted to making Love Parade a purely musical event, and by 1997 more than a million people from all over the world were descending upon the German capital each July to hear up to two hundred and fifty DJs from all genres play, and to soak up the vibrant carnival-like atmosphere. The closing hours of the Love Parade (known as the *Abschlusskundgebung*—try saying that ten times fast) feature back-to-back, thirty-minute sets from many of the world's top house DJs, and have included landmark performances by Tiesto, Sven Vath, and hometown hero Paul Van Dyk. There are spin-offs in Cape Town, Sydney, Tel Aviv, and beyond; San Francisco has staged three Love Parades to date.

Rock the Bells (www.guerillaunion.com/rockthebells)

The first Rock the Bells event was held in San Bernadino, California, in 2004, where the Wu-Tang Clan reunited. The same year, another Rock the Bells, this time in Anaheim, featured the newly reunited A Tribe Called Quest. The 2005 lineup featured DJ Muggs from Cypress Hill, Cut Chemist, and Q-Bert. The following year, DJ Big Whiz, Zion I, and Mos Def appeared. The 2007 Rock The Bells event was a tour that stopped in New York, San Bernadino, and San Francisco—Cypress Hill, The Roots, Rage Against the Machine, and Public Enemy headlined.

The Big Beach Boutique (www.myspace.com/fatboyslim)

Fatboy Slim DJed in front of a few thousand revelers on Brighton Beach, England, in 2001, at an event he dubbed The Big Beach Boutique. In 2002, sixty thousand people were expected to attend BBB2, but an estimated quarter million showed up, bringing the sleepy seaside town to a standstill for the biggest outdoor party in British history. Two years later, Slim played to around three hundred thousand people on Rio de Janeiro's Flamengo Beach. The third Brighton-based BBB3 event was held on New Year's Day 2007, with more than twenty thousand people braving the cold to hear Slim and his invited guests.

Coachella (www.coachella.com)

The first official Coachella Valley Music and Arts Festival was held in Empire Polo Fields in Indio, California, in 1999. DJs including Tom Rowland and Ed Simons from the Chemical Brothers, DJ Shadow Nightmares on Wax also played the inaugural event, and since then Cut Chemist, Paul Oakenfold, Pete Tong, Daft Punk, and many other house and hip hop DJs have been featured on Coachella lineups. The festival draws a crowd of more than twenty-five thousand to the desert each summer.

Miami Winter Music Conference
(www.wintermusicconference.com)

The Winter Music Conference has been held in Miami since 1975. It was originally a meeting of music professionals to hold seminars on new technology, share music, and cover business topics such as artist management and contracts. While sessions on these topics are still held, the event has become more about music fans, with every club and bar in South Beach hosting DJ events for one week each March. Running concurrently with all the other parties is the Ultra Music Festival, the biggest dance music concert in the United States, with more than one hundred and seventy-five DJs and live acts performing for over fifty thousand people.

Creamfields (www.creamfields.com)

Organized by the promoters of Liverpool superclub Cream, the Creamfields festival celebrated its tenth anniversary in 2008. The first event was held in a field outside Winchester, England, and featured Run-D.M.C. and Primal Scream alongside the world's top house DJs. Creamfields features eight to ten separate tents or outdoor stages, each corresponding to a different genre including house, drum & bass, and techno. The festival has now been staged in fifteen countries, including the United States, Argentina, and Portugal, attracting more than twenty-five thousand people in each location.

Lollapalooza (www.lollapalooza.com)

The inaugural Lollapalooza was held in 1991 in two California locations. Originally a rock festival, the event now welcomes acts from all musical genres. Muggs from Cypress Hill was the first DJ to play at the festival, appearing alongside his bandmates in 1992. Since then, many DJs, including Z-Trip, DJ Rashida, and Derrick Carter, have played alongside the biggest names in rock and indie music. Turntablists Craze and Klever performed acclaimed sets in 2007. The crowd at Lollapalooza is the most diverse you'll find at any U.S. festival, thanks to the wide range of DJs and acts featured.

THE TRAVEL

Once you've traveled outside your neighborhood to play, you start to tune your ear to what people want.

—Grandmaster Flash

For big-name DJs, crisscrossing the planet is the norm. When summer rolls around, Pete Tong, Carl Cox, and the rest of the British house music vanguard spend as much time in the clubs of Ibiza as they do in the U.K., as the entire island becomes awash with clubbers from May until September. They are joined by American DJ luminaries such as Roger Sanchez, Erick Morillo, and Danny Tenaglia, who all have residencies on the island.

But for the elite of the DJ world, travel is not merely a seasonal thing—it's a constant part of life. For pioneering techno DJ Richie Hawtin, travel is a balancing act throughout the year:

"Being a DJ is about being an entertainer, so while I may want to take a few weeks off, those people may be ready to party, so it's about when it's the right moment for them to enjoy what I do. That's why I'm out on the road so much. You have to balance being away for work and being closer to home. If I have a new album I may want to be away for six weeks to promote it and do interviews, whereas at other times, say if I'm recording the next album, I won't want to be away for more than a few days at a time."

Traveling is a two-way exchange for DJs. It allows them to spread their sounds and reputations across the world, but it also exposes them to new cultures, new musical genres, and new trends that they can bring back to their homelands. In this sense, travel is a way for DJs to stay on the cutting edge as a tastemaker, and provides inspiration for the continual musical evolution that is necessary to maintain a long and prosperous career.

In the early days of the house scene, DJs stayed close to home to build up loyal followings at local clubs and raves, and if they did travel to play it was only domestically. But when house music exploded, British spinners began to rack up frequent flyer miles. Pete Tong says:

> "The reputation of the elite DJs spread outside of England and that enabled them to travel more. Carl Cox was so well known in Scotland and England that people either loved or hated his music, so he had to travel to places like Spain and Germany where his music was popular. He was revered there and could play without the prejudice he faced in the U.K. The U.S. got popular and Oakenfold and Sasha and Digweed took advantage of that."

Sasha was one of the first U.K.-based house DJs to venture outside of Europe to play:

> "The turning point for me was being on the cover of *Mix-mag*. At the time, I just had gigs scheduled in England, and then I got an offer to play in Australia, which blew my mind. I was the first U.K.-based DJ to play there and it was amazing to be DJing on the other side of the world as a twenty-year-old. The travel was the most exciting part of it for me, the chance for us to spread our sound globally. John [Digweed] and I would do two-week tours

in America, to places such as Orlando, Miami, L.A., and San Francisco, and then eventually we got invited to play at Twilo in New York. The first couple of gigs into our residency there we played complex "trancey" records that we realized didn't sound right. Then we moved into playing more stripped-down trance tracks for a while and they sounded great in there. You have to be able to read the room. We'd do these epic twelve-hour sets at Twilo, and then I'd play once a month with Lee [Burridge] at Fabric in London. That was the most well-balanced I've ever been musically, as I was working with the best, most influential DJs who played completely different styles."

More recently, Sasha re-embraced international travel to escape the once-struggling London house scene. "I had to get out of London because there was a time around 2001 when the scene was going down and everyone there just accepted it," he says. "They were wrong though, because there were amazing opportunities in Eastern Europe and elsewhere. John and I would go to Japan and South America. We'd play in front of ten thousand people in Buenos Aires while people back home were saying house was dead."

Tong concurs, and believes that new, emerging technologies helped DJs emerge out from the post-2000 doldrums, enabling them to travel more and boost their profiles, and paychecks, abroad. "The next real boom in international travel was in 2000, when the bubble burst," he says. "Major labels were pulling funding, magazines and superclubs were closing. The Internet saved electronic music's arse really, because DJs could spread their message far and wide very quickly. There was a whole middle tier of U.K. and foreign DJs, not just the elite few, who began to travel. Anyone who was making music could travel anywhere to DJ."

Tom Middleton, who plays in dozens of countries each year, has a few tips for DJs who travel:

> "I take pictures of the crowd and put them on MySpace to connect people. When I'm going to countries such as Russia or Japan I print out a cheat sheet with a few phrases so I can communicate with the crowds, and that makes all the difference."

Unlike Sasha and Tong, DJ AM mostly plays in the United States, but his schedule is no less demanding than his colleagues who fly overseas regularly. While he tries to be at LAX, his club in Los Angeles, at least once a week, AM spends more time than he'd like waiting in boarding lines.

> "I take an average of five flights a week and I'm sick of flying, but it's worth it because I still love DJing. Even if I've taken a ten-hour flight and I'm dead tired, within the first five minutes of my next set I'm wide awake. I recently told my manager that I will not fly on Sunday, Monday, or Tuesday any more, because it's just too much. I'll work, I just won't travel on those days. I usually play at clubs from Tuesday or Wednesday through Saturday. Before I made that decision, it could be Tuesday in Detroit, Wednesday in Chicago, Thursday in New York or Miami, Friday in Vegas, and Saturday in Sacramento or San Francisco, and then back at LAX on Sunday."

Being a pro DJ is hard work, but who wouldn't want to devote their time to listening to, playing, and producing the tracks they love, and having the pleasure of connecting fans worldwide through music?

SIX

THE INFLUENCE *of the* DJ

You go to Japan and there are billboards with someone scratching, you look on commercials and there's a DJ, the video games coming out have DJs in them, the clubs; everything is DJ-oriented. —DJ Q-Bert

The culture of the DJ extends as far back as man has made music. Because, at the root of it all, a DJ is someone who brings other people together with music—who rallies those around them into a collective state of which he or she is overseer and director, and this, of course, is something many people aspire to. But many people want to be led, too. The Pied Piper was a DJ of sorts, albeit a creepy one, but, he seemed just as happy as those who danced their way happily into that mountain: people want to dance as much as some people want to make them do so. The DJ, as a result, has stayed at the center of a vast sphere of influence that ripples out from the booth across all aspects of popular culture—whether it's music, with rock bands and pop artists recruiting a DJ to amp-up their own sound or, sometimes, credibility; a gallery or an artist employing a DJ at an opening or exhibition; a fashion designer employing the services of a DJ rather than prerecorded music at a runway show; hoteliers installing turntables in their lobbies and restaurants. The Internet has also eradicated any limits the extension of a DJs brand might have had in the past, and DJs today are able to turn up in places most people have never heard of and still perform in front of a packed club thanks to a message board or blog on their Web site.

As we've seen, the interest in DJ culture reached something of an apex in the early '90s as the first superstar DJs, including Sasha, Oakenfold, and Carl Cox began gracing magazine covers and becoming familiar names outside of the clubs. Now it is peaking again, with DJs popping up in the most unlikely of places, whether it's in a video game or on the 2008 MTV VMAs, where DJ AM was literally the house band (the 2007 VMAs enlisted the talents of Mark Ronson). In this chapter we'll trace some of the key moments in the evolution of the DJ and its impact on all aspects of pop culture.

Music has always been a catalyst for subcultures: punks, mods, rockers, hippies, and the myriad other groups of people that identified themselves with a particular music scene. DJ culture, though, far transcends the parameters of the music the DJs are playing and here we're going to take a look at how, and why, that is.

DJ AS ENTERTAINER

As the superstar DJs emerged in the nineties, a new era of their craft was born. Gradually, people began going to clubs not because they liked the crowd or the atmosphere, but on the basis of whose name was on the bill that night. And while the DJ had always enjoyed some level of influence over clubbers while they were on the dancefloor, now they became celebrities in their own right. Their names were plastered on billboards, their faces

were on CD and magazine covers, and people began to identify
with them rather than just the music they were playing. Rather
than saying "I like trance" to a friend you might say, "I like Paul
Oakenfold" or "I like Paul van Dyk." Promoters, naturally,
jumped on the bandwagon and, particularly for special, one-off
events would try and one-up each other in composing "dream
lineups" of DJs who, in turn, began charging more and more
money to play. This, of course, just served to propel them to new
heights in the minds of the public and increased the distance between the audience and the DJ. There was a time when DJs
would finish a set and then go and dance their asses off on the
dancefloor. In the '90s, they were being whisked out of a back-
door and, often, to a first class seat on a plane or to a five-star
hotel. Clubs began being designed around this new beast—DJ
booths were elevated and expanded, and the lights designed to
focus on them as much as the dancefloor.

"If you look at pictures of any of the big guys now, the audience are always facing them," says Tony McGuinness, one third
of the globe-trotting trance trio, Above & Beyond, and a man
who, with his compatriots Jonathan "Jono" Grant and Paavo Sil-
jamäki, can claim the distinction of playing to a larger crowd
than any other DJ alive—an astonishing one million people, on a
beach in Rio, on New Year's Eve 2007. "When I used to go clubbing, I would be facing the nearest pretty girl, that's what I went
for," he continues. "But that doesn't happen now. There's a
whole room of people all facing one direction and they're all
looking for one thing and that's a performance from the DJ."
Last year, we were in the DJ booth of the main room with Above
& Beyond at Pacha in New York—it's about ten feet above the
dancefloor, and centrally located in the room. Sure enough, for
three hours, barely anyone in the room looked anywhere else
than at them as they held court, dropping melodic trance and often dancing around the space. For McGuinness, the treatment

of DJs today represents a transformation in the attitudes of clubgoers. "I never really wanted to be a DJ," he says, "because when I went clubbing the dancefloor area of the room was full of people having a fantastic time, and if I did happen to glance up to see what the DJ was doing, he looked like he was working pretty hard and not really enjoying it that much. There wasn't as much audience interaction with the DJ as there is now."

It's safe to say that McGuinness is quite happy where he is now, however, traveling the world and playing to packed clubs from Estonia to Uruguay. But DJs like McGuinness have not gotten to where they are today by resting on their laurels.

"If you look at the first wave of superstar DJs in the late '80s and early '90s most of them were playing other people's records, from vinyl," he goes on. "But now the formats are changing and most of the big DJs are producers as well. So, they're still playing other people's records but they have gained their reputations through their own productions, and whether it's Tiesto with his remix of "Silence," Paul van Dyk with his remix of "For An Angel," or us, what DJs have turned into is a kind of live incarnation of a studio artist. I'm not really sure that the original wave of superstar DJs—people who still play other people's records—is a phenomenon that is still with us. Increasingly, when you go and see a DJ play, what you get is a live experience, and with laptops you're able to change the nature of what you're playing as it's happening."

And that's the thing: while there are people that attack the popular DJs as commercializing their sound, they are where they are for a reason—in almost all cases, talent. "The term 'superstar DJ' is just that—a media term," says Paul Oakenfold, who should know—"just like how there used to be models and now there are 'supermodels.' [The label] didn't change anything for me because I'd been in the scene for years and was already successful. We were doing a Spectrum night on a Monday [started in 1987] and in just a few weeks the crowd was up to three thousand, so I was already playing to big crowds and getting booked to go abroad. I'd done remixes at that point for U2 and the Cure and a lot of production. It didn't change how seriously I took DJing or how professional I was in my approach."

When Oakenfold DJs he plays a lot of his own productions because the fans expect it, and it's the same with most of the most successful DJs today. "Nowadays going to see a big-name DJ is akin to seeing, say, Thom Yorke DJing and playing loads of Radiohead records among a bunch of other stuff he likes," says McGuiness. "If he didn't play 'Creep,' you'd be very upset because that's what you want: to be in a room full of people who love that music and, certainly in our case, want to sing along."

In the uppermost strata of the DJ world, just playing the same records as everyone else in your genre isn't enough anymore: "People will accuse us of just playing other people's music, but that's not true anymore," Oakenfold says. "We're creating music, and it's changing the perception of what a DJ does."

DO IT YOURSELF

When a DJ makes a track, they're not just adding to their own repetoire, they are spreading the essence of DJ culture further. When a DJ's tune breaks into the singles chart, or gets airplay on the radio, more people are likely to go see them play and so the community keeps getting built. Says Nic Fanciulli:

> "I started off as a DJ and then got into production later. Now though, it's the other way around. The days of a DJ just being a DJ are gone—you need production skills to back up your DJing. A well-produced track is

like a high-quality business card for a young DJ—it makes a great first impression. If you want to get into music production buy Cubase or Ableton and the tutorial books for them, and get online to look at the hundreds of music production forums that are out there. Then just start experimenting until you get the hang of it. It's not a science. You just need to get used to the tools and get in touch with your own unique style."

The DJ as a producer is definitely one of the main reasons that they have achieved the fame they have. "DJs have truly become pop stars," says Oakenfold. "Roger Sanchez had a number one single in the U.K. [Another Chance in 2001] and it was great, it also enables DJs to open for credible and big-name bands and musicians." As he says this, Oakenfold is preparing to take the stage in London in support of Madonna on her world tour (2008–2009). "All the big pop stars want some of that DJ cool factor to rub off on them," says Fanciulli.

Above & Beyond, who used to make a lot of money remixing other artists but have since concentrated on their own productions, have also had experience working with Madonna. In 2001 they remixed the song "What it Feels Like for a Girl" and it was the remix, rather than the original that Madonna (and her husband at the time, Guy Ritchie) decided to make the video for the single to. It was the first and (to date) last time she ever did that. "When we were doing the Madonna remix it was possible for a DJ or producer to get say £90,000 ($170,000) advance from a record company for a remix," says McGuiness. "Madonna saw us as the latest new thing, and for her it was always about trying to get that so she used us," he says. "It certainly did us a lot of good in terms of our profile, but for the amount of time you spend on a remix you might as well do your own track. We've found it rewarding artistically to concentrate on our own music."

Lars Sandberg, aka Funk D'Void, says simply: "I honestly think you need to have some productions out there in order to turn pro."

"Nowadays, if you're a young DJ, you're almost better off working on a track and getting DJs to play it," says John Digweed. "People want to book you if your records are being played by other DJs."

"The record industry is still going to have whoever's hot as a DJ remix their artists because they want to appeal to the broadest fan base possible," says Oakenfold. "Even though CD sales are down it's still about making money for the labels. We're not getting paid as much to do remixes now because of the sales drop-off, but there is still demand. The main reason I got this Madonna gig [as her tour DJ] was because they liked the last remix I did for her, and the U.S. radio stations played my mix instead of the single or album version." He summarizes succinctly: "If you're a young DJ starting out, you need to know your way around a recording studio."

BUILDING THE BRAND

As the spotlight has turned on them so the DJs have upped their game. McGuinness explains:

> "The emphasis is now on the DJ and his performance as the leader of the dance. This is an idea that goes back to prehistoric times; there's always been a figure in society who leads a mass dance. For me now, it has become much more of a performance."

Paul Oakenfold, a man who is used to being a focal point, says "Certain DJs command attention with their presence. Someone has to lead and it's the DJ. People look to the DJ as an entertainer and an educator."

With the profile of DJs increasing, so has their scope. "When I started out, the DJ was just another employee of the club," says Stéphane Pompougnac, the resident at Paris's famous Hotel Costes. "Back then, it was a full-time job, but now DJs are invited just once a week or for special events." Pompougnac's is an interesting case: he can be credited with starting the trend of lounge music on the back of his sets at the glitzy hotel. Pompougnac was one of the first DJs to play in a hotel regularly, a position that further extended the DJ's influence. By playing outside a club, he exposed a whole new clientele to his sun-drenched, deep house sound and, after a number of requests, he suggested to his boss at the glitzy Hotel Costes that he put a mix CD together as a "souvenir" for guests. That was in 2002, now the Costes mix series is on its eleventh (at press time) installment, is available all over the world, and Pompougnac is a common fixture at fashion events and runway shows. Now barely has a boutique hotel opened than it makes a mix CD bearing its name.

It's an interesting situation—as much as DJs such as Pompougnac have managed to maintain their integrity and sound, while reaping the benefits of an unbelievably popular franchise; other DJs, and other establishments don't have the same concerns. Rather, they see it as a money-making opportunity to be taken advantage of whenever, and wherever, possible. The DJ in the hospitality industry is one thing, but the lesson of Costes taught people around the world that there was serious money to be made not just from playing records, which is one thing, but from marketing the particular brand of cool that a DJ can lend to an endeavor. Lars Sandberg, better known as groundbreaking DJ and producer Funk D'Void, is none too happy about it:

"Today, you see DJs in all forms of advertising, movies,
and marketing," he says. "The only downside that I can
see is that as an art form it has been diluted through
mass-marketing and for me that has affected the image
of the DJ, and the quality of the music has suffered because of it. DJing in a fashion show and DJing in a club
are at complete opposite ends of the spectrum."

It's understandable that Sandberg, a pioneer of underground
electronic music, makes this distinction so clearly, but there are
DJs, like Gildas Loaëc of Paris-based record label, DJ partnership,
and fashion label Kitsuné, who get it spectacularly right. Kitsuné
(without the accent it means "fox" in Japanese), is a staple of the
current wave of electro disco-influenced house that has always been
big in Paris (think Daft Punk) and has, in the last few years, spread
around the world. Loaëc and his partner, Masaya Kuroki, have qui-
etly spearheaded this movement—holding down a monthly residency in Japan and another in Paris (more recently, they have taken
on a residency in Korea). From their offices, above the unmarked
Kitsuńe boutique on a quiet street in Paris, they and their small
staff manage the fashion and record label and are part of the vanguard of DJs who are involved with fashion. "We really loved fashion, and we really loved music," says Loaëc. "So for us it was about
having our hobby as our way of living. In one way music is selling as
much as before so it's a way of making income, and also artists can
have a great image and bring a lot of postive energy to an old fashion
house, like Amy Winehouse at Fendi. (The singer was featured in
the luxury brand's advertising campaign in 2008.) For the DJs it's
more of a niche market and it's another way to get noticed."

Pompougnac, who has DJed a number of fashion shows, including Gucci and Yves Saint Laurent, sees a considerable correlation
between fashion and DJing. "Fashion designers are avant-gardists

as much as DJs," he says. "DJs are setting trends like fashion designers and DJs involved in fashion need to find new atmospheres
and trends to bring to people." Paul Oakenfold has also played a
fair few fashion shows. "I think the main reason the fashion world
is tied to DJing is the cool factor," he says, simply.

Of course DJing and fashion have long gone hand in hand: in
the early 1980s Jam Master Jay was as well known for his forward-
thinking style, which bandmates Simmons and McDaniels
adopted, giving the group their unified, trademark look: black fe-
doras with black leather jackets and huge gold chains that would
make Mr. T. envious, combined with those unforgettable Adidas.
So while today's hip hop moguls may act like they're the first in
the genre to cross over into the world of fashion, they're actually
just guests recently arrived at a party Jam Master Jay started more
than twenty years ago.

"Jay was the reason Run and I didn't dress just like Flash, Bam,
and the other guys," McDaniels says. "He thought that we should
wear leather jackets, but rather than them being tight like most
people wore theirs, they'd be loose like the chains we had. We always had hats on, too. Jay told us that those godfather hats were
like crowns and represented us becoming the kings of the music
business." Run-D.M.C. also released the original ode to the
sneaker "My Adidas" in 1986. " 'My Adidas' was just a song about
the shoes we loved," says D.M.C. "If we wore red Adidas we'd
have to wear a red outfit to match, it was a style thing for us. We
did that song because the shoes were part of our lifestyle, not to
get a sponsorship deal."

The extension of the DJing brand not only includes hotels,
and the world of fashion, but also video games, TV, and films.
"My main job now is not DJing," says Oakenfold. "I still love it,
but my focus is on making music for films and video games. Because of DJing, I've realized that dream." Oakenfold's work in

Hollywood became so regular (he followed up 2001's *Swordfish* by working on *The Matrix, Collateral*, and some Bond movies), that he had to move there. "Clubbers or DJs who say I've sold out don't understand the scene or the business side of things," says Oakenfold. "A lot of the time it's just jealousy."

Like Tiësto, Sasha, and countless other members of DJing's upper echelon, Oakenfold and his team of publicists and managers carefully curate his image and every aspect of what is becoming a multimedia empire—from his logo to the distinctive packaging of his Perfecto label's CDs. He says:

> "I started marketing myself as a brand five or six years ago. If people like your brand, they'll go to see you at clubs, buy mix CDs, buy merchandise, buy the CDs you make, listen to your film soundtracks. I don't like to think of myself as a brand, but it's a question of understanding the marketplace and the way to get ahead."

The huge paycheck Oakenfold and his peers can earn in a night (upwards of $50,000) has received as much press as their DJing talents, but he isn't fazed by it:

> "The amount of money I make from a set never freaks me out, because it's just the nature of your value in the market. It's the same with actors or football players. If you buy a player and he helps you win a championship, it's money well spent. That's how it is with DJs, too. If a DJ packs a club with four thousand people he gets rewarded for that—it just reflects the business model now. Your value and popularity is based on putting butts on seats. What I'm paid is whatever the market dictates I'm worth."

AROUND THE WORLD

It might go without saying that the Internet is a primary reason for the prevalence of DJ culture around the world, but that culture itself is also changing and adapting to the medium. Many DJs, even those who were established long before the Web became the quotidian influence it is today, can barely conceive of a time before it. It allows DJs to communicate constantly with instant messaging; it enables fans to keep track of their favorite DJ's activities and movements and communicate with each other and the DJs themselves; and it provides an easy and obvious point of entry into what was once a seemingly closed world of DJs. The Internet has made possible a global network of DJ culture whereby people like Paul Oakenfold, Paul Van Dyk, and Above & Beyond can play to receptive crowds who know their music whether they're in Shanghai or Moscow, New York or Buenos Aires.

The familiar expression that "music knows no boundaries" might not always be so easy for bands and solo artists—think of how many bemoan not being able to "break America" or not being able to get the same reception outside of their home country—but for successful DJs it holds true. The best thing about this? You can do it, too. While in the club, that DJ might seem out of reach but the next day look them up on the Internet and try contacting them through their MySpace page or their Web site—you'll be surprised how many DJs will actually get back to you.

Above & Beyond are experts at utilizing the Web to its fullest potential and have a weekly radio show, *Trance Around The World,* that is broadcast online every week. McGuinness explains:

> "We can do our radio show on a Friday night and play in China on a Saturday and people will ask you to play a record that you played on the radio the day before. They even know the words! We can write a new song, play it

on our show, travel to South America and play it and people are singing along. That is ridiculous! It's the nature of
the world now—music travels so quickly. Within half an
hour of a set being finished the whole world can listen to
an exclusive track you just played. It used to take weeks
and months for a record to build and now it takes three
minutes. When we played in Rio on New Year's Eve
2007 to a million people—we went off for a bite to eat,
afterward back to the hotel, turned on the laptop, and
there are videos of our show on YouTube."

He continues:

"There is a fine network of accessibility that has spread
across the globe. You can play almost anywhere now.
It's always a surprise to me when we turn up in a country that we've never been to before and the reaction is
pretty much the same as it is anywhere. It could be
Greece or Detroit—you name it. It's true with any of
the big guys now. And it's not just what we're doing
proactively, it's what the fans do themselves. For in-
stance, we haven't been to Australia for a couple of
years now and there's a clamor on the forum to go back
that is ridiculous. The Internet just does it for you."

We put it to McGuinness that the same isn't necessarily true
for bands. "That's a very good point actually," he says. "But
you're going to the club for the club experience. One of the main
reasons that people go to clubs is to meet guys and girls. I would
argue you would go to see Coldplay or Radiohead in a very solitary, self-indulgent fashion. So I think clubs and DJs are keyed
into something more vital and much more important to human
beings than just music."

SOUNDING OFF—TURNTABLISTS: SONIC WIZARDS

*Being a DJ is basically all my life. I've made a career out of doing what I
love, and that's what I do everyday, that's who I am, and when I wake up
I'm thinking "Mixer, records, needles, turntables." That's me!*

—DJ Craze

As much as DJ culture is facilitated by the Web, there still exist
strong subcultures within the scene that thrive on the more
traditional forms of DJ interaction. Since the earliest days of hip
hop, the DJ battle has been a way for DJs to move their craft forward. Battling is a constructive outlet that provides DJs with a
forum to show the crowd and fellow competitors turntable routines they've never seen before.

"As turntablists we were trying to make the instrument of the
turntable do things it's not supposed to," Z-Trip says. "We developed our own decks, mixers, tone arms, needles, everything we
needed to facilitate experimentation. We took the baton from
the early hip hop and house DJs and ran with it. Pushing the
craft of DJing to new levels was the main thing for us—the only
thing. DJs now are so worried about getting to the big paychecks, but we were just focusing on the music."

Turntablists, such as DJ Craze, A-Trak, and DJ Shadow, are
the guys and girls that can spend twenty hours a day record shopping, practicing, jamming with fellow DJs—basically eating,
sleeping, and breathing DJing. They are the epitome of the term
perfectionist, putting hundreds of hours of rehearsals into a six-
minute performance at a DMC, ITF, or Skratchon event, and
showing the same level of dedication in getting ready for club or
party performances.

As New York DJ pioneer Jazzy Jay says in *Scratch* (2001),
"This wasn't just something we did for the money, we believed in
this. When I left, I could play for six or seven hours outside and

when I came home I set up my turntables and played for another six or seven hours. It was something I had to do." The turntablists shunned the mainstream hip hop scene that had left DJs out in the cold in the late '80s and early '90s, preferring to focus on technical innovation and a spirit of community that stayed true to the founding principles of the genre. DJ Klever breaks down the distinction between a turntablist and a regular DJ:

> "It's a mixture of creativity, hand control, confidence, and having just the skill to do it. Putting in the hours to be able to do these things. Whereas a DJ is just there mixing. I think what separates our personality from their personality is detail and hand control—detail about every little thing. You can always tell turntablists by their position on stage or in the booth. Turntablism is a lifestyle rather than just doing it for a few hours. It's more than what people see at the party. We're nerds, you know? We eat and sleep it. Whenever I get a chance I'm cutting it up or I'm working on some new patterns. It's in my blood, man."

The niche culture of turntablism is still about musical perfection and musical creativity, rather than chasing endorsement deals and Top 40 hits. DJ Craze elaborates:

> "Being a DJ is basically my life. I've made a career out of doing what I love and that's what I do every day, that's who I am, and when I wake up I'm thinking, 'Mixer, records, needles, turntables.' That's me!"

Turntablists have also made DJing visually appealing. Grandmaster Flash, Grand Wizard Theodore, and some of the other original hip hop DJs were the first to introduce body tricks into their sets to entertain the audience, and battle DJs have taken this discipline to another level: sometimes scratching with the elbows, feet, and even noses, mixing blindfolded, or spinning their bodies between the decks.

Outside of these body tricks, new techniques forward in scratching, such as the drum mimicking pioneered by Q-Bert, has kept the audience entranced by the DJ's performance. To get the full effect you have to see it live. Turntablists have made DJing into an art form that is as technically impressive and as innovative as anything that can be done on a traditional instrument. "People have taken DJing to levels us original DJs never thought possible," says Grandmaster Caz.

The DJ Crews: Power in Numbers

Although some turntablists prefer performing alone, others have formed collectives that have elevated the art of turntablism. Just like traditional bands or groups of guitarists jam with each other, turntablists get together to share new tricks, practice routines, and push each other musically.

"The advantages of being in a group are that you're around people who have a mutual love for what you do and therefore you're inspired constantly," says Rob Swift of the famous collective the X-Ecutioners.

Z-Trip explains the importance of being in the Bombshelter DJs collective with DJ Radar and DJ Emile:

> "Each crew had its own sound and skills. When we jammed together or played live, it was about *us*, not individuals. There was no money involved, we just wanted to hang out and play records. One guy would be better at scratching, another had a better record collection, so we all pushed each other to improve every day. All the other crews were focused on hip hop and battles."

Possibilities for innovation become almost limitless when using more decks and mixers in a group setting, and the collective offered more of a visual performance to crowds at clubs, parties, and DMC and ITF (International Turntablism Federation) events. Grandmaster Flash and the Furious Five and various subgroups from within Afrika Bambaataa's Zulu Nation were the pioneering crews, but turntablist collectives really came into their own in the late '80s and early '90s, when sponsored contests began offering these DJs ways to build a viable professional career. "DMC and the other competitions took the scene higher," says Z-Trip. "It was exciting to see DJs competing in a tournament environment in which they had just six minutes to show their skills."

The DMC World DJ Championships (formerly known as the DMC World Mixing Championships) was originally a house mixing contest, but at the 1986 event, champion DJ Cheese introduced scratching and the event was never the same again. DJs Jazzy Jeff and Cash Money (both from Philadelphia) were the forerunners of the U.S. turntablism scene in the late 1980s, taking DJ contests like DMC to newfound prominence in the scene.

The balance of turntablist power soon switched to the West Coast. The Shadow of the Profit group was formed in 1989 by Q-Bert, Mix Master Mike, and DJ Apollo. Three years later, Mike won the New Music Seminar DJ Battle for World Supremacy, the first West Coast DJ to claim this title, and with Apollo and Q-Bert (as the Rocksteady DJs) he also claimed the World DJ Champions team crown at DMC. The next year, Q-Bert and Mike entered DMC as the Dream Team and again took top honors.

"The group is taking scratching to another level, being a DJ band with instruments," says Q-Bert. "One guy would scratch a drum beat—bass, snare, cymbal—another guy would play a bassline. You can make different melodies by moving the pitch control. In '93 and '94 at DMC, I used a tone record, and tried to do a Hendrix thing with 'Voodoo Child.' We tried to copy other musical styles but on turntables."

In the 1990s, the Invisibl Skratch Piklz were the Harlem Globetrotters of turntablism. Their reputation was further enhanced in 1997 when Mike worked on the award-winning Beastie Boys comeback album *Hello Nasty* and then became the band's DJ. He was also hired by EA Sports to work on the soundtracks for their SSX snowboarding/skiing video games. Q-Bert recorded an ad for Apple's "Switch" campaign and provided the soundtrack for the video game *Tony Hawk's Underground*.

The 2001 animated film *The Wave Twisters* was made to synchronize with Q-Bert's groundbreaking 1998 album of the same name. He is considered by many of his peers to be the greatest scratch DJ of all time. "You think you've mastered scratching and then you listen to Q-Bert and are just blown away," says London's DJ Yoda [himself not exactly shabby behind the **ones and twos**]. "He's light-years ahead of everyone else and always has been."

Most other crews had little chance in battles against the Picklz, but New York collective the X-Ecutioners was one group equal to the task. Originally there were eleven members, but eventually a four-man lineup of Rob Swift, Roc Raida (the 1995 DMC World DJ Champion), Total Eclipse, and Mista Sinista took on the Piklz for turntablist supremacy, in contests that were as much for East Coast (X-Ecutioners) versus West Coast (Piklz) bragging rights as they were about music.

"I think that the beauty of the X-Ecutioners was that each of us had a distinct style and also our personalities were different," says Swift. "Fusing personality with style is what makes you unique." In 1995, the two collectives featured on *The Return of the DJ—Volume 1,* the first turntablism album that showed battle DJs everywhere that they could do more with their music than just compete, and that hip hop was more than just the rapper-dominated mainstream.

ROB SWIFT'S TOP TEN BATTLES OF ALL TIME

1. X-men (former name of X-Ecutioners) vs Invisibl Skratch Piklz. International Turntablist Federation 1996. (Winner: There was no winner declared. We left it up to the audience to decide for themselves.)

2. Aladdin vs Miz. New Music Seminar Battle for World Supremacy 1989. (Winner: Miz)

3. Steve D vs Francesco. New Music Seminar Battle for World Supremacy 1990. (Winner: Steve D)

4. Cash Money vs Joe Cooley. New Music Seminar Battle for World Supremacy 1987. (Winner: Cash Money)

5. Roc Raida vs Supreme. Clark Kent Battle for World Supremacy 1991. (Winner: Supreme)

6. Mista Sinista vs Eightball. Clark Kent Battle for World Supremacy 1993. (Winner: Eightball)

7. Mix Master Mike vs Supreme. Clark Kent Battle for World Supremacy 1992. (Winner: Mix Master Mike)

8. Flamboyant vs Francesco. New Music Seminar Battle for World Supremacy 1990. (Winner: Francesco)

9. Babu vs Total Eclipse. International Turntablist Federation 1996. (Winner: Total Eclipse)

10. East Coast DMC. 1992. (Winner: Rob Swift)

Out of the Basement, Into the Concert Hall

In 2001, DJ Radar broke the boundaries of turntablism when he performed the first movement of "Concerto for Turntable" (co-written by classical composer Raul Yanez) with the Arizona State University Symphony Orchestra in Tempe. He then went on a world tour with the Red Bull Artsechro (an orchestra of the finest young classical musicians handpicked from universities and colleges), which included a performance at Carnegie Hall in 2005. "Radar is a genius, a prodigy," says Z-Trip. "It took him years to come up with 'Concerto for Turntable' and he turned down a lot of gigs and CD opportunities to focus on it. When it came out many people in the DJ community were floored because it was just so different. London's DJ Yoda later worked with the Heritage Orchestra on a similar project. In addition to fusing hip hop with classical music, Radar also teamed up with Rob Carluccio on his invention of scratch notation, which allows turntablists to share compositions and performances via sheet music.

That's not to say that turntablism has become some sort of highbrow elitist club. On the contrary, it will remain *inclusive*. We asked Z-Trip to give us a look inside: "Back in the day all of us DJs were so tight," he says. "Q-Bert showed me how to put the needle in the wrong way so it sounded different on the record. I'm still tight with those guys now. If I'm working on a remix I'll call [DJ] Shadow to ask him about beats, or I can hit up one of the younger guys like A-Trak about vocal samples, and we'll end up talking music for hours. I played at Shadow's wedding, Golden and Romanowski played at mine. These guys are lifelong friends."

Klever, who has been close friends with Craze for over a decade, feels a similar unity with his fellow turntablists. "The other night Craze and I hooked up our computers because he wanted to hear the kind of music I was making and I wanted to hear the kind

of stuff he'd been writing on the road, and we're just loving it because it's from the heart," he says.

"It's all about fun, man, because we've made it this far and
we're just so blessed to be some of the lucky few," he continues.
"And the funny thing is I don't think we're some alpha fraternity, but it's a blessing for people to even think that way, because I remember being a kid and coming up and looking up to
people like Cut Chemist, Q, Z-Trip and I would be like 'Damn,
I wish I could hang out with them and not be looked at as some
little green-thumbed kid.' And sometimes I can't even believe
it. It's the best feeling ever to know that the people you looked
up to, or the people that you were battling against or were so
competitive against at one time are all just having a blast."

Along with U.K. collective the Scratch Perverts, the Bombshelter DJs, Allies, X-Ecutioners, and Invisbl Skratch Piklz have
extended the musical and commercial avenues of turntablists
everywhere, and breathed new life into the world of DJing. The
fact that recent DMC winners have been from France (C2C,
winners of four World Team Champions titles), Germany (Rafik,
2007 World DJ Champion), and Japan (Kireek, 2007 World
Team Champions) illustrates the fact that despite maintaining a
relatively underground presence, turntablism has become a universal passion for DJs worldwide. Klever explains:

> "I came from a background where there was a lot of nega-
> tive stuff, a lot of my buddies were dope dealers who
> loved to party, they were dropouts. Music saved me. If
> I didn't see a DJ play when I was fifteen I probably would
> be dead or in jail, because this world would've eaten me
> alive. It goes back to the gang mentality. We wouldn't
> have Herc or Baambaata and the Zulu Nation if it wasn't
> for this music turning violence into a positive force."

DJ CRAZE'S TOP 10 TIPS FOR WINNING THE DMC WORLD DJ CHAMPIONSHIPS

1. Watch all the DMC videos.
2. Learn as many styles as you can from watching those tapes.
3. Pick records that people like so you can get them on your side just with your selection.
4. Try to come up with something original.
5. Do some research on your opponents (what they're good at and what they're lacking).
6. Practice throughout year and try to come up with as many routines as you can.
7. Pick your five strongest routines that you've practiced.
8. Practice those routines . . . and keep practicing till you can't practice anymore.
9. Practice messing up and recovering.
10. *PRAY* that the day of the battle everything comes out all right!

A-TRAK'S TOP 10 BATTLE RECORDS

1. Turntablist—"Superduck Breaks"
2. Q-Bert—"Dirtstyle Deluxe Shampoo Edition"
3. D-Styles—"Skratch Fetishes of the 3rd Kind"
4. DJ Swamp—"Skip-proof" series
5. A-Trak—"Monkeyboy Breaks"
6. Ricci Rucker—"Utility Phonograph Record"
7. Mr Dibbs—"Unearthed Vol.3"

(continued)

8.   Q-Bert—"Toasted Marshmellow Feet Breaks"
9.   DJ Craze—"Bully Breaks 2"
10. Tittworth & DJ Ayres—"T&A Breaks"

Hip Hop DJs Hijack Hollywood

In the late '80s and early '90s, hip hop DJs were pushed out of the spotlight by rappers such as Jay-Z, Tupac, and Biggie Smalls, who often relied on studio-produced beats and samples rather than a live DJ. DJs came back to prominence through studio production and remixing, playing celebrity parties, and conquering the biggest entertainment media channels—radio, cable TV, the Internet, and the world's hottest clubs. Soon, DJs' opportunities were no longer restricted to knowledgeable underground crowds, but were expanded to include the mainstream. From Jazzy Jeff and Kid Capri's TV breakthroughs to Mark Ronson's Grammy Awards and DJ AM's rule of clubland, the DJ has become a pivotal cultural voice across all media. "The hip hop DJ is a star maker," says Grandmaster Flash. "There are a lot of big music stars out there who wouldn't have made it if it hadn't been for the DJs playing their records."

One of the earliest DJs to fashion the superstar hip hop DJ mold was DJ Jazzy Jeff. This Philadelphia native (real name Jeffrey Townes) got started by playing school and block parties. In the mid-'80s, Jeff and fellow Philadelphian DJ Cash Money were making names for themselves on the house party circuit, with Jeff taking DJ Spinbad's use of the **transform scratch (scratching while quickly moving the crossfader back and forth)** to a new level. "DJ Spinbad let a record play, then pulled it back while he moved the volume fader up and down," Jeff says. "I loved the sound that made, so I started experimenting with it at my house. I've always been rhythmic, so I tried to make it have a tune. One part of the transform, or scratching in general, is hand movement on the record, and the second part is hand movement on the crossfader. For my version of the transform, I'd move the record back and forward slowly while quickly moving the cross-fader from left to right. My friend was listening to me do it in my basement one day and he said it sounded like the intro to the *Transformers* cartoon. The name stuck. At the next party I played at the MC said, 'Here's my man Jazzy Jeff doing the transform.'"

In 1985, Jeff met up-and-coming MC Will Smith at a house party in Philadelphia. A year later, as DJ Jazzy Jeff and the Fresh Prince, they released their debut single "Girl's Ain't Nothing But Trouble," just after Jeff won the 1986 DMC New Music Seminar. Two years later, they put out their first album, *Rock the House*, on Jive records. It was the first LP to feature the transform scratch and also included Jeff's newest turntable invention—the **chirp scratch (which sounds like a chirping bird)**. The album went gold, cementing Smith and Jeff's reputation as the hottest DJ and MC duo in the land. Two years later, they dropped *Parents Just Don't Understand*. In 1989 this album won a Grammy in the new Best Rap Performance category, propelling the twosome to international renown. Jeff says:

> "DJ Jazzy Jeff and the Fresh Prince did a lot for people's perceptions of DJs. We tried to continue the legacy of Grandmaster Flash, in bringing the DJ back to the forefront. I was the band, Will was the singer—we got equal billing. The music industry had gone away from that but we helped bring it back. 'The Magnificent Jazzy Jeff' was the first time people had heard transforming and the chirp scratch on a record, and on every record we tried to show the artistry of the DJ. We put out *I'm the DJ, He's the Rapper* [1988] as a two-record release, and the whole second record was full of DJ cuts and rhythm tracks, just like we played at house parties. Whether

Will and I were playing in front of fifty people or fifty thousand people, we kept the essence of DJing—a DJ using two turntables and a mixer while the MC rhymes."

A year later, NBC cast Smith in *The Fresh Prince of Bel-Air*, and Jeff was featured as his best friend, Jazz. The show—the theme song of which featured Smith rapping—ran for six years, and was nominated for Emmys and Golden Globes. DJ Jazzy Jeff and the Fresh Prince went on to sell more than ten million records, and won three Grammys and an MTV Music Award. "After being on *The Fresh Prince of Bel-Air*, I realized that as a DJ you can't worry about which medium exposure comes from, you just have to be thankful for any exposure," Jeff says.

"When me and Will started making music, DJs and MCs knew about us, but after I was on that show eighty-year-old grandmothers knew who we were. We had the attention of fifteen million people and we realized that if we could reach 10 percent of them with our music that would be huge. We waited to drop *Summertime* until the show was at its peak, and that helped us reach the biggest possible audience."

When Smith went on to solo superstardom and to conquer the box office, Jeff returned to his first love—DJing. As well as spinning at clubs worldwide, he was the first corporately sponsored DJ and collaborated with Gemini on the first scratch mixer, the Gemini 2200 (aka Jazzy Jeff Signature Series). He also set up the Touch of Jazz production facility that has put out records for his old partner Will Smith, Michael Jackson, and Lil' Kim. In addition to his various hip hop productions, Jeff has worked on several house music projects, including the Defected Records mix CD *DJ Jazzy Jeff in the House* in 2004. Jeff's career is proof that a DJ can be commercially successful while maintaining street credibility. "Jazzy Jeff is one of the pioneers of DJing," says Z-Trip. "He gets overlooked sometimes because of his success but there's nobody better than him. He is, and always has been, way ahead of the game."

Kid Capri (David Love) was another early big name hip hop DJ who went beyond playing in clubs and introduced new audiences in other venues to the art of DJing. Capri began mixing at the age of eight and by his mid-teens was making a living selling mixtapes with Starchild. Soon promoters took notice and hired Capri to play at clubs across New York, including the infamous Studio 54. He was signed by Warner Bros. and produced records for Heavy D, Boogie Down Productions, and Quincy Jones. Then, in 1991, he released his debut album *The Tape*, which is regarded as one of the finest hip hop albums of all time. Although he was well-known on the hip hop circuit nationwide, Capri was still largely an underground presence. But in 1995, Capri got a call from Def Jam mogul Russell Simmons, who asked him to be the house DJ for the *Russell Simmons' Def Comedy Jam*, which ran on HBO. Of course, he accepted. This deal made Capri the first DJ to be an integral part of a cable TV show. *Def Comedy Jam* was a hit, running for seven years and distributed on TV stations worldwide. Since he started on the *Jam*, Capri has hosted such TV shows as MTV's *Beat Suite* and BET's *Tigga in the Basement*. Funkmaster Flex took note of how Capri and Jazzy Jeff had achieved stardom, and then set about becoming as influential as both of them; developing his skills in the boardroom as sharply as he honed his DJing moves. Flex was born in Brooklyn and started DJing as soon as he was old enough to reach his parents' turntable. He played parties across the district before becoming an assistant to legendary hip hop broadcaster Chuck Chillout on KISS FM. Flex then followed his mentor to WBLS and started making his name on New York's club scene. Among those paying attention were the bigwigs at HOT 97, who gave Flex his own show. His 1995 album, *The Mix Tape, Vol. 1: 60 Minutes of Funk*, was a hit, as were volumes two and three and his Def Jam release *The Tunnel,* a tribute to the seminal New York club. Flex's show has been number one on New York radio for more than a decade and pulls in an average of over two million listeners each week.

In 2000, Flex branched out into television, presenting *Direct Effect* on MTV. Three years later, he began hosting *Ride with Funkmaster Flex* on Spike TV, a show that focused on the customization of luxury cars (in 2007 Ford actually released a Funkmaster Flex edition of their Expedition—it was decked out in orange and red paint with a black pinstripe).

Following in Flex's footsteps is DJ AM (Adam Goldstein), one of the newest of the superstar hip hop DJs, who has mastereed the **mash-up** style—seamlessly blending snippets of records from various genres. He was born in Philadelphia and moved to L.A. in 1997, where he started playing at clubs such as Dragonfly in his teens and also became part of the band Crazy Town. The group worked with the Black Eyed Peas (then known as Divine Styler), fusing rock, pop, and hip hop, a musical medley that helped Goldstein to develop an eclectic musical taste and DJing style. When Crazy Town disbanded, Goldstein went back to DJing on the L.A. club and party circuit. His engagement to socialite Nicole Ritchie in 2004 made Goldstein a regular in celebrity tabloids that were (unfortunately) more interested in the relationship than his considerable DJing prowess. When Ritchie and Goldstein split up in 2005, Goldstein remained in the public eye, turning his club LAX into the hottest ticket in L.A. and soon agreeing to a reported seven-figure deal to host a weekly LAX night at Las Vegas club Pure.

In addition to his club endeavors, Goldstein has featured on albums by Madonna, Will Smith, and Shifty and regularly plays at celebrity parties, sometimes commanding more than $25,000 per appearance. He has also broken through with corporate America, DJing at T-Mobile events, designing a Diet Pepsi bottle, and launching a limited edition Air Force 1 sneaker with Nike. Goldstein says:

> "Seven nights a week there are club nights to go to, and it's DJs people are dancing to. People start noticing what the DJs are doing. Everyone wants to be a DJ."

According to urban legend, Sean "Diddy" Combs gave budding DJ Mark Ronson a $100 bill with his cell phone number on it after witnessing his genre-mashing setting the dancefloor alight at a New York club in 1997. A year later, Ronson played at Combs's 29th birthday party, setting this young DJ on a path to stardom. These days, Ronson is a hot ticket, playing premiere events for the movie *Blade* (for which he traveled around on a private jet with the movie's stars, Wesley Snipes and Stephen Dorff), Sean Combs's New York Fashion Week parties, and Hollywood uber-couple Tom Cruise and Katie Holmes's wedding reception. He also achieved success as a producer for the likes of Amy Winehouse, Robbie Williams, and Macy Gray, set up a record label, Allido, which has Kanye West collaborator Rhymefest on the roster, and released a critically hailed artist album, *Version*, made up of covers, most of which are collaborations with other artists-of-the-moment. The LP went to number two in the U.K. album chart and gave Ronson four Top 40 singles, including "Oh My God," (featuring Lily Allen), which has sold more than 300,000 copies. In 2008, Ronson won Producer of the Year, Pop Album of the Year, and Best Pop Album at the Grammy's and the same year was named Best Male Solo Artist at the Brit Awards.

The son of a socialite and stepson of Mick Jones, the guitarist for '70s band Foreigner, Ronson is, in many ways, the definitive "celebrity" DJ. He has stepped out from behind the decks to embrace a fame that now sees him sitting in the very same VIP lounges he once DJed for; his sister Samantha is a good friend of Lindsay Lohan and a DJ in her own right. There's something of the evanescent about all of this, of course. A sense that, by the time this book is published, the DJs' names now on the lips of event managers from Dior to Disney will have changed entirely. But although he got a good start in life, attending slumber parties with Sean Lennon and counting Mick Jagger as a family friend, Ronson is evidence that, done right, a DJ can achieve celebrity status while maintaining credibility and actually stick around for a while—something which takes more than the right pair of faded jeans and deliberately scruffy plaid shirt to achieve. What it takes is talent. Because while the very term "celebrity DJ" seems to have that slight undercurrent of condescension about it, the people that have achieved that status, and have ascended into that particular strata of the DJ spectrum are, almost without exception, extremely talented individuals.

That said, they are by no means more talented than figures like Grandmaster Flash and Luv Bug Starski (credited with coining the term hip hop), who, while definitely *stars* in their own right at the height of their success, were only so to fans of hip hop. In the hip hop community, you couldn't get any bigger than people like Flash and Starski. The same is true for seminal DJs like Larry Levan and Frankie Knuckles—while house-music pioneers and the kings of the nightlife in New York and Chicago respectively, they never achieved widespread fame while they were changing the musical landscape. Indeed, Knuckles achieved widespread popular attention not on the strength of his genre-defining sets at the Warehouse, but on the back of his 1987 Trax Records single "Your Love."

In the '90s, however, everything changed. As musicians saw

the rising popularity of DJs, they stepped out of the parameters of their bands to take a place behind the turntables, often with no prior experience. Boy George of Culture Club, Prince Paul of De la Soul, Q-Tip from a Tribe Called Quest, and Perry Farrell of Jane's Addiction all began to play "sets"—often just as figureheads, names to sell tickets to an event, or to mark a particular party out as cooler than the next one. "I came downstairs to the DJ booth and Perry was standing there wondering why there was no sound coming out," said Ronson in 1998, remembering a party he played at with Farrell. "He had forgotten to lower the arm onto the record." The trend of musicians as wannabe DJs exists today, and it's easy to see why it's so popular. For one, they don't have to lug around amps, guitars, drums, and the other paraphernalia that usually encumber them and can instead just pull their iPods out of their pockets, plug them in to the mixer, and just stand there looking good for a while. However, DJs like AM, Ronson, and DJ Vice have proved that you can be famous and still be a talented spinner. And if they never got another Page Six mention, their DJ abilities that they possess would ensure that they were still celebrated by fans and fellow DJs alike. DJ AM says, "I really believe I was born to DJ. I'll always do this, even when I'm eighty years old, because I need to DJ, I have to do it."

EXTRAS: CITY GUIDES

Now that you've learned about the culture of DJing, here's a bit about the cities whose scenes have pushed it found.

New York
Clubs such as Arthur, Sanctuary, The Loft, and Studio 54 created the sound and style of disco in the early to mid-'70s. At The Paradise Garage, Larry Levan invented garage—and this influenced

the development of the house sound that was later brought to an enthusiastic New York audience at The Tunnel by Danny Tenaglia (who also had a residency at Twilo) and Junior Vasquez, at Twilo and at Devil's Nest and Roseland by Lil' Louie Vega. Today, New York is undoubtedly the home of hip hop radio, with the biggest names in hip hop guesting on shows with superstar Funkmaster Flex, DJ Mister Cee, and Cipha Sounds at HOT 97, radio legends Kool DJ Red Alert and Chuck Chillout at KISS FM, and DJ Clue, DJ Spinbad, and Marley Marl on Power 105.1.

Chicago

Frankie Knuckles invented house music at the Warehouse in the late '70s and early '80s and DJ Ron Hardy carried on the torch at the club, which was renamed Music Box when Knuckles left to start Power Plant in 1982. DJ collective the Hot Mix 5, which included Farley "Jackmaster" Funk, Ralphi Rosario, and Steve "Silk" Hurley, introduced house to the masses on WBMX radio. The first house track, "On and On" by Jesse Saunders and Vince Lawrence, was cut in Chicago and the first two big house labels, Trax Records and DJ International records, were based there. In 1997, Marshall Jefferson, DJ Pierre, and Herb Jackson's collective Phuture released "Acid Tracks," on Trax, creating the subgenre acid house. The same year Hurley released "Jack Your Body" on RCA under the pseudonym JM Silk and it went straight into the U.K. Top 40 at number one.

San Francisco/Bay Area

Along with the X-Ecutioners from New York, San Francisco crews the Invisibl Skratch Picklz (DJ Apollo, Mix Master Mike, Q-Bert), the Bullet Proof Scratch Hamsters (Eddie Def, DJ Quest, DJ Cue, DJ Marz), and the World Famous Beat Junkies

(J.Rocc, DJ Curse, Rhettmatic, Babu, Melo-D, "DJ What?!", Mr. Choc, and Shortkut) took the art of turntablism to new levels from the mid-'90s onward by applying the old school hip hop collective model to DJ battles and competitions. If you've got a spare five minutes, check out these guys on YouTube, and see the movie *Scratch*.

Miami

Since 1975, Miami has been host to the world's largest dance music industry event, the Winter Music Conference, which attracts hundreds of DJs and thousands of clubbers to the white sands of South Beach each March. It was also the place where Miami Bass, an influential form of U.S. house music, was created in the late '80s. DJ Laz, Triple M DJs, Space Funk DJs, and Ghetto Style DJs were all influential in developing the sound, which combined rapping with hard drums and warped rhythms. Miami Bass was popularized at clubs such as Studio 183, Pac-Jam, and the aptly named Bass Station. Miami is also the hometown of DJ Irie, who plays nationwide when he's not performing for the Miami Heat NBA team, and three-time DMC World DJ Champion Craze lives there.

DJ CRAZE'S TOP TEN MIAMI BASS DJS/PRODUCERS:

1. Magic Mike
2. Beat Master Clay D
3. Jealous J & Jock D
4. Danny D
5. Amos Larkin
6. Mr. Mixx
7. DJ Laz

(continued)

8. Dynamixx 2
9. Disco Rick
10. DJ Uncle Al

London

DJs Danny Rampling, Paul Oakenfold, Johnny Walker, and Nicky Holloway brought the sound of Ibiza to London in 1987 and fused it with U.S. house to make the distinctive British house vibe that changed the face of global dance music. Shoom (opened by Rampling), Sanctuary and Spectrum (Oakenfold), and Trip (Holloway) introduced the British public to house, along with Jazzy M's show on LWR. The rave scene later began in London warehouses. In 1989, Pete Tong started influential house label FFRR, launching his Essential Selection show on BBC Radio 1 in 1991 and the Essential Mix two years later. Superclubs Ministry of Sound, Home, and Fabric influenced a new generation of clubbers in the '90s, and London is still home to one of the most vibrant club scenes in the world.

Ibiza

OK, so it's an island (50 miles off Spain's southeast coast), not a city, but indulge us anyway. Ibiza was in some ways the birthplace of house music as we know it. Clubs such as Pacha and Amnesia introduced the pioneers of the British house scene to a new type of electronic music in 1987 and 1988, and before long they started DJing there each summer and bringing legions of fans with them. Ibiza (for better or worse) went from being a sleepy little island with a couple of great clubs that catered to Spanish royalty, local residents, and music industry insiders to a focal point of the house scene that attracts hundreds of thousands of clubbers from across the globe each summer. In addition to checking out the superclubs such as Space and Privilege and the incredible white sand beach at Las Salinas on the south of the island, visiting the intimate terrace at the Café Del Mar is a must. Island veteran DJ Jose Padilla and guest spinners create a laid-back soundtrack that perfectly complements the spectacular sunset over the Calo des Moro bay.

PART THREE

BE THE DJ

SEVEN

DJ 101

We've taken a look at the history of DJing, DJ culture, and the life of the DJ, and now we're onto the main event—how to DJ. In this chapter, we'll show you how to choose and set up equipment, introduce you to fundamental skills such as mixing and scratching, and explain building a set and a mixtape, all with help from the experts at Scratch DJ Academy and some of the most famous DJs in the world. We'll explore how DJing is half technique and half taste, and how this applies to picking tracks, crafting a mix, and applying personal style to your music.

While the content of this chapter will give you a solid foundation, by its very nature, DJing is an instinctive art, and the only way to do it right is to practice over and over again. So, if this stuff doesn't seem natural at first, stick with it. Get yourself the basic equipment, have a read of this chapter, and then lock yourself in your bedroom, basement, or wherever else you decide to set it up and get to it. Now!

TOOLS OF THE TRADE

Many of the world's top DJs started on equipment that was pre-historic by today's standards for a lot of them, hardware now seen as basic, such as a DJ mixer, was unavailable. "There was no mixing, so we had to go up to get the sound up and down using the volume fader," says Q-Bert. Eventually Q-Bert bought a mixer, making it much easier to switch between records and to listen to tracks on his headphones before unleashing the mix on the dancefloor.

Now, DJs are in the opposite situation—there is almost too much equipment to understand and use, let alone become proficient with. The introduction of the **direct drive turntable (in which a motor powers electromagnets that deliver steady power to spin the platter)** in the late '70s was significant. Previously, all turntables had been **belt-driven (meaning that a motor drives a belt, which spins the platter).** Over time, the belt stretched, causing records to rotate at inconsistent speeds. Thankfully, the good folks at Technics (commonly pronounced in the United States as "techniques") debuted the SL 1200, the first mass-produced direct drive deck.

The next leap forward in DJ equipment evolution was the introduction of the CD turntable in the late '90s. Decks such as Pioneer's CDJ series mimic the functionality of standard turntables, but include extra features such as the ability to add and trigger **cue points (these allow the DJ to automatically start a CD at a predesignated spot),** monitor BPM counts (an analog or digital display of how many beats per minute the song is playing at), play a track backwards, **loop (repeat)** sections of a track, and much more.

Many manufacturers' CD decks also support MP3s, memory cards, and DVD content, utilized to great effect by acts like Daft Punk and Coldcut. Because CD decks are smaller than their analog counterparts and CDs are more portable than records, this technology has made the DJ more mobile. In addition to making travel easier, using CDs also enables DJs to copy and share tracks and remixes more simply than when they used to press and distribute vinyl test pressings.

At first, CD decks were rejected as a gimmick by much of the DJing community, but now clubs and the pros alike embrace them as a useful medium. Annie Nightingale told us why she favors CDs over vinyl: "CDs have made my life a lot easier, because that format is more convenient than vinyl, even though vinyl sounds better," she says. "Flying and lugging records through airports is just too much hassle for most DJs now, so I just carry CD wallets. Particularly with weight limits on planes now—you don't want to fork over extra cash for taking your vinyl with you."

Final Scratch was the next major advance, soon to be followed by Serato, Traktor, and a whole host of other proprietary systems, which use time-coded vinyl to enable DJs to control MP3s as if they were records. Software programs such as Ableton Live, Pro Tools, and Cubase empower DJs to not just synchronize tracks but also to deconstruct and rebuild them—a step beyond the traditional mix versions, as Sasha did on his *Fundacion: NYC*, *Involver* and *Involver 2* CDs. "When I was coming up we would take twelve boxes of records and check them in at the airport, whereas now kids have laptops," says DJ Skribble, who has become one of America's better-known DJs by being the resident DJ for MTV's *Total Request Live* and *Spring Break* shows. "It's given more people the chance to be a DJ. I have an old-school mentality with new-school technology—I use Serato because it's like using vinyl."

Matt Black from Coldcut explains the importance of DJ software in moving the art of DJing forward: "Time-coded vinyl systems like Serato or Virtual Vinyl can be combined with drum trigger pads and you can set cues in each song and jump around the cues using the drum pads, and then scratch it and mix it using the turntables, and you can do it twice per laptop."

With mixing software, DJs have more flexibility than ever before, which is important as their schedules are becoming increasingly packed with travel, recording, and remixing. "With Ableton you can push yourself and there's a convenience factor—I can work on a set on the plane or download tracks to work on later at my hotel," says Sasha. "The thing about Ableton is that you can use it in an unlimited number of ways. James Zabiela uses it as an effects unit to complement his CDs."

For DJ Yoda, switching to Serato was a logical choice. "My DJ style has always been to flip records quickly—I might just spend twenty seconds on each track, so I'd have to carry four crates of vinyl everywhere," he says. DJ Nu-Mark from Jurassic 5 explains the power of using a computer and Serato to build a set instead of turntables and a mixer: "For me, Serato has opened up endless possibilities of creativity, because I'm making up my own versions of songs and really clean crisp and defined parts of my mixes," he says "I'm able to get to songs quicker and I have eight thousand tracks with me at any given time."

Before you can jump in and learn how to DJ on any of this technology, you need to understand how everything works on the most basic DJing setup—two turntables, a mixer, and a pair of headphones. DJ Yoda explains:

> "There are so many different options for DJs these days—they can use vinyl, Serato, Ableton, CD decks—but I think it's important to get used to working with vinyl first. It's crucial to have that basis, because the new technology just emulates two turntables and a mixer. Then when you've mastered turntables, you can take full advantage of the new toys."

Sasha agrees, warning DJs who are just getting started not to bypass vinyl in favor of newer technology. He says:

> "Starting a DJ career on Ableton is a terrible idea. You've got to know how to mix two pieces of vinyl together—to build a set without any bells and whistles—before you can move onto CDs or Ableton."

Black is also convinced that turntables still have a place for DJs working in any medium, in spite of the introduction of CD and digital mixing technology. "Ten years ago we did [seminal album] *More Beats & Pieces* to explore the idea that a turntable and pieces of vinyl were still the best direct interface for a DJ to make music," he says. "We made our own sample piece of vinyl and used the turntables to manipulate it. Ten years on and we're using turntables again, not Ableton Live, to do audio visual scratching on four turntables with four channels of music and visuals. That's what I call 'Re-turntablism,' which proves that turntables are still an amazing and enjoyable interface to use."

TWO TURNTABLES, ONE MIXER

Now it's time to introduce you to this setup. The key to understanding the equipment is knowing how it works together to produce sound that makes people dance.

Turntable
The thing that plays your records. Technics SL 1200s and 1210s have long been the gold standard, but Vestax, Numark, Gemini, and Stanton are also turning out high quality turntables that offer USB connectivity, recording direct to your iPod and featuring Gracenote software that auto identifies artist, album, and

track, and many other flashy features. Whatever make and model you choose, we suggest going for a direct drive system, which offers a more powerful and stable motor than cheaper belt drive alternatives, which decrease in performance as the belt that drives the platter stretches. You'll also want to pick a turntable that has a metal platter, because it is more durable and absorbs more vibration than the cheaper plastic alternatives. The pitch control should have a range of at least −8 percent to +8 percent, so that you can adjust the tempo of records enough to beat match effectively.

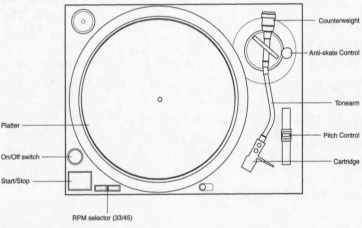

Credit: Steve Woodzell

Record

A piece of vinyl cut with one long groove that contains the sound. Smooth lines are the silence in between the tracks.

Platter

The platter is the circular plate on the turntable that spins the record. You'll need to buy a pair of **slipmats** made from felt, to go on top of the platters, to allow manipulation of vinyl that the rubber mat that comes with the turntable doesn't. Slipmats are cheap—$20 a pair, at most.

Needle

The needle, also known as the **stylus**, is housed in the **cartridge** (usually abbreviated to **"cart"**), and allows the turntable to capture the sound from the record, channelling the sound back through the tone arm and into the turntable. Turntablists and hip hop DJs generally use thicker, more robust needles that can handle scratching, whereas house DJs prefer a finer, more sensitive stylus. The best cartridges and styli are made by Ortofon, Stanton and Shure. They range in price from $50 to $400. The more expensive the cartridge, the more resistant it will be to skipping, and the better the sound quality it will convey.

Tone Arm

The tone arm is an extension of the needle, capturing the sound from the record and bringing the sound back into the turntable. When you're testing out turntables, make sure the tone arm feels solid, as a flimsy one indicates a poor quality turntable that won't be durable enough for hours of practice and gigs.

RCA Wires

The sound travels through RCA wires that extend out of the back of the turntables and into the back of the mixer.

Mixer

Think of the mixer as the bridge between the turntables and your audio setup. It lets you switch between turntables and blend the sounds from both (using the crossfader), change the levels—such as bass, mid-range, and treble—alter input and output volume, and much more. You can get a mixer for as little as $100, but if you're serious about DJing, $300 to $450 will get you a high-quality model that delivers superior sound. You can't go wrong with a mixer from Numark, Raine, or Vestax.

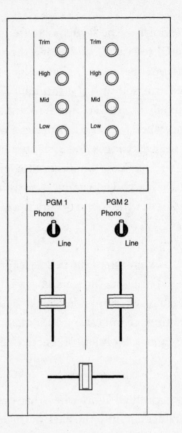

Credit: Steve Woodzell

Back of Mixer (Inputs)

The RCA wires from the turntables plug into the inputs on the back of the mixer. The wires from turntable #1 hook into the channel one phono inputs. (Turntables are plugged into "phono" because they are "phonographs.")

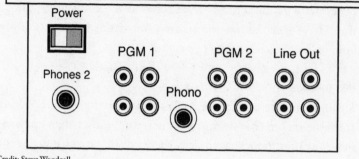

Credit: Steve Woodzell

Back of Mixer (Outputs)

The sound travels out of the outputs at the back of the mixer and into the speakers. Outputs are generally labeled "Master" and "Booth."

Crossfader

The crossfader lets you switch between and combine sound coming from the left and right turntables. The crossfader position determines sound output.

Sound channels

The sound travels into the mixer and down the sound channel. The mixer levels, from gain, to EQ, to upfader, to phono/line switches and more, control the sound for that channel.

Speakers

In the DJ booth of most clubs, there are smaller speakers called monitors that let the DJ keep tabs on what's playing over the main sound system while still listening to headphones. For your bedroom setup, you can start by just connecting the mixer to your stereo system. If you want a more high fidelity sound, buy an amplifier and speaker package. JBL and some of the other main manufacturers create self-powered speakers, so you don't have to shell out for an amp (most mixeres contain pre amps).

Headphones

Headphones are usually used only to listen to the sounds coming from the record that he or she is cueing up, rather than all channels. The best models have swivel ear cups that make it easier for the DJ to adjust them while listening to the monitors, and many fold down for easy transportation. You can get a decent pair from Sony, Sennheiser, or Technics for around $100.

EXERCISES—THE BASICS IN ACTION

We've compiled a few basic DJing exercises that will help you become familiar with your DJ setup.

Needle Placement Exercise

The point of this exercise is to get you comfortable manually placing the tone arm and needle on the record (and then removing them). Make sure to place and remove the needle by the little arm on the needle.

First, place a record on a turntable and press the Start button. Now practice *gently* placing the needle on the record and then removing it, without touching the vinyl with your thumbs or fingers. First aim for the very beginning of the record, and then try dropping the needle at the beginning of the different tracks (when we say "dropping," it sounds careless, but finesse is the aim of the game here). One way to needle drop is to listen to the record several times in advance and to add a visual marker, such as a pen or pencil mark on the record label, at the point where you want the music to begin.

You can then just place the needle when the record rotates to this indicator.

Pitch Control and rpm Speed Exercises

Pitch control and the rpm functions alter the speed of the record. Begin playing a record on a turntable. Speed up and slow down the record by adjusting the pitch control and alternately switching between 33⅓ rpm and 45 rpm.

Listen for even the slightest differences in speed and tone as you move the pitch control up or down and switch from lower and higher rpms. Repeat this exercise until your ear is trained to detect what speed a track is being played at, whether a track is pitched up or pitched down, and ultimately, by how much.

The Science of BPMing

One of the most important DJ fundamentals is learning how to properly mix two records together. Pull off a solid mix, and life is good. A bad mix and you've got your work cut out for you. We'll get into more of this later, as it's a critical element to the art form. The main building block in understanding this skill though is knowing how to measure the speed or tempo of a record. The academic term for this is **bpm (beats per minute).** The bpm is a measure of—you guessed it—how many beats there are in a 60 second period.

Measuring BPM

First, get a stopwatch or a regular watch with a second hand. Then play a record on a turntable. Start the watch and begin counting beats (you may choose to start counting at the beginning of the song or you may prefer to get a feel for counting the beats first and start timing in the middle of the song). Then after 30 seconds, take the number of beats you have counted and double them. Now you know the record's bpm.

Guessing Record Speeds

The goal of this exercise is to develop a good ear for guessing record speeds. First, grab four to six records, preferably of different genres. Then play each of the records and see if you can immediately determine if some are slower or faster than others. *Practice trying to mix the records.* When you drop the incoming record, listen for whether it is slower or faster. Then after you have guessed their order, count each record's bpm and see how close you were.

FREQUENTLY ASKED QUESTIONS

If two records don't have the same BPM, can I mix them?
Yes, the pitch control on the turntables allows you to adjust the beats per minute of each record. That said, two records must be in the same range of bpm for them to be mixed easily—a 92 bpm record will *not* mix with a 140 bpm record. Usually, if there is less than a 15 bpm difference between records, or the bpm of one record is close to double that of the other, they are able to be mixed. Also, remember that if the bpms are wildly different, even though you might be able to adjust the pitch control to get them in time, it won't sound good.

How can I tell whether to speed up or slow down records?
The first step is to find the bpm for your records. This will give you a sense of which record is faster. Then you'll need to develop an ear for just how far to adjust the pitch controls.

BUILDING BLOCKS—BEATS, BARS, AND PHRASES

Now that you have a good understanding of how the equipment works, let's move on to how to manipulate and identify tempo and how sound is produced. We're going to take a much closer look at that sound. Seeing that every track from every genre is different, the ability to identify common components will enable you to determine which fit well together and which don't. Here, we'll break down music into its basic structural elements, helping you not only to listen to music more effectively but also to improve your blending and mixing (when we get there, of course).

Making the Beat
The beat is created by three drum sounds: the kick, the snare, and the high hat.

The Structure of Bars
Beats are organized into bars. Bars (also known as "measures") are groups of four beats counted out, "1, 2, 3, 4, 1, 2, 3, 4" and so on. Bars are then grouped into phrases. Generally, the kick drum (the low-pitched drum known as the bass), falls on the 1st and 3rd beat of every bar, and the snare drum (the high-pitched drum), falls on the 2nd and 4th beat of every bar. When you clap to a song, you will usually clap on the 2nd and 4th beat of every bar.

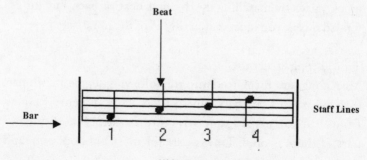

4/4 bar/measure of music

Phrases Defined

Bars are then grouped into phrases that are generally two, four, or eight bars long, which are counted out, "**1**, 2, 3, 4, **2**, 2, 3, 4, **3**, 2, 3, 4 . . ." and so on with the number in bold representing the first beat of a bar within the phrase.

16-Beat (Four bar) Phrase

Identifying the "1" Beat

The first beat of a phrase is also known as the "1" beat. Most producers make it easy to identify the "1" by using some sort of musical signature, including cymbals, an extra piano or guitar riff, an extra drum element, or removing the vocals.

Importance of the "1" Beat

In order to mix, you must be able to identify the first beat of a phrase—this is the beat that you mix the songs on. You can do quick mixes by matching up the first beat of bars, but for extended mixes, you must match the "1" of the phrases.

Typical Song Structure

Most songs are formatted into the following segments: chorus (8 bars), verses (16 bars), intro (bars vary by genre ranging from 0 to 16), extro (same structure as intro), and bridge (8 bars, if there is one). This is true for most hip hop, pop, and rock songs.

Identify the Beat

The beat of the song should come naturally to the listener. You won't need to actively listen for certain elements of the song to distinguish the beat. First start playing a record. Second, and rather simply, start bobbing your head or tapping your foot when you feel the beat. It is okay to pick up on audio cues at first, but then see if you can carry the beat without having to listen for specific sounds.

Beat Sounds Exercise

In order to manipulate the record, whether you're interested in blending, scratching, or beat juggling, you must understand the different sounds.

First, play a record on turntable #1. Then find the kick. You can increase the bass by turning the low EQ on your mixer all the way up and reducing the high EQs. Now find the snare. Turn up the middle and high EQs while turning the low EQ down. Lastly, find the high hat. Now make it stand out by turning the high EQ up and cutting the low EQ.

Counting Bars Exercise

Now that you can bob your head to the beat, try counting out the bars. Counting a bar is simply a four count, "1, 2, 3, 4, 1, 2, 3, 4" and so on. To get started, play any instrumental song.

Then count the bars, starting with the first downbeat (kick sound), "1, 2, 3, 4, 1, 2, 3, 4, etc." until you've made it through the first chorus.

Once you're comfortable counting the bars, try dropping the needle in the middle of the song, and see if you can pick up the bar count.

Phrase Exercise

Listen to different songs and identify the phrases. As a DJ, you should always be listening for phrases. Again, to get started, play any instrumental song.

Then count out the phrase (1, 2, 3, 4—2, 2, 3, 4—3, 2, 3, 4—4, 2, 3, 4 and again assuming a 16-beat phrase). Pay attention to the hints that identify the "1" beat.

Once you are comfortable that you have feel for the song, drop the needle down in the middle of the song and try to pick up the phrase just by listening to it. The key is to listen for the instrumental flourish that will happen just before the "1" beat.

MIXING, BLENDING, AND CUTTING

Now that we've covered how songs are structured, let's start to do things with them. This section is about the techniques that enable you to blend and mix tracks. Your ear will tell you which song is slower and which is faster, pitch control allows you to adjust the bpm accordingly, the fader will enable you to blend the records, and headphones will help you listen to the mix to make sure it's right on before you play it out over the speakers.

Mixing
How you transition from song A to song B—the very technique that differentiates a DJ from an iPod Shuffle. You need to match the tempo and the beats (beat matching) to mix two tracks successfully and a common way to introduce a second track is to "drop on the one" (explained below).

Blending
Generally refers to combining the acapella (just the vocal track) with the instrumental of another track of your choice to create a new and combined sound.

Cutting
Fading in a few bars from the record on turntable #2 while playing the track on turntable #1.

Dropping on the One
What is dropping on the "1"?

It's the act of cueing up the "1" beat of the incoming record and releasing it on top of the "1" beat of the outgoing record.

Why is dropping on the "1" important?

In order to mix two songs together seamlessly, and thus avoid the dreaded "hoof beats" (so called because a bad mix sounds like galloping horses' hooves on tarmac), the DJ must be able to identify the "1" beat of the incoming record, cue it up, and drop it in on time with the "1" beat of the outgoing record.

What is the action of dropping on the "1"?

Dropping on the "1" is the key to making the incoming and outgoing beats line up when you're mixing two records together. Simply put, its the standard template for the mix. It works like this: cue the "1" beat of the incoming record (generally the kick drum) and then release it on the "1" beat of the outgoing record. If done properly, the kick drums will line up on top of each other and create a seamless mix (as opposed to the kick drum lining up on top of a snare drum, creating a bad mix).

Below is an example of two 16-beat phrases that are lined up incorrectly, with the "1" beats unaligned. This would be the result of dropping in the incoming record at the incorrect moment (not dropping the record on the "1"). The result is two tracks in time, that will sound out of sync.

Below is an example of two 16-beat phrases that are lined up correctly, with the "1" beats aligned. This would be the result of dropping in the incoming record at the correct moment, leading to mixed music that will sound in sync.

EXERCISES

For all of the exercises below, make sure that the pitch control is at "0" on both turntables.

Dropping on the "1" Exercises: # 1

The goal of this exercise is to make sure you are comfortable with releasing the record at exactly the right moment and with precisely the right speed. For this exercise, you should use two copies of the same record. Count out loud "1, 2, 3, 4, 1, 2, 3, 4". Move the crossfader to the center position. Start the right turntable and cue up the "1" beat. Hold the record so that the platter is spinning beneath the record. Release the record immediately after counting a "4". If done correctly, the record should not sound too fast or too slow. Repeat. After you feel comfortable on the right turntable, practice on the left turntable. And then do it again.

Dropping on the "1" Exercises: # 2

Here you'll take what you've learned from the previous exercise, but instead of counting your own beat, you'll drop the incoming record on the "1" of a playing song on the opposite turntable. Again, you should use two copies of the same track. Note that you should aim to drop on the "1" of a bar—do not worry about lining up the phrases yet. After you become comfortable with bars, aim to drop on the "1" of phrases.

1.   Move the crossfader to the center position.
2.   Start the right turntable and cue up the "1" beat (and create a visual cue).
3.   Hold the record so that the platter is spinning beneath it.
4.   Next, play the exact same track on the left turntable.

5. Scratch the cued-up "1" beat to the beat of the playing record.

6. Release the cued record on the "1" of the playing record. If you do it right, they should sound smooth as they play over the top of each other.

7. Repeat. After you feel comfortable on the right turntable, practice on the left turntable.

Before scratching, make sure you are counting along to it. A big problem many people have with this exercise is that, even though they properly scratch for four beats and release it, they don't necessarily do it within the bar structure of the track. For example, their scratches fall on the 2-3-4-1 beats of the song, resulting in a release on the "2."

Dropping on the "1" Exercises: # 3

This exercise is exactly the same as the last one, except this time you will start with the crossfader in the Left position and you will move it to the Center position. You will have to incorporate the use of your headphones. For this exercise, you should again use two copies of the same track.

1. Move the crossfader to the left position.

2. Start the right turntable and cue up the "1" beat in your headphones (and create a visual cue).

3. Hold the record so that the platter is spinning beneath it.

4. Next, play the exact same track on the left turntable.

5. Baby scratch the cued-up "1" beat to the beat of the playing record.

6. Release the cued record on the "1" of the playing record and move the crossfader to the center position. If

you've done it right, they should sound smooth as they play over each other.

7. Repeat. After you feel comfortable on the right turntable, practice on the left turntable.

Dropping on the "1" Exercises: # 4

You're going to do the same things again, except this time, you will use two different records and cut the crossfader from the left to the right position.

1. Move the crossfader to the left position.
2. Start the right turntable and cue up the "1" beat in your headphones (create a visual cue).
3. Hold the record so that the platter is spinning beneath it.
4. Next, play the track on the left turntable.
5. Scratch the cued-up "1" beat to the playing beat of other track.
6. Release the cued record on the "1" of the playing record and cut the crossfader to the right position.
7. Repeat. After you feel comfortable on the right turntable, practice on the left one.

Bringing the Mix Together

As the other half of mixing is matching tempos, below are some exercises to bring it all home. Step one is identifying the incoming and outgoing records' bpm (which we've covered) and the second is identifying the "1." Once you've done this, follow the chart on the next page.

STEPS	CROSSFADER	RECORD 1	RECORD 2
1	Left		Line up the "1". You can simply line up the first beat of the song.
2	Left		Knowing the record's bpm in relation to the bpm on record one, adjust the pitch up or down to either make the record faster or slower.
3	Left	Play this record through the main speakers and count the bar: "1, 2, 3, 4, 1, 2, 3, 4" and so on.	Hold this record with the platter running beneath it. Feel free to scratch as you count to the beat, but don't lose your placement.
4	Left	Playing.	As soon as you count "4" on record one, release record two and listen to it in your headphones. Determine whether it is slower or faster than record one.
5	Left	Playing.	Pull back the record to a "1," adjust the pitch up or down, and repeat.
6	Right		When you drop the record and it sounds like it has the same bpm as the record one, release it and move the crossfader.

Altering BPM Exercises: # 1

This exercise is just like the dropping on the "1" exercise part 4, except that this time you will make pitch adjustments on the cued record until cut is playing at about the same bpm.

1. Move the crossfader to the center position.
2. Start the right turntable and cue up the "1" beat (and create a visual cue).
3. Hold the record so that the platter is spinning beneath it.
4. Next, play the track on the left turntable.
5. Baby scratch the cued up "1" beat of the second turntable to the beat of the first.
6. Release the cued record on the "1" of the playing record.
7. Is it too fast or too slow? Make a decision.
8. Stop the track on the right turntable, move the record backwards to a "1" beat, and adjust the pitch up or down accordingly.
9. Repeat until you have beat matched the record.

Altering BPM: Part 2

The goal of this exercise is to work on matching beats, except this time you will do it through your headphones.

1. Move the crossfader to the center position.
2. Start the right turntable and cue up the "1" beat (create a visual cue) in your headphones.
3. Hold the record so that the platter is spinning beneath it.
4. Next, play a track on the left turntable.
5. Baby scratch the cued-up "1" beat of the right turntable to the playing beat of the left.
6. Release the cued record (right turntable) on the "1" of the playing record (left turntable) so that it only plays in your headphones.
7. Is the right turntable's track too fast or too slow? Make a decision. If you need to, move the crossfader to the center position to check.

8. Stop the right turntable, backspin to a "1" beat, and adjust the pitch up or down accordingly.

9. Repeat until you have beat matched the record. Once you have, move the crossfader to the center position.

MIXING TIPS AND TRICKS

Follow the Snares

A common mixing tip is to follow the snares inside of a song, so you can determine how best to bring in the next song. Kick-drum patterns, while generally on the 1 and 3 beats of each bar, can change throughout a song. Snares offer a consistent sound to follow and always fall on the 2 and 4 beat count. House music offers a more reliable kick drum to follow, but other genres can present difficulties. As such, the snare is a good sound to follow when beat matching.

EQing

During a song that has a very identifiable and common chorus or hook, some DJs will cut off the sound or the bass in order to allow the crowd to hear themselves sing. If you cut out the bass, you will allow the crowd to still hear the song but without the lows that can fill up the sound box. Or you can just cut the sound out completely. For example, in Black Sheep's "The Choice is Yours," a DJ will play the chorus . . . *"Engine, engine number"* (and then cut out the sound and let the crowd say) . . . *"On the New York transit* (and then cut out the sound and let the crowd say *line*). DJs try to not use this more than three times per night so it doesn't lose its effect. EQing serves to bring out the energy of the crowd, and can give people a good surprise when they hear themselves singing unexpectedly.

Doubles/Looping

When a DJ takes a chorus or hook and repeats it on another turntable to extend it. This is particularly effective for tracks that contain catchy lyrics.

Quick Mixing

There's a general club rule that anything old school (including '80s and classic hip hop) should not be played for too long. This follows Grandmaster Flash's Quick Mix Theory.

THE ART OF SCRATCHING

If you don't think scratching qualifies as art, check out a Q-Bert routine on YouTube sometime. Grandmaster Flash, Theodore, and the early pioneers began to use scratching and cutting on recorded tracks as well as in their live sets, and first Grandmixer D.ST and then Jam Master Jay showed that scratching could make a group sound and look cool.

Then in the mid- to late-'80s came the transform and other new scratching variations from turntablists such as Cash Money and DJ Jazzy Jeff, whose rise to prominence coincided with the beginning of mixing tournaments such as DMC, Skratchon, and the International Turntablist Federation. Q-Bert and the other Invisibl Skratch Piklz and other crews like the X-Ecutioners, Bullet Proof Space Travelers, and Bombshelter DJs took scratching to another level in the '90s, and today scratch DJing is as popular in Europe and Asia as it is in the U.S..

While house and traditional hip hop DJs focus on creating the perfect mix and have to be careful not to beat clash or risk alienating the dancefloor with anything too daring, the turntablist is generally more experimental. As such, turntablists have an

unspoken bond with each other that acknowledges and appreciates scratch routines for their difficulty and the time spent
preparing and practicing them. Scratching can be heard in clubs
to help transition between records, but you generally won't hear
scratching routines on the mainstream club circuit as it's not
something the masses understands or appreciates. While many
DJs ultimately hope for commercial success, turntablists are
happy spending hours honing their scratching craft in
anonymity and look forward to showing their skills to other like
minds via communal practice sessions, battles, and competitions. Scratching does feature, in its most basic form, in pop music, TV ads, and other mediums, but those who are on the
cutting edge care more about their work behind the decks than
about getting in a magazine or on TV. In some ways, this makes
them true artists, obsessed with being the best manipulators of
sound they can be. We're going to show you how to perform the
basic scratches and to use the crossfader to help, but, at the risk
of sounding like a broken record (pun intended), you'll need
to practice scratching regularly over the course of a career to
master it.

CROSSFADER CONTROL

The crossfader is essential in scratching—while one hand ma-
nipulates the record the other controls the crossfader.

Why is crossfader control important?
For a number of scratches, the crossfader is an integral part of
the sounds you can make, allowing you to make record sounds
audible or inaudible. The way in which you grip the crossfader
determines the speed and control you'll have in manipulating it.

What is the fader slope?

The fader slope determines the speed with which the crossfader opens the sound with respect to a given turntable. When mixing and blending, the traditional fader slope allows for a gradual blend as the crossfader moves from left to right or vice versa (the option on the left). However, when scratching, most DJs prefer a fader slope that allows them to instantaneously open or close the sound of a given turntable (the option on the right).

What is the cut-on point?

The cut-on point is the point at which a crossfader opens the sound with respect to a given turntable (the fader slope of the crossfader determines the cut on point). The cut-on point is essential to scratching because instead of having to move the crossfader all the way from the right position to the left position, or vice versa, an instantaneous cut-on point allows the DJ to open and close the fader with respect to a given turntable in a fraction of the amount of time that it would normally take to open or close the fader.

How do I control the crossfader with quick movements?

Two ways: finger control and wrist control.

By limiting control of the fader to the fingers, you can greatly increase speed and accuracy. The key to controlling the fader in this fashion is to begin with the crossfader closed, either in the right or left position, and to then use your fingers to tap the crossfader back and forth over the cut-on point. This greatly increases your speed by cutting out the need to use the arm to move the crossfader back and forth.

Next comes wrist control.

The only difference between finger control and wrist control is that you use the wrist to move the fader back and forth, instead of using your fingers to tap the fader. Holding the fader at the top is essential when using the wrist to move it back and forth.

What is the best way to use finger control?

When practicing finger control of the crossfader, please keep the following in mind: First, the crossfader should begin and end in the closed position. Next, place your thumb against the inside wall of the crossfader. It is important to rest your thumb against the crossfader and to not push your thumb against the crossfader. The most important concept here is to think of the joint of the thumb as a spring, at rest against the crossfader when it is in the closed position. The opposing fingers should not touch the outside wall of the crossfader.

CROSSFADER EXERCISES

Crossfader Cut-On Exercise

This exercise will help you recognize the location of the crossfader's cut-on points. Make sure to pay attention to the visual location of the point, as well as the physical feel of where the point is on the mixer, since you shouldn't have to look at your crossfader when you mix or scratch records! Also, make sure to check the slope control on the fader first.

1. Play a record on turntable #1.
2. Move the fader to the right position (at this point, the music should not be playing through the speakers).
3. Move the fader slowly towards the left position.
4. When the music starts playing through the speakers, you've found that mixer's cut-on point for turntable #1.
5. Repeat the exercise to find the cut-on point for turntable #2 starting with the crossfader at the L position.

Finger Control Exercise

Follow the steps above to help guide you through this exercise. Also, make sure to switch the slope control on the fader to the "mountain" option. First, play any record on turntable #1. Then move the fader to the right position (at this point, the music should not be playing through the speakers) and rest your thumb against the inside wall (as seen above). Tap the fader with your opposing fingers. Then, experiment with quick taps and more extended taps. These will be essential for other scratches like forwards, stabs, and transforms, which are more advanced.

BABY SCRATCH

What is it?
Pushing and pulling the record over the tip (the beginning) of the sample. You simply move your hand on the record back and forth. This is the original scratch and DJs frequently use it even in the club setting to add to their mixes.

What noise am I trying to make?
You are trying to create the sound of pushing and pulling the record over the tip of the sample.

How do I do it?
Line up the record at the tip of the sample and push the record until you hear the "Aa" of the "Aaaahhh" sample. Then pull the record back and hear the sound in reverse: "aA"

Is there anything else I should know?
There are three things to keep in mind when performing the baby scratch (and other record scratches). First, find a sample and line it up at the needle. Create a visual marker on the record's label

that you can use to make sure the sample stays lined up. Second, pretend your fingers are glued to the record at 9 o'clock. *Don't take your fingers off the record.*

Baby Scratch Exercise

Cue the tip of the "Aaaahhh" sample. Use a sticker or pen to mark the record at 12 o'clock. Play a beat on the other turntable. Baby scratch to the beat. Focus on scratching to a steady rhythm.

Drag Scratch

What is it?

Slowly pushing and slowly pulling the record over a sample.

What noise am I trying to make?

It should sound like you are dragging the record slowly over a sound, hearing both the push and the pull.

Is it similar to anything I already know?

This is the exact same scratch as the baby scratch, except done more slowly and over the course of the entire sample.

How do I do it?

Line up the record at the tip of the sample and slowly push the record until you hear the "A a a a h h h " of the "Aaaahhh" sample. Then slowly pull the record back and hear the sound in reverse "h h h a a a A".

Drag Scratch Exercise

Cue the tip of the "Aaaahhh" sample. Then use a sticker or pen to mark the record at 12 o'clock. Next, play a beat on the other turntable. Finally, drag scratch to the beat. Focus on scratching to a steady rhythm.

Scribble Scratch

What is it?
Pulling and pushing the record very quickly over the tip of a sample.

What noise am I trying to make?
It should sound like a higher pitched baby scratch.

Is it similar to anything I already know?
This is very similar to the baby scratch, except done more quickly. It is usually performed twice as fast.

How do I do it?
Line up the record at the tip of the sample and push the record fast until you hear the "Aaa" of the "Aaaahhh" sample. Then quickly pull the record back and hear the sound in reverse "aaA."

Scribble Scratch Exercise

Cue the tip of the "Aaaahhh" sample. Then use a sticker or pen to mark the record at 12 o'clock. Play a beat on the other turntable. Finally, scribble scratch to the beat. Focus on scratching to a steady rhythm.

BACKSPIN

The backspin can be used in several ways, but here we're going to focus on it as a mixing tool. This radical transition creates an in-your-face sound that gives you the ability to switch between records without having to mix them. The backspin is simply pulling hard on the playing record so that it backspins on its own and then cutting the fader over to the cued record to come in immediately. Hip hop and reggae DJs frequently use this technique to switch between records, favoring a fast and sometimes abrupt transition over a slower more gradual one.

Slow Repeat Backspin

The slow repeat backspin is the process of turning off the turntable playing the outgoing record and then consecutively pulling back and releasing the record to replay a particular sample or beat. The volume control is used to cut out the sound when pulling back the record. The sample or beat will then play consecutively, but play more slowly each time until it dies.

Note that the volume control movement occurs a split second before the record movement even though it looks like it is done in tandem. This type of backspin effect will make it sound as if the outgoing record is dying. In turn, this will increase the impact of the incoming record.

MIXING FOR HOUSE VS. MIXING FOR HIP HOP

A lot of hip hop DJing is about instant crowd reaction and satisfaction, and so the philosophy of the DJ has to be one of openmindedness and flexibility. Hip hop DJs do plan to use certain tracks and may order their sets based on the venue and time of performance, but they can only plan their sets to a certain extent. It all comes down to the crowd that night at that one gig.

DJ GEOMETRIX (WASHINGTON, D.C.—TROOPERZ CREW) TOP 10 SONGS THAT WILL GET A REACTION 10 YEARS FROM NOW

1. Juvenile — "Back that Azz Up"
2. Lil Jon & East Side Boyz — "Get Low"

3.   Ying Yang Twins—"Salt Shaker"
4.   50 Cent—"In Da Club"
5.   Usher—"Yeah"
6.   Mystikal—"Shake Ya Ass"
7.   Nelly—"Hot In Herre"
8.   2Pac—"California Love"
9.   House of Pain—"Jump Around"
10. Rob Base and DJ Easy Rock—"It Takes Two"

With today's hip hop DJ, or those who favor the mash-up style in particular, that's not very long—anywhere from twenty seconds to two minutes of each song is played before mixing into or cutting to the next. These DJs tend to be more spontaneous, responsive, and open, and are not afraid to blend in house, reggae, and any other style that they feel will complement a set.

House DJs tend to play entire songs more often. Therefore, they can really plan their sets ahead of time and many put a lot of effort into doing just that. They are open for adaptation based on crowd reaction or instinct, but the house DJ usually has a fairly solid idea of track selection and order before stepping into the booth. The perfect house set builds across several hours until, at its peak, the crowd is completely at the disposal of the DJ. The best house DJs match not only beats but also harmonies and key, so that tracks flow even more smoothly, without the crowd even knowing when the songs are changing. The ability to wind down a night or set is as important to the house DJ as the power to build to a crescendo at the right moment. It's all about track selection, timing, and knowing the crowd.

THE ART OF THE MIXTAPE

Back out of the lab and into the classroom again. So, if you don't
have access to turntables, now is the time to start paying attention. Actors use a head shot photo with their résumé on the back
when attempting to get auditions. For aspiring DJs, the mixtape
is their head shot; a way of showing their skills to radio stations,
club promoters, potential managers, and to music fans. In the
early days of house music, more established DJs who had earned
club residencies also used the mixtape to distribute their live
sets, this had the dual purpose of raising their profiles and earning extra money on the side. The mixtape was also popular in the
early days of hip hop, when DJ sets were a permanent fixture in
Sony Walkmans and boom boxes. Some of today's DJs, such as
Atlanta's finest turntablist Klever, still produce mixtapes that
generate buzz in the underground hip hop scene. Now that
we've shown you how to mix, you can put your newfound skills
to work by creating your own musical calling card—your own
mixtape.

Nowadays, of course, the mixtape will probably not be a tape
at all, but rather an MP3 file or CD. Regardless of the format,
the DJ must meticulously plan the track list that's included on a
mixtape, demonstrating an ear for hot tracks, technical prowess,
and the ability to craft a set people would pay to hear. The mixtape is an advertisement that on average gets listened to for no
more than two minutes by promoters who could receive dozens
or even hundreds of mixes each week, so having a compelling intro that will catch people's attention and make them listen for
longer is essential.

The mixtape can also be a DJ's only chance to connect with
the person who could launch their career, so it must be meaningful. The mixtape should be raw, energetic, and representa-
tive of a DJ's unique style and personality. If it just sounds like

everyone else's work it will be going into a promoter's or agent's trash can.

To learn more about the art of making and distributing mixtapes, we turned to London's DJ Yoda (Duncan Beiny), who was named by ℚ magazine as "One of the 10 DJs to See Before You Die." Before he started playing clubs, Yoda made a name for himself by making killer mixtapes.

> "I was making tapes for myself of music I was into at the start. Then I started making copies for friends. Then I began taking 50, 100, 200 copies into London record shops. Then it took off and they were selling well— 1,000 copies or more—and I got picked up by a record label. I had sheets of paper with record shop listings and would call them asking if they would sell my tapes. We'd do it on a sale-or-return basis, so if they couldn't have sold them they'd have given them back, but luckily that didn't happen."

Yoda believes that the advent of digital music has changed the game of creating and distributing mixes. "It's a different age now," he says. "The covers and presentation aren't important any more—it's about making something original that will grab people's attention. Just be yourself and don't copy anyone. I get sent a lot of mixes and most people are trying to sound like someone else. I don't know why people don't just play the music *they* like and put their own stamp of originality on the mix."

Another Brit, James Zabiela, who plays at clubs across the globe, took a more cerebral attitude to crafting the mixtapes that earned him his big break. He reveals that hours of work went into crafting his early recorded mixes in the mid-'90s. "I actually broke about four tape decks because I used to copy so many tapes and the heads would wear out. I was such a perfectionist and would take ages getting the tape right, so I'd often break the tape player because I'd keep pressing the record button and rewinding it and re-recording until I got the mix just perfect," he says. "Obviously, when you're recording a mix on a computer and make a mistake, you can go back and quickly correct it but back then it was one take, recorded for forty-five minutes, and it was stressful. I never had a computer, I never had the Internet or anything like that, and the only way of getting a gig was to make a mixtape."

Zabiela advises budding DJs to put as much time and effort into the presentation of a mix CD as into the actual mixing. While this differs from Yoda's approach, both DJs made it big on the strength of their mixtapes, so you've got to find what works for you. "I did a graphic design course in college and worked for a design company that was owned by the same guy who ran the record store I worked at," Zabiela says. "I'd use my graphic design skills to make my own sleeves and make my mixtapes and CDs look really cool before I sent them off to promoters and magazines. Everything was channeled into DJing. When I was designing flyers for promoters I would say 'Can I put my name on the flyer?' and occasionally that worked. That was a good way of getting a gig and it was also a great way of establishing a relationship with club promoters."

Zabiela's big break came when he entered *Mixmag* magazine's Bedroom Bedlam competition and won.

> "[My] tape ended up in Sasha's car," he says. "He used to listen to it on the way to gigs and so he called me in for a meeting at his agency."

Zabiela and Yoda are just two of the many DJs whose careers were launched by creating quality mixtapes and peddling them to anyone who would listen. Wait until you're completely satisfied before putting out a mix, as a bad one can set back a career before it has really started. When you're happy with your mix, send it to promoters who would think about booking an unknown name for their clubs, give it to any industry contacts you may have, distribute it to as many friends as will play it, and then get working on the follow-up!

BUILDING A SET

> *If you play a big record when people aren't ready, the effect of it is lost. Knowing how to do things properly is a craft.*
>
> —John Digweed

To be a successful DJ, merely knowing how to use the equipment and how to scratch, beat match, and accomplish the other tricks of the trade is not enough. Although being able to select tracks that will engage your audience is also important, you have to know how to structure them in a way that will entertain from the first bar of your set to the last. This involves knowledge of the genre you'll be playing (classic hits, the latest big tracks, future favorites, and everything in between), the venue and the time of the set, plus a hundred other variables. Z-Trip explains that the advances in DJ technology and changes in fans' expectations are creating new challenges for DJs looking to craft and deliver engaging sets.

"People are less and less focused on music. I'll play at a festival, and instead of dancing there are kids watching something on a huge TV screen. They're not communicating on the dancefloor like fans used to. As a DJ, the way to overcome that is to challenge yourself and the crowd. If you know you'll be playing at a venue where people may stand and watch you instead of dancing, you've got to have a set that is visually engaging, so pick tracks that you'll do a lot of scratching on. It's your job as the DJ to retrain people's ears. You're in control when you're DJing, so you need to step up."

No need to be intimidated—we've broken down every aspect of building a set for you.

Before we really get going, here's what house music legend John Digweed has to say about delivering a set. "If you play a big record when people aren't ready, the effect of it is lost," he says. "Pacing a night conserves energy for later on, so that people want the big tunes later. Knowing how to do things properly is a craft."

Location, Location, Location

Geography is the first factor to consider when planning a set. The regulars at a rural Nebraska bar, it's safe to say, will not want to hear the same tracks as the party crowd in Miami Beach. While you can't be coerced or controlled by the audience's expectation, as the role of the DJ is to decide upon and deliver the music, you can't discount where you are and who you're playing too, either. The crowd's reaction will ultimately determine whether the promoter asks you back.

"Each set has different rules," says Z-Trip. "I don't ever play all the same records at two different venues, but there will be elements that people can tell sound like me, familiar tracks or mixing techniques. If I'm in the South I know they love crunk, so I'll get those type of tracks lined up, or if I'm in Hollywood it's more of a party vibe so I'll buy more of the commercial songs that are big right now. Your location is very important."

It's the same for house DJs, hip hop DJs, and any other style of DJ—you have to think about how the locale will influence the taste of the crowd. "No matter where I go, the venue is very important in determining what I play," says Sasha. "If you're playing an open-air club in Romania, a boat party in Miami, or a tiny, dark club in New York you're going to play three different sets."

While quality mixing is paramount in a club or at a festival, the clientele at other venues may well be looking for something other than a beautifully constructed set. "In a wine bar or lounge, beat mixing isn't important—it's all about a smooth blend," says Tom Middleton. "You can find tracks with similar tempos and as the record you're playing is trailing off just move the crossfader across to bring in the opening beats of the next track. It's not really mixing but a crowd like that won't care—it's all about a soundtrack that's a narrative to their evening. In that environment, the priorities are your choice of music and the order you present it. The DJing techniques employed by Kissy Sell Out and Boyz Noise are what I did when I started. You turn everything up, use abrupt mixing to chop and change between tracks. It's not smooth like the traditional house sound. I went to a house party last weekend, and what the kids there loved was that the DJ's mix was high-energy and dramatic. They aren't concerned with hearing a subtle and smooth blend."

Genre

DJs can't play one style of music. The masses want to hear it all—hip hop, house, rock—all under one roof.   —*DJ Skribble*

If you're a hip hop junkie, understanding the roots of breaks, scratching, and rapping and the fundamentals of song structure (see chapter 7) will help you identify the best new songs. It's the same for any other genre—there is not only subjectivity but also quality benchmarks set by the likes of Grandmaster Flash, Afrika Bambaataa and Run-D.M.C. for hip hop, and Leftfield,

Underworld, and the Chemical Brothers for house, and today's music can be measured against them.

Another reason to research classic tracks in your chosen genres is that a sprinkling of these musical gems in a set connects you and the audience with something they'll remember fondly. And if what you're playing isn't going over well, pulling out a classic from the record crate is always a reliable back-up plan to recapture the crowd's attention.

DJ EXCEL'S (PHILADELPHIA—SKRATCH MAKANIKZ) TOP 10 "OH, CRAP, I JUST CLEARED THE DANCE FLOOR, HELP ME GET THEM BACK" SONGS

1. Bell Biv Devoe—"Poison"
2. Rob Base & DJ EZ Rock—"It Takes 2"
3. Michael Jackson—"Wanna B Startin' Somethin'"
4. Daft Punk—"One More Time"
5. Sean Paul—"Temperature"
6. Stardust—"Music Sounds Better With You"
7. AC/DC—"All Night Long"
8. Beyonce—"Crazy in Love"
9. 50 Cent—"I Get Money"
10. Enur fa Natasja—"Calabria"

But knowing your genre doesn't stop with an appreciation of musical history. To be relevant among the ever-swelling ranks of DJs, you need to know what's big right now. Listening to traditional or satellite radio, from underground shows to the Top 40, is a great way to do this. The Internet is also a useful tool. From podcasts to online music communities to buzz charts on DJs' Web sites, you need never feel out of touch with the scene. Going to clubs, lounges, or bars is also essential. If you're going to know what works on the dancefloor, the best way is to see the physical reaction of a crowd when a new track comes in. Just because a record sells well doesn't mean it's club friendly or suitable for a party. Checking out music via all these mediums will also help you get a sense of where your favorite genre is heading.

"As a DJ there's the social responsibility of introducing people to new music, and blending familiarity with unfamiliarity for the crowd," says Tom Middleton. "I love the energy of being able to start somewhere and take people through a complete range of styles and genres while maintaining the groove that keeps them dancing."

Sticking to one genre is the easiest way for a beginner to build a set, as the records you'll play will have a similar sound, tempo, and song structure. If you're a hip hop DJ, you're going to want to plan on playing just part of each record, as the typical crowd is not as patient as a house audience. You're going to be expected to play a lot of the current jams. The mash-up DJ has an even greater challenge, as he or she must be familiar with multiple genres and be able to combine tracks from them all into one cohesive set that balances creativity with crowd appeal. Once you're comfortable with constructing and playing a set within one genre, pick another couple of musical styles that you're into. Then start listening to your own music and the new hits in those genres to see which sound like they'll complement the tracks from your preferred style (for a lot more on this, see the next chapter). DJ Skribble is the epitome of the mash-up DJ, varying his sets to suit the audience and venue. "Now, DJs can't play one style of music. The masses want to hear it all—hip hop, house, rock—all under one roof, which is what Louie Vega used to do at Fun House back in the day," he says. "You can put me into any situation, into a college bar or an underground rave and I'm going to rock it. I love all music and all aspects of DJing so I never want my craft to stay in one place."

If you are going to mix, for example, a house record into a hip hop record, you'll need to make sure they're two tracks that work together, from the tempo to the vocals to the key they're in. A well-performed mash-up is about fusing musical styles, but there has to be some method to it, or it will just be a mess. If you can't find two records that go perfectly that's OK—you can use one track that just has a beat. DJ AM explains how he puts this into practice for gigs at his club LAX: "My default drum beat has been [Afrika Bambaataa's] 'Planet Rock.' So, if I have a song that may not fit I'll play it alongside 'Planet Rock'—you can't do mash-up tracks in isolation." Practice small parts of the mash-up set before you play it out, and have a back-up plan for each track combination. What you think sounds good in your bedroom may be awful at the club. Basically, keep a few classic and current hits that you know any crowd will love close at hand, and if you screw up a mash-up, get one of them on as quickly as possible to recapture the dancefloor.

Throwing a Themed Party

Another way to build a set is to pick a theme and choose records that fit with it. For example, it could be a New York theme. Just pick tracks that have lyrics about the city and reference it. It could be hip hop, funk, jazz—anything and everything that ties back to the theme. Making a set thematic will help you prepare and deliver the mix and cause it to be memorable in the minds of the attendees. DJ Yoda explains how the theme works great for a mixtape and club night alike. "I like the idea of a tight theme. I did a country-and-western-inspired compilation and an '80s-infused compilation. A-Trak did a great Dirty South, hip hop mix combined with electro and house. A theme will structure your mix and make it unique."

To start understanding themes, pick a few of your favorite tracks from several genres and listen to them all the way through until you can identify at least one driving message per song. Then look through your music collection for other tracks with the same theme. Genre is not important here—you can tie together songs in a set by a common message they feature. This not only benefits you as the DJ but also gives the crowd a way to identify with what you're playing, whether they're on the floor from the first track onward, walk in halfway through the night, or just catching the last few tracks. A lot of people that go to clubs and parties attend so many that the DJ sets they hear become blurred together and almost indistinguishable. Creating a mix around a theme will help your set stand out both when it's first heard and also months later in the recollections of those who heard it. Mash-up DJs such as British outfit 2 Many DJs, Annie Mac, and Mr. Mash-Up himself, DJ AM, frequently use themes to create fresh and engaging sets.

Rob Swift explained how he's using that theme of a particular musical legend to inspire track selection for an upcoming set. "Later this month I'm spinning at a club and the theme is Miles Davis," he says. "I'm going through my Miles Davis collection, getting back in touch with tunes that will fit well. Then I'll go to the record stores to get other tracks I've listened to that will work. I'll probably play a jazz track like "Melting Pot" by Booker T and the MGs. Even though it's not by Miles Davis, it's up-tempo, makes you want to move, and it will fit with the Miles stuff. I know it will work because I know the Miles vibe."

Another reason that mash-up DJs are successful is because they offer something for everyone. A guy might not like the two hip hop songs you played back-to-back, but may dig the disco classic you brought in next. And the fact that you're keeping a theme going throughout the night will make your sound coherent, even if you play records from ten or twelve different genres.

DJ Yoda says that whether you're using a theme or any other method to organize a set, you've got to put your own imprint on it to stand out. "What's important is having your own style—I can spot my favorite DJs just by listening to their sets—their music sounds like their personality," he says.

Based on Beats

Whether you're playing music from just one genre or from ten different ones a simple way to craft a set is to determine a bpm range for all the tracks you're going to play. That will mean you need to use the pitch control and record manipulation minimally, simplifying beat matching and enabling you to maintain the tempo of the set so the crowd can keep dancing without having to adjust to a change in rhythm. Whether you use some of the manual methods we suggested earlier in the chapter for measuring bpm, or rely on a digital beat counter or beat counting software, once you've been DJing for a while you will instinctively know the rough bpm of each track, or at least whether they're of comparable speed. We suggest going with a fairly narrow bpm range, such as only picking tracks that are between 95 and 105 bpm, but if you insist on using a slightly larger span, you can label the tracks by bpm and arrange them in your CD case/record box accordingly. "Back in the day I'd play any track that'd make people dance if it was between 110 and 125 bpm," says legendary house DJ Tony Humphries. "Now I've expanded that a little, but it's still a good way to choose tracks, and it makes it easier for you to mix them."

TAKING THE TASTE TEST

Being a good DJ is about balancing what your ego wants with what the audience you're playing to wants. —Matt Black from Coldcut

You can have top-of-the-range equipment and impeccable mixing skills and still be an awful DJ. How? Simple. An inability to select tracks your audience will like and play them in a sensible order. So, playing one big hit after another is out. So is playing a whole set of unfamiliar material. "Digital software puts tracks in line, but it doesn't choose the records you play—that's something you gain from years of experience," says John Digweed. "The DJ is still making the choices. If you get the selection wrong it won't matter how perfectly it's mixed. Good DJs play records that make sense when you hear them together. That's what people said about Larry Levan, that he was talking to you through what he played. I'd rather hear a DJ play good music and mix it badly than the other way round." "I spend all my time between shows searching for and listening to new music," says Annie Nightingale. "I have to keep my show on the cutting edge. What I do well is introducing listeners to the best of new music. I listen to hundreds of new tunes a week, and there could be three good new tracks in a week, thirteen the next, twenty-five the next. You just never know so you have to listen to everything and anything. The genre doesn't matter—a good track is a good track. I don't care about bpm or how a song sounds, and actually I prefer playing all sorts because people won't listen to a show for two hours if all the tracks sound the same. My job is just to find the best music and share it with my audience."

To Digweed, the reaction of the crowd is the ultimate judge of a set. "I played a show in Greece and a guy was giving me a hard time about how CDs were soulless and don't have the same effect as vinyl," he says. "But to me, it's what comes out of the speaker that's important, not the format. If people are dancing it doesn't matter."

DJ RASTA ROOT'S (ATLANTA—SMOKIN' NEEDLES) TOP 10 CLUB RECORDS

1. Pharoah Monch—"Simon Says"
2. MOP—"Ante Up"
3. Red & Meth—"Rockwilda"
4. Kanye West ft. T-Pain—"Good Life"

(continued)

5. Mobb Deep—"Quiet Storm"
6. Frankie Beverly ft. Maze—"Before I Let Go"
7. Audio 2/50 Cent—"Top Billin'/I Get Money" (Rootzilla live mash-up)
8. Goapele—"Closer"
9. Nas—"Made You Look"
10. Chubb Rock—"Treat 'Em Right"

New York house legend Junior Sanchez agrees that what you play is the primary factor that will determine if the set is successful. "It's all about taste and selection—I'd rather hear a guy play great music and mess the mix up than hear a great mix of crap records," he says.

Selecting tracks a crowd will react to is not just about knowing your classics and keeping up-to-date on current hits. You also have to be willing to experiment with new songs from unproven artists and producers. We asked Z-Trip how he uses unknown tracks to enliven sets.

"I always have twenty tracks with me that I love but which may be too cutting edge for most crowds. If the opening of my set goes well, I'll pull out a few of those tracks and just hit them with it. When I do it and people go nuts, I know that's one of my best nights on the tour. As a DJ, you have to get to that point, where the crowd feels comfortable with you and knows that you're going to lead them where they want to go. I'm always thinking of giving them something new, because it keeps them interested and me excited, even if it's the last show of a long tour."

RECIPE BOOK TIME

> *To get people dancing you have to be subtle—you can't just throw on all*
> *the big classics early. You have to introduce different elements gradually*
> *and build the set.*
> —DJ Yoda

There is no infallible format for putting tracks in order, as every genre, venue, and DJ will influence how it's done. However, we do have a few simple pointers for you to follow.

If you're a hip hop DJ, take the advice of many of the top DJs and make your set preparation into a personal experience. Imagine there's just one girl or guy on the dancefloor, who epitomises what that venue is about. As you're picking out tracks, keep in mind that you're trying to get and keep her or him dancing. A few classics, a lot of new tracks, whatever you think will work for that one special person. That's it. If you can apply that mentality to your track selection and order, you'll be fine. DJ Nu-Mark says:

> "For me a party is about texture. I don't start out and say
> I'm gonna build it from this artist or this age to this age
> or go from rock to hip-hop or any of that. I blend tex-
> tures, so if the texture of a hip hop song matches the
> texture of a funk song then I'm gonna blend them."

If you're a house DJ, you need to incorporate the peaks and valleys in your set, which for a house crowd culminate in a crescendo in the middle of the headliner's set and then goes back down to a still danceable, but not as euphoric, level. To hook the crowd, you'll need to build complexity as you progress. Aim to start and finish with more simple tracks, with classics and current hits sandwiched on either side by more minimal tracks. The big tunes are the peaks of the waves. Pick out the ul-

timate record that you know will rip the roof off and make that
the track that you'll unleash in the middle of the set. If you really
want to keep the crowd going, two copies or two different mixes
of the same track can work perfectly.

Preparing for a Set—The Trick of Timing

*For a two- or three-hour set you build up a momentum and an energy that
carries you. For six- or eight-hour sets there's more of a richness and deep-
ness. It's like getting lost in a good novel, whereas a shorter set is like flick-
ing through a magazine.*
                                      —Richie Hawtin

Even before you start thinking about record selection, you've got to
be aware of what time of day or night you'll be playing. If your set
will be at a club, go to it on a different night during your designated
time slot and see what type of music is being played and how the
crowd reacts to the DJs who are used to playing then. A 9:00 P.M.
warmup set is going to differ wildly from the headlining midnight
slot, which will be different again from the after-hours final slot.

    The length of your set will also help determine what tracks
you select and their order. Sasha explains how he works a long
mix: "With a nine-hour set you can't just bring people up and up.
You've got to take them up, bring them down, and go back up
again to keep things interesting—keep people dancing. But then
you can't go so low that they leave because they think you're
done. There's an art to it."

DJ ANI QUINN'S (NYC) TOP 11 QUESTIONS DJS DON'T WANT TO HEAR WHILE DJING

1. "Can you play something good?"
2. "If you play such and such, I promise everyone's going to start dancing!"

3.   "If you play such and such, my friends and I will start dancing and we'll really get the party started!"

4.   "Can you make an announcement? I can't find my friend (keys, cellphone, purse, jacket, hat, etc.)."

5.   "I know you just played such and such, but could you play it again for me?"

6.   "I missed it. I was in the bathroom."

7.   "You said you'd play such and such. Can you play it now? My friends and I are leaving."

8.   "It's my brithday! Can you play 50 Cent's, 'It's Your Birthday?'" (The name of the song is "In Da Club!" At least get that right.)

9.   "Can you play something faster?"

10.   "Is this what you're playing all night?"

11.   "Can I leave my coat with you?"

At the other end of the spectrum is the mini mix, which can be just thirty minutes or less. For this, you're not going to get away with playing nine-minute house epics, but will need to use parts of your records. Go through your tracks and seek out individual elements, such as catchy vocal hooks, powerful basslines, and funky breaks, that you can use to make up a short set. In some ways, you'll need to spend longer preparing for a brief set, because there's less time for experimentation when you hit the DJ booth. You can write out your set list, or just pack the tracks you'll need in order, as you won't be able to use many.

Digweed told us about the differences between warmup and peak-time sets. "A few nights ago I played a club and had the volume on low," he says. "The sound guy came up to me and asked me if there was something wrong with the sound system. Ten minutes later the manager asked the same question, because he thought it was too quiet. I told him it wouldn't be in an hour. There's no point in walking into a club and red-lining the volume when nobody's in there. When the place filled up I cranked it up and the dancefloor was rocking. Sometimes you go to clubs and DJs are playing the biggest records of the night first, but nobody's ready to dance. It's wrong. The hardest job for a DJ is doing an opening set."

In case you're wondering what the difference is between warming up, headlining, and playing the last set of the night, we've put together this quick guide.

9:00 P.M–12:00 P.M.—You have to get the audience prepared and set the mood for the rest of the night. It's a bit of cat-and-mouse type of game. You want to tease them a bit, win their loyalty. Music in this warmup slot can be just a backdrop for the crowd, so you're able to experiment more than you would during a peak hours set.

James Zabiela, one of the most popular and proficient U.K. house DJs, told us that warming up for his mentor, Sasha, helped him understand the importance of the warmup DJ.

> "I got to be very respectful of what I played and warming up I would sound much more mellow, rather than going in and smashing the room to pieces. You have to get people on the dancefloor, keep them grooving, keep them happy, but without stealing the limelight from the headline DJ. You can't be the dessert before the main course. You have to be very wary of what bpm you're playing, you can't play too fast and you can't play any massive records too early in the night."

COSMO BAKER'S (NYC—THE RUB)—TOP TEN SONGS TO END THE NIGHT WITH (AKA "FINISHING OFF STRONG")

1. M.F.S.B.—"Love Is The Message"
2. Eddie Kendricks—"Date With The Rain" Extended Disco Version
3. Womack & Womack—"Baby I'm Scared Of You"
4. LTD—"Love To The World" Extended Edit
5. John Paul Young—"Love Is In The Air"
6. Billy Paul—"East"
7. The Chi-Lites—"My First Mistake"
8. Billy Stewart—"Summertime"
9. Marvin Gaye—"Got To Give It Up"
10. Roy Ayres—"Everybody Loves The Sunshine"

12:00 P.M.–2:00 A.M.—You're in your peak set, but still need peaks and valleys inside this period. You can't just play back-to-back hits for three full hours. You want the set to climax about halfway through.

2:00 A.M.–3:00 A.M.—Give it all you've got. At this stage, the promoter wants you to keep people in the club, so you have to keep them engaged. This set is coming off the back of the headlining DJ, so the crowd will be ready for fireworks from your turntables.

3:00 A.M.–4:00 A.M.—Winding it down. You need to get people out the door, and don't want them too amped up during this time. The whole process needs to be a bell-shaped curve—you welcome them in, interact with them at a high-energy level, and then say your good-byes. A good approach for the closing set is to return to the bpm principle we explored earlier. Set aside a few mellow tracks that you can put on to calm people and wind things down. People want to go away from a club with a smile, and picking high-quality, low-tempo tunes is the best way to achieve this. DJ Yoda suggests calming things down if you're the last DJ in the booth on any given night. "I am a big fan of playing a slow song at the end of the set," he says.

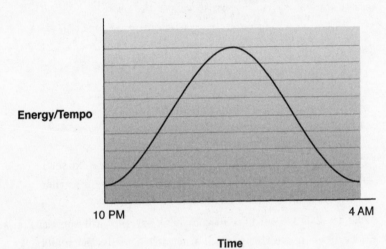

Club Set Energy Flow

Energy/Tempo

10 PM   4 AM

Time

Credit: Steve Woodzell

INSIDER INFORMATION

For me a party is about texture. I don't start out and say "I'm gonna build it from this artist or this age to this age or go from rock to hip hop" or any of that. I blend textures, so if the texture of a hip hop song matches the texture of a funk song then I'm gonna blend them.

—DJ Nu-Mark

"For a commercial crowd, I start big, with two or three absolute smashes that everyone will now," says Z-Trip. "Then I've got the dancefloor hooked, and people will trust me, so I can do my own thing, experiment for a while. Then I will end the set even bigger than how I started it. I look at it like a gymnast's routine—I want to blow the judges—the audience at a club, party, or wherever—away at the end so they leave thinking, Wow!" For Z-Trip, making such an impact may look easy, but it's the result of hours of preparation and practice.

> "My trick is that, no matter where I'm playing, I always have five or six mini sets planned out. Even if you research the crowd and the venue things can go wrong— a crap warmup DJ, an awful sound system. But if you're prepared with your mini sets and each one has a different vibe, you can pull out of almost any situation. If I start to lose the dancefloor I just go to one of my crates or Serato playlists and play the first track from another mini set. If that doesn't work, I'll hit up the next set I have. Just organize your records, CDs, or MP3s so that they're divided in that way, and you'll do fine. The funny thing is that it makes you look like this amazing guy who can cook something up on the fly, but really you've been ready all along."

Tony Humphries learned the fundamentals of building a set when he started on New York's KISS FM in 1981. "Barry Mayo at KISS taught me how to arrange power records, filler tracks, and classics, and I've followed his guidelines to this day," Humphries says. "He figured out that whether it's radio, TV, or in a club, a form of entertainment can keep your attention for fifteen minutes. For me, that meant I had three records to appeal to a broad section of listeners. There'd be no more than three power records per hour, or they lost their effect. I'd play a female vocal track, a male vocal track, and then an instrumental. That way they'd get one story from a female perspective, another from a male, and have time to digest those, before I went into the next story. That's what DJing is—storytelling through music."

"When you're a dance DJ, your primary objective is just to make people dance, to take them on a voyage essentially," says. A-Trak:

> "If you're a good DJ you must have your personal stamp
> that's recognizable in the way that you mix your songs
> and the progression and intensity of your sets through-
> out the night. It's a lot more subtle then hip hop, of
> course, and is entirely focused on the music itself. You
> can't play Baltimore house at 9:30 when you have to see
> people walking into your club. When I see a new DJ
> whose mixes are really clean, plays the right thing at
> the right time in a set that sits well at the time of the
> night he's playing and also brings in a selection that I
> wouldn't have thought of, that's when I get most ex-
> cited about someone. The progression of the songs and
> the relationship between that and what your audience
> is anticipating is an art form."

Even with all this advice, becoming a successful DJ (whatever your definition of success is) is going to take effort, persistence, and the ability to bounce back from disappointment. However, if you apply what you've learned in this chapter, love music, and have a passion for DJing, you will meet your goals. Just remember that whether you're a seasoned pro like DJ AM, Sasha, or Q-Bert, a complete novice or somewhere in between, you can never practice too much or stop improving. Back to the decks with you!

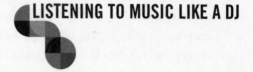

EIGHT

LISTENING TO MUSIC LIKE A DJ

*DJs finding new music and introducing other people to it is what keeps
the music industry alive.* —DJ Z-Trip

As much as this book is about DJing, it is, at its core, about music. About listening to it, selecting it, playing it, playing *with* it, appreciating it, and as cliché as it might sound, finding it within yourself. It's the ultimate uniting force—something that transcends geographical and ideological parameters and infiltrates every aspect of society. Music is why the Scratch DJ Academy was founded, why we're writing this book, and, of course, why you're reading it.

T.S. Eliot once said, "You are the music while the music lasts." This book is for anyone for whom that sentiment holds true. Because while we've spoken to some of the most respected DJs in the business, who get paid a lot of money to play the music they love, it's our belief that there is a DJ in everyone. It's our hope that this book can help you find, explore, and release that inner DJ. Because, before the first gig, before the turntables, before the mixer, before the headphones, before anything, a DJ is someone with a love for music and that, we like to think, is pretty much everyone.

What sets a DJ apart from someone who just likes music? Is there a difference? Certainly DJing is intuitive, and skilled DJs can create moods as much as he or she can reflect or enhance them, but what does this take? Well, a sense of timing helps, and an ability to read the atmosphere of a room or the attitude of a crowd won't hurt either. How do DJs find and select new tracks? This chapter will help you answer these questions. By the time you're done reading it, you should be able to hear music in a new, more attuned way, which will help in identifying the best tracks and combining them in a mix or playlist. And this section will give you a better grasp of the different music genres and how they are related. We'll also discuss how understanding the skills that professionals use can translate into daily life, enhance your overall appreciation of music and ultimately, bring out your inner DJ. DJ Hapa, who appears daily on the Emmy Award winning KTLA Morning News show in L.A. explains:

> "Everyone has the potential to be a DJ. I've taught
> everyone from a six-year-old girl to a sixty-two-year-old
> guy how to DJ, and while they might never become pro
> DJs, just learning more about how to appreciate music
> and select tracks has given them the most important
> principle of DJing: We all have music inside us."

The profession of DJing conjures up a certain mystique in many people's minds, but while it's true that most pro DJs do have some innate musical ability, most of the skills that make them successful can be learned (eventually) by anyone. The first, and arguably most important, part of being a successful DJ is the knack of selecting a track that will evoke a response (whether it's physical, emotional, or both) and then picking another song that complements it. Repeat this simple process several times, and you have a DJ set, mix CD, or an iTunes playlist. Interpreting music is in some respects subjective, but there are objective standards to be applied to song selection, too.

Music is all around us. Listening to it can be personal, such as in your car, on your MP3 player, on TV, or on your computer at school or work. It can also be shared—at a movie theater, a concert, or a Broadway musical. Because we're bombarded with music all day and night, it's very easy to zone out and become ambivalent to everything we hear, even that which we profess to like. To distinguish which tracks have merit, as DJs on every level do, we need to re-educate ourselves, retraining our minds and ears to become more like the DJs'.

"We're in a microwave culture where we want everything right now, and that extends to music," says DJ Hapa. "Having instant access to so much music has tipped the quality versus quantity balance too far toward quantity, and this over-consumption has killed many people's ability to see the beauty in music. You may have 250 GB of music but you can't listen to all of it. DJs are just the opposite—we're searching for quality tracks that work well together in a set to create a connection with our audiences. We're the people who read the sleeve notes on records and CDs to find out who the bass players and pianists are so we can find more of their work."

The first part of releasing your inner DJ is to evaluate the reasons why you're listening to music. If you're just listening for relaxation you will have one set of selection criteria—maybe you're after songs that are downtempo with positive lyrics. Or if you're compiling a playlist to listen to while working out, you'll want something very different—tracks that are high energy and pump you up (check out A-Trak's "Running Man" Nike + Mix mix). For a DJ, the intention could be to get a track for a themed party, finding a record that will get people dancing, or locating a song that will get fans off the dancefloor at the end of the night. Learning to identify a purpose for listening to music is a key part of selecting the correct tracks. DJs are always actively listening, whether it's in a club, at a record store, or online.

The second factor involved in listening to music like a DJ is considering your audience. While the audience shouldn't dictate what is played and when, it cannot be discounted. If you're playing in a club that mostly features Top 40 tracks and you come in and play a deep house set, you're going to be in trouble. Equally, if you use the same track list for a festival that you used the previous night at a family wedding reception, it is unlikely to go over well. If you're able to accurately analyze your audience you will be one step closer to accessing your inner DJ.

"When listening to music I compartmentalize," says Z-Trip. "If I'm working on a remix I'll be honing in on just one part of each track, looking for a horn or vocal I can sample, or just the right beat. At other times I'm looking for tracks that will fit with a festival vibe, or a Dirty South vibe, depending on the shows I have coming up. And sometimes I'm just looking out for songs I can drop anywhere, on any dancefloor."

MAJOR TAYLOR'S (CHICAGO) TOP 10 MOST REQUESTED CLUB SONGS

1. Michael Jackson—"Billie Jean"
2. Prince—"Kiss"
3. Cajmer—"The Percolator"
4. Salt & Pepper—"Push It"
5. Journey—"Don't Stop Believing"
6. Biggie Smalls—"Juicy"
7. Michael Jackson—"PYT"

(continued)

8.   Anything by Jay-Z
9.   Anything by A Tribe Called Quest
10. I'm going to leave this last slot open for whatever
     pop song is huge in the last 2-month period

THE TIMELESS SKILL OF THE SELECTA

Flash, Bambaataa, and the other early hip hop DJs were cutting breaks from artists like Chicago, AC/DC, and Johnny Cash. They'd play whatever made people move.   —Jazzy Jeff

Before the birth of hip hop and house music, the DJ pioneers were to be found in Kingston, Jamaica, in the yards and streets where Bob Marley, Peter Tosh, and Bunny Wailer crafted reggae out of the country's existing ska sound. There were guys, most notably the legendary Lee "Scratch" Perry, who played tracks from these genres alongside rock-steady beats, rock riffs, and soul vocals, but they weren't called DJs—they were known as selectas. This name inferred their ability to choose tracks that people wanted to hear over the incredibly powerful sound systems that gave life to a vibrant, seven-days-a-week party scene.

When Kool Herc took these principles to New York in the early '70s there was no hip hop music as we know it today. Herc and the other New York DJs played whatever records they could find from the history vaults of rock, soul, funk, jazz, and current disco and punk and combined them in the type of eclectic sets we now call mash-ups. "The records we played weren't Top 40, they weren't on the radio," says Grandmaster Caz, Herc's peer. "We were reaching back into the past to find beats and a special something in old classics and hard-to-find tracks."

Beyond their technical ability or mastery of new technology, the best DJs of today stand out because of their encyclopedic knowledge of music, and an innate ability to find tracks from all styles that work together to convey energy and emotion to a crowd. "Flash, Bambaataa, and the other early hip hop DJs were cutting breaks from artists like Chicago, AC/DC, and Johnny Cash," says Jazzy Jeff. "They'd play whatever made people move. The DJ who went above and beyond to find rare tracks was respected, which is why Bambaataa was called 'Master of Records.' Then the other guys would have to up their game to stay competitive. Innovation by one DJ still raises the bar for everyone else."

MUSICAL COMPOSITION 101

> When I listen to regular music I'm listening to the vibe. To everything: the vibes, the melodies, vocals. I listen to it how everyone listens to it. The only difference is I'm thinking, 'Can I use this in my set?'
>
> —DJ Craze

A lot of people think they can cook, but to become a chef, you need culinary school training to understand ingredients, timing, taste, techniques, and texture. When chefs graduate, they view cooking as not merely a household chore or job but as an art form, because they appreciate the different elements that go into it. It's the same with music—the more you learn about the building blocks of music, the better you'll be at listening to, selecting it and playing it so others can share your enjoyment.

"I mainly just listen to music how everyone else listens to music—I just feel alive," says DJ Craze. "Whatever life comes out of the song, that's all I'm paying attention to. When I listen to regular music I'm listening to the vibe, to everything: the vibes, the melodies, vocals. I listen to it how everyone listens to it. The only difference is I'm thinking, 'Can I use this in my set?' "

VERSE, CHORUS, BRIDGE, REPEAT

To be able to select and combine songs effectively, you need to know how the lyrics and music are laid out.

Although each song is different in instrumentation and vocals, a lot of hip hop, rock, and pop music follow the same basic formatting. With almost every song, there are main definable parts:

- **Intro:** The beginning of the song, where the beat comes in and leads in to either the first verse or the chorus. Usually, it doesn't have any lyrics or features the musician talking with or without music. Tracks with longer intros are easier to mix, as you have more time before blending them with the song that's already playing.
- **Verse:** A group of several lyrical sentences that convey the theme(s) of a song. Verses usually have the same melody, but the lyrics are different. Each verse is generally sixteen bars long.
- **Chorus:** The melodic part of the song that repeats throughout it, between the verses, and is sometimes repeated at the end of the track. The chorus usually, but not always, contains the title of the song. It is generally eight bars long.
- **Bridge:** A departure from the general theme of the song. The bridge breaks up the repetitiveness of a song. The bridge is generally 8 bars long. There isn't always a bridge.
- **Outro/Extro:** The outro is the ending of the song.

Here are a few typical song structures (each block below represents 8 bars):

1) Song One

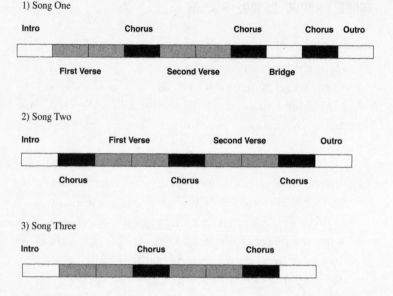

2) Song Two

3) Song Three

The Song Structure of House

As with most hip hop, rock, and pop songs, house music tracks also have some sort of intro and outro, but the body of the song is somewhat different. House music generally has a 16-bar introduction; the duration of the outro varies depending on the song.

The main difference is that, unlike other genres, house music typically builds up, adding instrumentation, vocals, and other elements until reaching a crescendo, and then deconstructs gradually. The intro and outro usually consist of just drum tracks, making them the ideal mixing points. Below is a generic outline of a house song (each block represents eight bars):

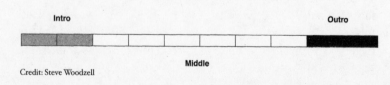

Credit: Steve Woodzell

Song Structure Exercise

Listen to different songs and identify their different song structures.

1. Play a song with vocals.
2. Next, listen to it all the way through and try to identify the intro, verse, chorus, and bridge (if there is a bridge).
3. Now, listen to the song again and count the bars for each segment. Then repeat the process with a different record.

Stay on Frequency

> *A lot of DJs don't listen to music as much as I do. Many of them will get a set they like and keep it the same for four months. With the Radio 1 shows I can't do that even if I wanted to—it has to be fresh.*
>
> —Pete Tong

Regardless of the genre, every song is comprised of three sound frequency ranges—high, low, and mid-range. Mixers allow you to adjust these to alter the dynamics of a song with sliders, knobs, or buttons (also called kill switches), with the purpose of enhancing the track in the context of your mix. Lows are the beats (kick drums and bass sounds). The mids are melodies and vocals, and the highs are instrumental extras such as high hats and tambourines.

A good way to retune your ears is to listen to songs in multiple genres and just focus on identifying the lows—what they sound like, their patterns, how they affect the sound of the track. Then move onto the mids, then the highs. With practice, you'll be able to not just deconstruct individual tracks, but also to instinctively know which songs will complement others, and so will work well together in your MP3 playlists or DJ mixes. DJ/producers use this listening technique to identify tracks that can be combined to make a hot remix—for example Danger Mouse fusing the Beatles' *The White Album* with Jay-Z's

The Black Album to create *The Grey Album,* which catapulted him into the upper echelon of the DJ/producer community.

DJ EXCESS'S TOP TEN CLUB TRACKS

1. Eric B. & Rakim—"Paid In Full"
2. The Pharcyde—"Runnin'"
3. A Tribe Called Quest—"Electric Relaxation"
4. Black Sheep—"The Choice Is Yours (Remix)"
5. De La Soul—"Buddy"
6. Busta Rhymes—"What It Is"
7. 50 Cent—"Just A Lil' Bit"
8. Dr. Dre ft. Snoop Dogg—"The Next Episode"
9. Jay-Z—"Public Service Announcement"
10. The Notorious B.I.G.—"Hypnotize"

The fact that the two components of this mash-up—rock and hip hop—could not be more different shows the vast potential for melding musical styles. DJing and a love of music in general is about instinct and intuition, not logic. Pete Tong has stayed ahead of the game by constantly seeking out the new music that excites him. "I'm twenty years older than most of these new up-and-coming DJs, but I've been able to regenerate and stay in their world," he says. "A lot of DJs don't listen to music as much as I do. Many of them will get a set they like and keep it the same for four months. With the Radio 1 shows I can't do that even if I wanted to—it has to be fresh."

GO YOUR OWN WAY

Entertaining people is the ultimate reason for DJing. To set yourself apart. It's not about inserting something, but just taking what's out there, mixing it with your knowledge of music history, and putting your twist on it.   —Harry "Choo Choo" Romero

The great thing about developing a true DJ's listening acumen is being able to put your own mark on the music you select and the playlists and DJ sets you craft from it. It's almost better if you select an eclectic range of music for your sets—because then you'll have mastered the ability to surprise and excite a crowd and yourself. "I respect DJs such as DJ AM and Z-Trip because they have the courage to play anything," says Jazzy Jeff, himself no stranger to playing the full musical gambit. "Their musical taste is what makes their sets interesting. Each one of these guys takes you to a different musical destination. Too many DJs are playing it safe and just playing what's popular. That's killing the art of DJing. To stand out you need to take your audience on a ride, and there has to be no doubt that as the DJ, you're driving. Otherwise club owners will stop hiring DJs and will just put an iPod in the DJ booth. The task for me, AM, Z-Trip, and other DJs is to keep giving fans our interpretations of what we feel through the tracks we play, and to compel people to groove to what we play. That's what being a DJ means."

When looking for songs and putting your mix together, put yourself in the listener's place. Would you be excited to hear this collection of tracks, and feel like you'd got your money's worth if you heard it at a club or festival? Is this mix CD you just made for your girlfriend or boyfriend or whomever different from anything you've given her or him before? Then maybe ask yourself: Does this selection of songs get *you* excited? If the answer to even one of these questions is no, you'll know it's time to start again.

Balancing Act

> *I get a lot of tracks each day and they're each six or seven minutes long, so even if I skip through them, I'm listening to music for six or seven hours a day. I get at least a hundred and fifty tracks a week now—I'm constantly getting new music.*
>
> —John Digweed

Once you understand how to analyze a song—from the high, low, and mid-frequency ranges to the verses, bridges, and choruses to the beats, bars, and phrases—you're able to listen to it with more critical ears. You'll no longer say you like a song just because it "sounds good," but will rather be judging tracks on their true musical merit and on the basis of the elements they contain. So building a set or playlist, which used to be a chore, becomes a musical adventure.

Harry "Choo Choo" Romero fills us in on getting the balance right:

> "Entertaining people is the ultimate reason for DJing. To set yourself apart it's not about inventing something, but just taking what's out there, mixing it with your knowledge of music history, and putting your twist in it. You've got to step out of your comfort zone to grow as a DJ and an artist."

But remember, the most important thing—more important than the graphs and frequencies and basslines—is just that you're listening to music—avidly, devotedly, passionately. You can't do it incorrectly. If you're paying attention and actively listening, then you're a good way along the road to becoming a DJ. And, if you weren't someone who paid attention to music, who wasn't interested in concentrating on its nuances and inflections, its highs, lows, mid-points, and everything in between, then we doubt you would've read this far.

Going on a Musical Safari

When I was growing up there was none of this genre obsession you find now in the music industry. Hip hop DJs played rock, soul, funk; anything and everything with a good beat, a powerful rhythm that people could vibe to.
—DJ Jazzy Jeff

Most of us have a particular musical style we identify with. For some, it could be tied to where we grew up, or what our parents listened to. But the pioneering hip hop and house DJs played music from all genres. "When I was growing up there was none of this genre obsession you find now in the music industry," says Jazzy Jeff. "Hip hop DJs played rock, soul, funk; anything and everything with a good beat and a powerful rhythm that people could vibe to. It's the same with Frankie Knuckles and the other early house DJs—they played house, hip hop, R&B. Before scratching and the other technical stuff you had to be able to mix tracks together, knowing how each record would fit with the next. I'm trying to get people back to viewing music as music, regardless of genre. I won't be pressured to play just certain styles or the hottest new tracks. I'm the DJ and I control the music."

The time you were just starting to get into music is also an influential factor. Why else would we pay to hear bad '80s cover bands? (well not *us*, of course, but you get the idea). Whatever the reason, a lot of people stick to listening to and learning about just one genre their entire lives, blinkered to the world of musical possibilities around them, and a lot of DJs can be the same way. It's the very nature of music to evolve and fans' tastes to progress with this evolution. DJ Skribble believes that the current DJ scene favors those who can incorporate multiple genres into their sets to have a long shelf life. "Now it's like it was back in 1994, when [Erick, of Subliminal Records fame] Morillo dropped 'I Like to Move It,' because

DJs aren't just sticking to one style," he says. And if you're not a DJ and you just buy one type of music to listen to because that's what you're used to, aren't you getting a little bored of those same old songs?

"I look for something that sounds like something I've heard before, but know I haven't," says DJ Nu-Mark from Jurassic 5. "That's why I like covers of old funk tracks so much, like these James Brown remixes I bought recently. And any cover of Al Green is a winner to me because you can play that for a very Hollywood crowd and for a very deep underground crowd."

DJ NU-MARK'S TOP TEN FUNK SAMPLES

1. Joann Garrett—"It's No Secret." Cadet Records. Produced by Andre Williams.

2. Skip Easterling—"I'm Your Hoochie Coochie Man." Instant Records. Produced by Huey Smith and Tex Liuzza.

3. Soul Rhythm Band—"Mamma's Little Baby." Pelikin Record Company. Produced by Artie Fields.

4. Linda Mackey—"Gotta Find My Man." VJ International Records. Produced by Gabriel Flemmings.

5. Deniece Chandler & Lee Sain—"Hey Baby." Toddlin' Town Records. Produced by C. Johnson & Vineyard.

6. The Battered Ornaments—"Late Into The Night." Harvest Records. Produced by Andrew King.

7. Film Vertonungs Platte—"Get Up." Golden Ring Records. Produced by Klaus Weiss. 1977.

8. The Romeos — "Precious Memories." Revue Records. Produced by N. Montague.
9. Bill Moss — "Keep On Using Me Jesus." Bilesse Recordings. Produced by Bill Moss.
10. Jimmy Takeuch — "Dock of the Bay." SRM Records. Produced by S. Cropper.

As a DJ and a music fan, developing an appreciation of other genres will open your mind to what's out there and teach you more about how your genre of choice fits into the bigger musical picture. You can start by asking music-savvy friends to compile a playlist or recommend a favorite radio show. Or go to a club, festival, or anywhere you'll be in new musical territory.

"The first records I bought with my own money had nothing to do with DJing, like Fleetwood Mac *Rumors*, Elton John's *Greatest Hits*," says Stretch Armstrong. He has a rich and diverse musical background, and it helped him develop the love of music that would propel him into a professional DJing career. "Then I started playing the drums when I was about four, because I loved the Beatles and I liked Ringo's name, and because of all the instruments that appealed to me the most. "When 'Rapper's Delight' came out the fifth graders were imitating it, so I went out and bought it. My sister was obsessed with the poppy side of disco and she also turned me onto reggae. She was my window into black music when I was too young to go to clubs." DJ AM was also exposed to a wide range of music early on. "When I grew up in Philly I went to public school where hip hop was all there was. My sister was a full-on punk rocker, and my parents listened to Elton John, Bob Marley, and Billy Joel, and I loved it all. Back in the '80s, we had Power 99 FM, which gave hip hop love before it was mainstream, playing doubles of Whodini tracks. I wanted to do that."

Embracing the Mash-Up

The rule at my nights at LAX is "play whatever you want to play. Be brave." On certain nights I'll play the Beatles, James Brown, Erick Morillo, everything you can think of in an hour, because I like it all.

—DJ AM

There's a reason that the mash-up style is so popular in so many clubs—people want to listen to all the genres they love without hopping between the house room, the hip hop room, and so on. You don't have to become a mash-up DJ, but occasionally dropping a song from a different genre into your sets or playlist will help you create a connection with a crowd and keep your interest.

The lines we draw between musical types are really nonexistent—while there are characteristics that typify genres the names for each style are imposed by us. As time goes on, genres fragment into subsets, so that now there are so many categories that it's hard to tell what tracks fit where. But music is music, and if you like a track and think a crowd will enjoy it too, why not throw it into your record crate or your playlist? Says Z-Trip:

> "Looking for new music is one of the best things about being a DJ. DJs finding new music and introducing other people to it is what keeps the music industry alive."

"The rule for my nights at LAX is 'play whatever you want to play. Be brave.' On certain nights I'll play the Beatles, James Brown, Erick Morillo, everything you can think of in an hour, because I like it all," says DJ AM.

Mo' Music, Mo' Problems?

Now it's easier to receive, listen to, and play music by new or up-and-coming artists, which makes it more interesting for me. The end result is a more open and inspiring scene with endless possibilities.

—Richie Hawtin

Ten years ago, 99 percent of DJs got their music from record shops. These were not just places for buying music, but also communities where DJs would talk about their upcoming gigs, hot tracks, and what was new on the scene. There was also a competitive element, with DJs trying desperately to get their hands on rare classics and the best recent joints. While they didn't always earn much, record store owners and staff were treated like royalty by DJs, because they held the keys to the music. Cultivating a relationship with all the best record shops in town was the only way for a DJ to stay ahead of the game, and a lot of U.K.-based spinners would think nothing of driving a hundred miles or more to make a pilgrimage to such vinyl emporiums as Blackmarket Records in London's Soho and Hard to Find Records in Birmingham, while any self-respecting DJ in the greater New York area would spend as much time as possible rifling through the racks at Vinyl Mania and Music Factory (stores which, at press time, have thankfully survived the switch to CDs and MP3s).

To afford buying records, many smart young DJs took jobs in record stores, realizing that working both sides of the counter was a fast track to getting the tracks they craved, absorbing the knowledge of the older DJs in the area and meeting club owners and promoters that maybe could offer that elusive first gig. James Zabiela was one of these. "My dad worked at Movement Records in Southampton, and I did my work experience there with school when I was fifteen," he says. "The guy who owned the shop used to pay like £15 a day, but if you took records you got the equivalent of £20 worth. So, I worked there for records. It really became sort of an addiction. I spent my girlfriend's money on vinyl and got into debt because of it. That's kind of how I fell in love with dance music." Today, while there are still some successful record shops, many DJs have turned to CD and MP3 mixing. DJs in the '80s and early '90s had no idea that just a few years later online music sites would overtake their beloved record stores as the default option for finding new tracks, and that online forums and social networking sites would resign the community aspect of all but a few stores to the history books. With the rise of the Internet as a tool for finding tunes, the modern music fan has access to more songs than ever before. This can be a good thing, as there's an almost unlimited selection of old and new music available for listening and purchasing. Techno legend Richie Hawtin tells us about how the availability of music online affects him:

> "There is an avalanche of new music. Every couple of days I go through hundreds of downloads, e-mail links, CDs, and records to figure out what I'll be playing in my next set. There used to be a certain elitism to the scene, because only people with enough money could get all the best tracks, and it was a hassle for artists to get records to the DJs they wanted to play them. Now it's easier to receive, listen to, and play music by new or up-and-coming artists, which makes it more interesting for me. The end result is a more open and inspiring scene with endless possibilities."

While the Web has facilitated access to music, this can create difficulties for the DJ and music lover alike. How can you distinguish between thousands of new tracks and select the best ones?

Here, Sasha compares how he used to acquire music when he was on his way to stardom in the '90s, with how he listens to and buys music today:

> "I developed a relationship with the guys at [Manchester's] Eastern Bloc, the most influential record shop in the country," he says. "I was in there four days a week looking for new tracks. Massive Records was also very influential. They would save me white labels, and that special relationship kept me ahead of the game. Now it's all different. Boomkat [an online music store, found at www.boomkat.com] is my favorite record shop, and I get a lot of my stuff sent digitally. Everyone has access to the same tracks, so it's hard to stay ahead. I used to play an exclusive record for nine months or the whole year. Some of my sets were recorded, but there was no Internet so those tapes weren't everywhere. Now even the most exclusive tracks don't stay exclusive for long."

Harry "Choo Choo" Romero has also embraced the Web as a source for listening to and acquiring new tracks and old classics, but emphasizes the need to listen selectively and critically to the plethora of new tunes he's exposed to each week. "There's such a barrage of music," he says. "I can get thirty e-mails a day with links to thirty tracks per e-mail. I recommend hiring a personal assistant, if you can, just to handle e-mail! A lot of people send me promo copies and I buy a lot of music on [MP3 download stores] Traxsource (www.traxsource.com) and Beatport."

Looking at editors' picks on the music sites and more generic Web outlets like Amazon, iTunes and Rhapsody (www.mp3 .rhapsody.com) are other good starting points, as are browsing forums and DJ community pages, and even MySpace.

The Music Community

*Instant messaging is a primary source for great new music. It comes from
DJs—tastemakers who have good sets of musical ears. There's so much
music now that DJing is about filtering, so you need contacts you trust to
recommend good tracks.*   —Tom Middleton

One way for DJs and music fans to acquire music is to become part of a community, whether that's in person, breaking
down the nights' sets with fellow DJs in a diner at 5:00 A.M., or
with fellow music enthusiasts worldwide via the Internet.

Other than their dedication to the craft of DJing, the main
reason that DJs spend so much time carefully listening to, buying, and putting tracks in their sets is the increasing demands of
today's fans. "Everything moves so fast now," says John Digweed.
"The time between getting a record, putting it in your set, and
playing it is much shorter. You don't promote a record for two
months anymore, because when people hear a track they like,
they want it immediately. They'll take videos on their phones
and put them on YouTube, and that can do a lot for a new track.
The video not only shows the big track, but also the crowd going
nuts. As a record label you have to use all the new channels to get
your stuff out there."

It was Leo Tolstoy who said that "music is the shorthand of
emotion," and we must say, we're inclined to agree. There's music
out there for everyone to find expression in and to express themselves through. You just have to have the inclination to find it, and
the understanding to know when you have it. Once you've discovered *your* music, whether it's jazz, hip hop, house, or a combination of styles then you might want to think about sharing it with
others. And once you've decided to do that, then we're hoping
you'll want to do it in creative ways. And lo! You're a DJ.

NINE

TALES FROM *the* CRATE

In the chapter "The Life of the DJ" we took you inside the world of the DJs, and in the chapter "The Influence of the DJ," we examined both the historical significance and current impact of the ever-evolving DJ community. But we've saved the best for last and here it is—a collection of anecdotes on everything from playing to Prince, warming up a crowd of 450,000 people for the Rolling Stones, and being deported at gunpoint from the U.K.

DIGGING FOR VINYL GOLD

> *I get the opportunity when going to Japan or Europe to get rare and exclusive tracks that DJs who don't travel can't get, and that makes my collection unique.*
> —Rob Swift

Few DJs are respected by their peers unless they have a passion for finding new music and a solid record collection to reflect this. Almost every DJ we talked to shared a story about spending too much on vinyl, staying in a record store for twelve hours, or listening to music until they were incoherent. "I spent close to two grand on vinyl in one trip to Japan," says Z-Trip.

"The stores had a bunch of rare and exclusive tracks that I just had to buy, even though a lot of them were fifty bucks a pop. It's sad to see a lot of the old record stores closing. For me, going into these places was like going to church—I was going there to be cleansed and take refuge. I'd go in with an open mind, and an open wallet because I never knew what I'd find, or who'd be in there. I've sacrificed buying gas, even buying food, to buy new vinyl. I've spent all day in a record shop, just indulging in the art of digging for tracks. And then, when I found that perfect piece of vinyl, it was like it was destined for me. Going into a record store is like going on a journey and never being sure where you'll end up. I always leave better off than when I came in—with more knowledge, more music, and more friends."

In addition to becoming the first DJ to work on a network news show, DJ Hapa runs the Rehab record store. He explains his motivation for starting such a venture in an age when so many record stores are closing. "Rehab was an online store to begin with, but we decided to open a physical space to bring music lovers together in community," he says.

"The record shop is the barber shop of the music industry, a place where DJs, producers, promoters, and other people who care about music can congregate with like minds and talk about music, politics, sports, anything. It's also a place of business where we find new DJing tools and share musical knowledge."

Rob Swift gave us his scoop on the best record stores, past and present, in New York:

> "When I was fourteen or fifteen I'd go to the old Music Factory in Times Square. Guys used to sell records on the street so I'd just stop for a while and rifle through their stuff. I used to hit up the Sound Library often, and Big City Records is another favorite. Fat Beats is a great place, and Rockin' Soul is another. These shops will always be around because, even though the digital revolution is going on, they're timeless. They're still keeping the doors open for music lovers like me and it's still a great atmosphere."

Pete Tong told us about how the decline of record stores and co-incidental rise of the Internet has changed the way he finds new music and interacts with fellow DJs:

> "Twenty years ago we were standing at a record counter and that was the connection—not just with new music, but with owners, club promoters, and other DJs—it was a community. Now it's all online—blogs and download sites. I get a lot of music, but a lot of it is very good because of the sources I get it from. I don't throw much away. The computer is central to every DJs world, whether it's playing music on it, downloading music on it, or chatting with other DJs on it. I send a lot of music on to other DJs."

Jazzy Jeff also thinks that online music sites can help DJs shop intelligently for new music and old classics alike. "Not everybody is this lucky, but Kenny 'Dope' Gonzalez [from house duo Masters at Work] gave me a hard drive with a hundred and sixty thousand tracks on it," he says. "You don't need that hookup to get great songs though. I know guys that use the iTunes Music Store exclusively." The Internet, of course, provides an almost unlimited source of new music. "When I'm at airports and hotels or before and after gigs I trawl through blogs and use search aggregators like Elbows [http://elbo.ws] and Hypem [hypem.com] to find new promos, just get up to date on what's new," says Tom Middleton.

DJ CRAZE'S TOP 10 PLACES TO FIND MUSIC

1. iTunes
2. Beatport
3. Digiwaxx
4. Discobelle
5. Palms Out Sounds
6. Mad Decent Blog
7. Missingtoof
8. The Sexy Result
9. OnSmash
10. Last but not least, your local record store, if you still have one!

Once they find the tracks they want to put in their sets, DJs need to be able to play them on equipment that's responsive. Back in the day, when the pioneering hip hop DJs were honing their craft, there was a problem with the techniques of cutting, scratching, and backspinning—the turntable platter gripped the vinyl too tightly. "I realized that there had to be a buffer between the metal platter and the vinyl so I could move records back and forth," says Grandmaster Flash. "I bought a piece of felt, cut it into a circle that fit onto the platter, and then sprinkled starch all over it. Then I turned my iron up high and ironed it until it became a hard wafer. I put that between the platter and the record, and it did the job." While no longer starch-based, the slipmat Flash invented is now used by the majority of DJs on the planet.

LIVING THE GOOD LIFE—CLUBS, COMPETITIONS, AND CEREMONIES

I was in the middle of my set and I started scratching. It was the first time I'd done it in public. . . soon everyone was just going nuts, waving their hands in the air and screaming. — Grand Wizard Theodore

As you've learned throughout this book, every DJ has to pay his or her dues to achieve success. Once they've got to the upper echelon, DJs have access to a unique perspective on parties, club nights, and live events—on the other side of the dancefloor or stage to the rest of us. We asked a few of the world's best to highlight their most memorable DJing experiences.

Who better to start with other than one of the pioneers of hip hop, Grand Wizard Theodore? "My favorite DJing memory is putting on a night at the Sparkle club," he says. "I was in the middle of my set and I started scratching. It was the first time I'd done it in public. Some people stopped dancing and stared at me, but soon everyone was just going nuts, waving their hands in the air and screaming. To get that reaction was very special."

Grandmaster Caz was featured in the generation-defining film *Wild Style,* which was filmed in the EBB Park that's just yards from his home in the Bronx. After the unexpected global success of the film, Caz and his Cold Crush Brothers crew became part of a landmark tour of Europe and the Far East. He has fond memories of the trip:

"The *Wild Style* tour of Japan in 1982 was the first time another country was exposed to a live, hip hop experience. We had DJs, MCs, the graffiti guys, b-boys, and b-girls—basically everyone who was in the movie. There were stages set up for us in the middle of city squares, and we had thousands of people watching us. We were on TV and radio shows, going to movie premieres—it was nuts. When we went to play at clubs, the Japanese DJs had never seen scratching or messing with breaks so they were just in awe. The coolest part of the whole trip was on the night before we left, because when we went back to those same clubs, the DJs were trying to scratch like we did. They totally got the sound and the culture. Now Tokyo has one of the biggest hip hop scenes in the world. To have been part of starting that is very special."

In 2007, the culture-changing influence of hip hop DJs was memorialized when Grandmaster Flash and the Furious Five were inducted into the Rock and Roll Hall of Fame. "It was a wonderful feeling and I hope many other DJs follow me in having that honor," Flash says. "I'm still in awe of being alongside the Beatles, Jimi Hendrix, and Michael Jackson. I'm on a level playing field, standing next to them with my turntables."

As the '80s drew to a close, house music exploded in England. In 1989, U.K. house pioneer Danny Rampling decided to introduce the faithful at his landmark club Shoom to the real sound of U.S. house music and bring over one of the godfathers of the scene. Tony Humphries explains:

"Danny came to Zanzibar, the New Jersey club where I had my residency. After my set finished he invited me to to play at Shoom. I didn't want to because I was playing seven days a week on KISS FM in New York, spinning at Zanzibar, and doing a lot of remixes. He stayed for four days and eventually convinced me to come. I'd never been out of the country, let alone to the U.K., so I had no idea what to expect. Some people at Zanzibar told me it was a waste of time to go because the Brits didn't know anything about house. I took my calzone case, which is a big metal record crate, full of about three hundred records, and Danny had to pay an excess baggage fee for it. When we pulled up to Shoom I couldn't believe what I saw—there were kids lining up around the block to get in. We got in there and I started playing the same stuff I dropped every week at Zanzibar, tracks from Ten City, Kevin Saunderson, Talking Heads. The crowd went bananas to every track. I'd never seen anything like it. When I got home the same people who'd given me crap for going to England asked me how it was. I told them, 'You guys think you're cool, but you have no idea. You need to check out these cats in London.' The next time Danny had me over to play I paid for eleven of the Zanzibar regulars to come with me. They were floored by what they saw, by how huge house music had become in England. After that, nobody at Zanzibar said anything to me because I had these guys tell the crazy stories for me."

Nick Warren plays at clubs all over the world, but one particular gig stands out. "I was asked to play at the Fun Factory in New York before it turned into Twilo," he says. "Junior Vasquez was the resident DJ there, and he wouldn't let anyone play in the main booth; he made them play on the floor because it was *his* booth. But he actually asked me to play in the booth, which I didn't think anything of at the time, but looking back now it's like, 'Wow,' because that was a seminal club. Vasquez came up while I was playing a break beat record and said, 'Nick, that's the first time a break beat record has ever been played at the Fun Factory.' I just said, 'okay' and didn't think much of it, but I remember it now as an amazing time."

DJ Craze has won multiple turntablist battles and titles, played at the world's biggest clubs, and been part of the Allies, one of most influential and celebrated DJ collectives. But, there's one moment in his career that stands out above the rest: "The greatest experience was winning the [DMC] World Championship for the third time," he says. "It felt great because no one had done it at the time, and still hasn't. And that was the greatest feeling to know that I'd be remembered. When they announced my name that was the time where I was like 'Damn, dude. I did something with my life.'"

For many of the DJs we talked to, their most exhilarating sets occurred before they turned professional. Jahi Sundance shared the story of the craziest gig he played at. "In college, I was DJing at a thousand-person party and it was the hottest show on campus," he says. "It was 1:30 A.M. and the party was ending soon. I played the theme song from *The Godfather,* which was on a two-and-a-half-minute LP. The song has no beat, just instrumentals, and DJs know how any song without a beat seems like it goes on forever. So I was really nervous about the crowd reaction when I dropped it. Well, the crowd went nuts. Right afterwards I played 'All About the Benjamins'—the Biggie Remix. The place exploded." But, he adds, "We tried to do it again at the next party and it bombed."

THE LIVE DJ EXPERIENCE—WHO NEEDS A BAND?

I had no idea how many people were watching me because my head was down looking at the decks, but when I glanced up there must have been 70,000 lighters shining out there.... The video of that show will be on my MySpace page until the day I die.   —Z-Trip

Arenas and festivals were designed to showcase the talents of rock bands. While this genre is still at the core of the live music scene, DJs have demonstrated that they have the technical prowess and performance abilities to share the bill with any conventional band, and in some cases, provide an even more dynamic and visceral experience.

The Beastie Boys, Jurassic 5, and other hip hop groups have all used live DJs to great effect. But it was Run-D.M.C. that started it all back in the mid-80s. Darryl "D.M.C." McDaniels explains how his band and its DJ, Jam Master Jay, changed the face of the live hip hop experience:

"Run, Jay, and I were on tour with Marvin Gaye and seven other bands in the summer of '84, just after we'd released our first album. It was an open air gig in Alabama and we were the opening act. It was a rock crowd, so when Jay came out behind his turntables they were like 'Where's the band?' Then he played our intro—'I'm Jam, Jam, Jam Master Jay'—and was scratching. They had no idea what was going on. He introduced me—'D, D, D.M.C.' and then 'R,R,R, Run'— just cutting that intro up. Then we got into our first song and the audience went nuts. We just had twenty minutes, so we only played Jay's intro, 'Here We Go,' 'It's Like That,' and 'Sucker MCs,' but we got everyone into it, even though they didn't have any idea about hip hop or DJs. The next group came on, and they just had a traditional band instead of a DJ. They got no reaction from the fans, because people wanted more of the hip hop band with the DJ. Jay made that show for us. After their first song the sky clouded over and it started raining so hard that they stopped the show. Afterwards we thought it was a sign from above that we were going to take over the music industry, which we did. Later in the tour, the band managers and tour promoter got together and decided that because we were tearing it up and bands couldn't follow us, we'd have to close each gig."

Several DJs, including A-Trak and Paul Oakenfold, have warmed up for music heavyweights during arena tours, but Z-Trip played a particularly well-attended gig once, too: "My best gig has to be opening for the Rolling Stones outdoors in Toronto in front of 450,000 people. It was a rock crowd, so I knew I had to do something different so I wouldn't get booed off stage. I wanted to win them over early, so I played Janis Joplin's 'O Lord' and then a few other classics to show them I knew rock music and wasn't up there just jacking around. Once they'd cheered three or four times I knew I had them hooked. Halfway through the set I was playing drum and bass. I'm a big fan of throwing a few curveballs in the middle of my sets because if I've won over the crowd early, they'll let me get away with anything."

Z-Trip also has happy memories of playing at the Bonnaroo festival. "The other show that stands out was playing on the last day of Bonnaroo in 2003 while the sun was setting," he says. "At the end of my set, I played my remix of 'Dust in the Wind' and told the crowd to pull out their lighters and hold them up. Until that point I had no idea how many people were watching me because my head was down looking at the decks, but when I glanced up there must have been 70,000 lighters shining out there. At the end of the song I told them I wanted to make a wish and blow out the candles. I counted to three and blew into my headphones, and all the lights went out—it was pitch black. The feeling I had, the connection with the crowd, was indescribable. The video of that show will be on my MySpace page until the day I die."

Z-Trip is not the only DJ we talked to who recounted playing to a massive crowd. On New Year's Eve 2007, Tony McGuinness and his Above & Beyond cohorts DJed in front of a million people on a Rio de Janeiro beach. He recalls: "I remember standing backstage in Rio looking up at the stars—it was a beautiful night, the middle of their summer, the sea was washing in on the sand—and I thought this could be one of the most amazing nights of my life. There was a significant chunk of that city's population just standing on the beach waiting for us to go on. Most people were dressed in white, which gave the whole thing quite an eerie vibe. After we did the countdown to twelve o'clock I grabbed the mic and yelled 'Happy New Year,' and there was a huge cheer as we started the first record. When you play for that many people for whom music is such an important thing, it's special—and playing to a million such people was phenomenal. It was an extraordinary night."

For Annie Nightingale, Eastern Europe provided a surprising but welcome vibe:

> "I played at a festival in Hungary and the girl who DJed before me played almost every tune I had in my set. On one hand I was thinking 'Oh crap, what am I going to play now?' but I was also excited because we were both dialed into the same scene, even though we lived in different countries that were hundreds of miles apart."

Steve Lawler counts the renowned Glastonbury Festival, which attracts about 100,000 people to a farm in South West England each summer, among his favorite DJing experiences. "I played Glastonbury last year and noticed there were only two DJs on the bill for the tent I was to be in—the rest were bands," he says. "I thought the arena would be empty because Sasha and I were competing against Amy Winehouse and the Who, so I'd made up my mind it would be a crap night. But when I got there it was jam packed with more than nine thousand people. I played my heart out and they really got into it. It went so well that I ended up playing another set for Annie Mac's Radio 1 show."

James Zabiela shares his favorite festival experience: "A couple of years ago I was at a festival and played the closing set, which finished at 8:00 A.M. It was just a really electric and magical atmosphere and there were 10,000 people in front of me. Goldie was playing at the other stage and that closed early, and while I was on my encore, on my last record, he got on the mic and said, 'Big up for the Southampton massive!' [a reference to Zabiela's hometown]. It was quite funny as I had never met the guy. Suddenly, I had a moment of inspiration. I had my iPod and a mini jack cable in my bag and I plugged it into the mixer and played [Goldie's hit] 'Inner City Life.' It was one of the best sets of my life, if not *the* best. The festival's at an old fortress so it's a really beautiful landscape as well. Goldie was pretty happy that I dropped his record and it was one of those things where you're almost moved to tears because it was such an epic situation."

PANIC STATIONS: WHEN GOOD SETS GO BAD

I had to reboot my computer on stage at a festival in front of five thousand people and there was silence for a minute—the longest minute of my life. I had to pretend it was an encore.

—DJ Yoda

While a lot of DJs find it hard to identify their best gigs from so many good memories, none of those that we talked to had any trouble recalling their worst. We asked Z-Trip to tell us about a time when he wasn't well known enough to pick and choose his shows. "I was booked to play a wedding and my equipment was broken, so I borrowed decks, a mixer, an amp, and speakers from a friend. I went to the house where the reception was being held and started setting up. It was all fine until I went to hook up the amp to the speakers—there were no speaker cables. I called another friend and then hot-wheeled it to his house to pick up his cables. I had to get there and back in thirty minutes, and he lived way across town. The wedding party was already at the house when I got back, waiting for me to announce them. I got out of the car, and stumbled across the lawn, getting my suit all messed up, with the cables tucked under my arm. It was so humiliating."

Rob Swift was a little further along in his career when he had one of his worst DJing experiences. "One X-Ecutioners gig we did in Kentucky was at a place that wasn't set up for hip hop. There were bass bins under the stage, and every sound messed with the turntables, and there was horrible hum and feedback through the speakers. It threw us off, and we were really paranoid about it, but the crowd still enjoyed it, I think."

DJ Craze has also had his fair share of bad luck. Once, when he was performing a Serato set, his laptop died because he had forgotten to plug the power cord in. "Whenever it crashes I just get on the mic and I tell the crowd, 'Yo! We have some technical difficulties and as soon as that computer turns on it's about to get crazy in here!' I don't like to freak out—I just get on the mic and tell them to hold tight, it's not the end of the world. As soon as the music comes back on, I'm gonna make up for it."

DJ Yoda has also had Serato issues. "When I used Serato live the first five or six times, I'd load a certain track when on stage and it crashed," he says. "I had to reboot my computer on stage at a festival in front of five thousand people and there was silence for a minute—the longest minute of my life. I had to pretend it was an encore."

It's not just DJs who use new technology that have equipment problems. Turntables can and do go wrong just as often as CD decks and DJ software. Richie Hawtin told us about a particularly diabolical experience. "I had a problem with the decks once and had to use just one turntable for a two-hour set," he says. "Luckily I had a small sampler with me so I'd sample 8 or 16 bars of the record that was playing, then play the sample through the mixer so I had something to mix the next record into."

EARLY MUSIC MEMORIES

> *There was a New Year's Eve gig at my dad's friend's house and they had him set up in the corner of the living room. He controlled a crowd of fifty or sixty people for the whole night and I was, like, "Wow I want to do that."*
> —Rob Swift

Usually when people say a guy was born to do something, it's a cliché. However, in the case of Q-Bert, it may just be true. "I've played around with records since I was a toddler," he says. "My parents got me a children's record player, a Fisher-Price thing I think, and I messed around with the different speeds." Annie Nightingale also had music hardwired into her. "Music has been the passion of my life," she says. "The first word I remember saying, even though I couldn't say it right, was music. I realized that I couldn't sing and although I had piano lessons, my hand-eye coordination was too bad to play a traditional instrument, so I turned to DJing as a way to express myself."

It was a family connection that spurred A-Trak to become a DJ. "My older brother and his friends messed around with my dad's records after school. When I was twelve I tried it one day and picked scratching up really quickly," he says. "My brother encouraged me and told me I should practice, and that's why I began taking it seriously." Rob Swift was also ushered into a love of music and appreciation of DJing by a family member. "My introduction to DJing was through my dad DJing for weddings, Christmas parties, and New Year's Eve parties for his friends," he says. "It made me want to be like him and do that. There was a New Year's Eve gig at my dad's friend's house and they had him set up in the corner of the living room. He controlled a crowd of fifty or sixty people for the whole night and I was like, 'Wow, I want to do that.'"

Another DJ impacted by his family's musical interests was Jazzy Jeff:

> "I grew up in a musical household. My father was an MC for Count Basie, so I knew the great jazz guitarist Wes Montgomery and organist Jimmy Smith. My brothers and sisters played all sorts of styles—Motown, funk, rock, and soul, and as I was the youngest of the six of us I just had to listen to whatever records they brought home." Jeff also found early hip hop records to be influential.
>
> "When 'Rapper's Delight' came out I felt like someone had made a record just for me. After that there seemed to be great new hip hop tracks coming out every week. I'd turn on the radio before school and listen to

them, and then again in the school bus. In class we'd be
writing out lyrics and trying to memorize them, because
you were cool if you could say the rhymes all the way
through. Soon, it wasn't enough for me just to know the
words—I wanted to play those songs, to control them.
That gave me a certain kudos. Guys wanting to throw a
party would come to me and ask me to DJ. And if I liked
a girl and she was at a party I DJed at, I was getting ahead
with her. Everyone at our school looked up to the DJs."

Despite the fact that he lived in London, which doesn't exactly have New York's hip hop pedigree, DJ Yoda was influenced
by early imports from the States. "The music I was surrounded
by at age eleven and twelve was pop and bits of hip hop," he says.
"An older cousin lent me a Public Enemy tape and then I got Salt
N' Pepper records. I heard scratching in the music I was listening to, especially with Jazzy Jeff and the Fresh Prince. It inspired
me to start messing around with scratching records."

Other DJs got into traditional types of music that helped them
appreciate song structure and composition in a way that furthered
their DJing careers. Tom Middleton is one such DJ. "My first
memory of music is from when I was five. It was Tomita's
'Snowflakes are Dancing,' which had been recommended to my
dad to test his high-end stereo system," he says. "He sat me down
between the speakers and we were blown away by this blend of
synthetic sounds that were covers of classical compositions by
Debussy played by this Japanese whiz kid. I played cello and piano
and listened to BBC Radio 3 on my dad's radio so that classical
background has provided a good basis for what I've done with
music—a classical influence merged with this other-worldly syn-
thesizer sound from people like Jean-Michel Jarre and Vangelis."

A GIG'S A GIG

I couldn't wait to DJ after hours at The Boiler Room. It was ghetto, and completely illegal, because you can't serve alcohol in L.A. after 2:00 A.M. and we opened then. I showed up with my decks, my home stereo, and speakers. That was the sound system and for a bar we sold cans of Bud. It was nuts and I made forty bucks a night. —DJ AM

The world's best DJs may have lives that seem unimaginable to someone who's just starting out, but they all have something in common with everyone else—beginning their DJing careers somewhere. Rob Swift recollects his debut behind the decks at a junior high prom. "Up until then I was used to DJing in my bedroom and was having these dreams of people watching me play and dancing, and then suddenly I was doing it. People looked at me differently, like I was a god up there for that one night."

DJ AM's paychecks, too, used to be at the opposite end of the scale. "I couldn't wait to DJ after-hours at the Boiler Room," AM says. "It was ghetto, and completely illegal, because you can't serve alcohol in L.A. after 2:00 A.M. and we opened then. I showed up with my decks, my home stereo, my own speakers. That was the sound system, and for a bar we sold cans of Bud. It was nuts and I made forty bucks a night. Later I did a night called Dragonfly, where I earned $150 a night. I was broke, and couldn't even afford a home phone. But if you're happy and you know that you're enough, then you're successful. DJing makes me happy, I get to make other people happy doing what I do, so I'm the luckiest guy on Earth."

There was a time when Z-Trip's gigs weren't quite so glamorous, either. "My first residency was at Bobby McGee's restaurant in Arizona," he says. "The waiters and waitresses dressed up, so you had Captain Hook, Little Bo Peep, Davy Crocket, and so on. It was the cheesiest thing in the world but I learned so

much—how to read a crowd, how to turn a room if it wasn't going well, and how to use the mic to interact with the crowd. The
managers were only interested in sales so they put me through
this program that was designed to drive people to the bar. They
had me play a hip-hop record, then a mellower R&B song, then
an indie rock/alternative song, which took about fifteen minutes. Then I'd start again with another hip hop song. At the end
of half an hour I'd give the crowd a complete musical experience.
It taught me about aiming for a goal with a set, rather than focusing on the music. When I left there, I took that idea and in-
verted it, so my primary goal was getting the most out of music.
While I was having fun, my days at Bobby McGee's were num-
bered. This one night I played 'Can't Trust It' by Public Enemy,
even though I knew the ownership was prejudiced and hated
anything like that. The owner was outraged, and as well as chew-
ing me out he sent out a memo to the other franchise locations
saying that all music had to be approved by him in advance, and
that DJs couldn't play Public Enemy tracks. I quit soon after
that, but I kept that memo for years. When I made a record with
Chuck D, I put it on the inside of the CD sleeve. It was perfect."

DJ Hapa's career also had humble roots. "I started DJing
when I was sixteen and two years later I moved south to go to
UCLA," he says. "In those days it was hard to find other DJs to
hang out with, but I came across two guys on campus that were
from the Exquisite Sounds crew. They invited me to their next
practice and it was me and nine other DJs crammed into this
tiny apartment. Our first gig was in the huge basement of the
Bonaventure Hotel. Because I was the new guy I had to start
carrying in equipment—forty speakers, all the wires, decks, and
other gear—at 10:00 A.M. It took me all day. We had the party
and it was a great vibe because there were over 5,000 wild college kids packed in. Like a lot of other gigs we did, I didn't get to

play for more than a few minutes because I was the tenth guy on the crew's roster. I was bored, so I started picking up the mic and hyping up the crowd between the other guys' sets." While at the time he would have preferred to just be DJing, Hapa's stints on the mic soon paid dividends:

> "After one gig, a producer from a new cable TV network came up to me and said she liked my style. She asked if I'd ever thought about TV work and I told her, 'No, I'm a DJ.' She convinced me to audition for the role of the DJ on a show and I got the part. Two jobs later I landed the KTLA job. I never thought picking up the mic would do anything other than hype up the crowd, but it shows that as a DJ you've got to be versatile because you never know what skills promoters are looking for."

Darryl McDaniels is one of the best known MCs in the game, but he began his hip hop career as a DJ in his home neighborhood of Queens. He told us about his first gig. "I began DJing in my basement and my first gig came about after I started hanging out with Joseph 'Run' Simmons. He hosted a party over on Douglas Hays's block and got on the mic to introduce me. He started rhyming over the track, 'Drummer's Beat,' and his rhyme finished 'On the way back from San Francisco, I picked up Easy D and we came to rock this disco.' Then I started DJing and people went nuts."

TEARING THE ROOF OFF—TRACKS THAT ROCK

> *"Billie Jean" by Michael Jackson has it all: strong drums, funky melody, and it's up tempo. Everyone knows every word, whether they like it or not.*
> —DJ Daddy Dog

As a member of the Allies, J-Smoke has played in battles and clubs all over the world and has no trouble identifying the track that never fails to light up the dancefloor.

"The vocals and the beat in Dr. Dre's 'Nuthing But a G Thang' are independently superb and perfect when combined," he says. "It's the type of song that never gets old—everyone loves it. The tempo is slower and more laid back then the usual hip-hop track, but I can still play it in primetime and get the desired reaction."

We asked mixtape and club DJ Jesse Felluss about the most dramatic response he's seen to a song in a club. "I played 'Born in the U.S.A.' by Bruce Springsteen, which was an unusual twist to my normal set," Fellus says. "Throughout the night I noticed this drunk dude passed out and slouched in his chair in the corner of the club. He was out cold until I dropped the song. After the first few bars, he sprung to his feet, made his way to the dance floor, where he promptly face planted. The club manager and bouncers immediately put him back in his chair but this time moved the chair to the back corner of the club until he sobered up. I guess he was very patriotic, but also very drunk."

When it comes to parties, Felluss turns to Prince's "Kiss" to get the crowd rocking. "It has a great intro (universally recognized), the beat is fun (it's upbeat and funky) and hard hitting (drums or old rap), the subject matter involves a situation that everyone can relate to ('You don't have to be rich to be my girl . . .') and it works for any crowd and any kind of party," he says.

DJ Daddy Dog, who has played for Eminem, Ludacris, and Public Enemy, also reaches back into the '80s when he needs to get people jumping. "'Billie Jean' by Michael Jackson has it all: strong drums, funky melody, and it's uptempo," he says. "Everyone knows every word, whether they like it or not. I think this song is such a classic because it helped define Michael Jackson's style and success."

DJ MAJOR TAYLOR'S [CHICAGO] TOP 3 DJING RULES

1. **No requests.** That's what jukeboxes and iPods are for.
2. **Don't touch me or the equipment.** If I'm ignoring you' it's because I'm in the mix. Don't start tugging and tapping me because you think your request is more important than anything else jumping off in the room at the time. What the hell are you doing in the booth anyway?
3. **Always floss after meals.** It's a great way to prevent gum disease.

DJ GRAFFITI'S [ANN ARBOR, MICHIGAN] TOP 3 DON'T MESS WITH THE DJ RULES

1. No bumping the DJ table/booth!
2. Stop sending your friends up to request the same song you just asked for.
3. Touch the turntable and you might lose your hand.

BEST CELEBRITY GIGS

It was the oddest mix of people—musicians, celebrities such as Tom Hanks, Spielberg, and Brad Pitt, and then a bunch of country folks. I was freaked out for a moment because I wasn't sure how to make all these people happy. But then I realized certain music is universal and will always work, and that changed everything for me.

—DJ AM

DJ AM is a regular on the Hollywood party circuit, which presents a completely different challenge to his nights at his LAX club in L.A. and residency in Las Vegas. He told us about a memorable A-list show. "One of my most important gigs was playing Melissa Etheridge's birthday party," AM says. "It was the oddest mix of people—musicians, celebrities such as Tom Hanks, Spielberg, and Brad Pitt, and then a bunch of country folks. I was freaked out for a moment because I wasn't sure how to make all these people happy. But then I realized certain music is universal and will always work, and that changed everything for me. I played Rupert Holmes's 'The Escape Song,' and it was one of the biggest records of the night."

DJ Zander, former resident at hot New York clubs Vela and Stitch, has played his fair share of celebrity gigs for the likes of Marilyn Manson and Slash. We asked him to recount his favorite celebrity encounter:

"I was spinning at Bungalow 8 in New York, which is a venue famous for its high-end atmosphere and impossible door policy. And with any impossible door policy comes celebrities. The DJ booth is up on the second floor with the main space largely blocked by railings. It makes a DJ's job very challenging when he can't see the people he's spinning for. I was fifteen minutes into a

Prince megaset with 'Raspberry Beret,' 'I Wanna Be Your Lover,' and 'Erotic City,' when someone told me Prince was downstairs. I had unknowingly been giving him a tour of his past hits and former glories. It made the news the next day and I still can't believe it—I played a set for Prince!"

WELCOME TO THE CRAZY SHOW

One time there was a shooting at a venue I was going to be playing at with the Cold Crush Brothers. Once the crowd saw that we were about to get going everyone calmed down and came back into the club, because they were so eager for the show to start. That was the power of the DJs.

—Grandmaster Caz

Whether playing at a party to 40 people, a club for 400, or a festival in front of 40,000, DJs have to respect the crowd, who are the lifeblood of their careers. However, there are times when fans cross the line. DJ Daddy Dog explains:

"I used to have a Friday night residency at this New York City hotspot named One51. The dress code was so strict that even I had to comply. So every Friday night, I'd throw on real shoes, a shirt, and a pair of pants. I used to spin the VIP room and at about midnight each week, the same guy would walk in wearing shorts, flip flops, and a baseball hat. Who let this guy in? Invariably, not long after the first bottle brought over to his table was done, he would get up on the dancefloor and do the same thing each week. He'd reach into his pocket and pull out a thousand dollars in twenties. With wads of cash in each hand, he'd throw it up in the air, lottery-winning style. People at the bar and the staff, waiters and waitresses would run over, fight over it, and pick it up. It was a disgrace all the way around. The worst was one week when I brought in a new up-and-coming DJ to open up for me. This dude went straight after the dough as well. Now at least I understand why they eased up on the dress code for him."

Z-Trip also had an encounter with an odd character at a gig, although the situation was a little more dangerous than a guy throwing money at the staff. "I DJed at a lot of parties in bad neighborhoods," he says.

> "One time a guy came up to me with his arms crossed while I was playing and I saw he had a can of mace tucked under one arm, like he was going to spray me. I quickly whispered a warning to my friend and he grabbed the guy, took him outside, and beat the hell out of him. At those parties I'd be playing for $20 or $50 just so I could buy a few more records, but I'm not sure I would've carried on if that dude had sprayed mace in my face."

Grandmaster Caz has also had a few crazy club and party experiences in more than thirty years of performing. "One time there was a shooting at a venue I was going to be playing at with the Cold Crush Brothers," he says. "Once the crowd saw that we were about to get going everyone calmed down and came back into the club, because they were so eager for the show to start. That was the power of the DJs."

GOING ABOVE AND BEYOND

At 9:00 A.M. the next day people were wasted, so some of them were wandering across the motorway and others were just sitting in fields staring at the sky. Cars were stuck in the mud. It was pure havoc. The police threatened to put me in jail if I threw another party. I realized then that it had gone too far so we had to stop.　　　　　　　—Steve Lawler

Some DJs risk everything from prosecution to violence and possibly death for the sake of music.

We start with one of the founding fathers of hip hop— Grandmaster Flash, who put everything on the line for music. "My father collected records obsessively," he says. "I was never to touch them or his turntable, which was in the living room. When I was six I started disobeying that. I'd drag a chair into his bedroom, get up on it, and open the closet. Then I'd grab the record I wanted to hear and take it to the living room, get up on another chair, and play it. When he got back, the records would be out of order, and he'd beat me. Still, the next day, as soon as he went to work, I'd be back in that closet. I ended up in the hospital several times from his beatings, and once he took my hands and held them on a radiator until they burned. It still didn't stop me. I risked my life for the love of music."

Ten years after Flash took hip hop to new heights, it was the rave scene that was on the cutting edge of music. Steve Lawler clearly remembers his most outrageous rave experience. "When I lived in Warwickshire my friends and I found a tunnel that was between two farms and under the M42 motorway," he says. "Ten friends chipped in to help me hire equipment and we had a hundred and fifty people show up to the first party in that tunnel, then more and more started coming as word got around. The police turned up every time but because we only sent out the flyers on the day of the gig only a few of them came. They always said,

'We'll give you an hour to dismantle the sound system and get everyone out or we'll come back and arrest you all,' but we knew they didn't have enough of them to do it, so we just carried on. We'd hand out flyers that had a mobile phone number on them. The person with the phone was sitting outside a pub on the route and would tell people who called how to get to him. Once he had twenty or thirty cars show up he'd lead them to where we were. We put on the flyers, 'Bring your own torch' because it was pitch black out there. At the last party we had seven hundred people show up. The vibe was incredible. I played for ten hours and people were just dancing the whole time. At 9:00 A.M. the next day, people were wasted so some of them were wandering across the motorway and others were just sitting in fields staring at the sky. Cars were stuck in the mud. It was pure havoc. The police threatened to put me in jail if I threw another party. I realized then that it had gone too far so we had to stop."

While most of the top DJs employ assistants to coordinate travel plans, that doesn't mean that everything always goes smoothly. "Craze and I were going to Ireland from London Heathrow," says DJ Klever. "He had an expired visa and I didn't have one. We decided to come up with some line about him being from a hip hop magazine and me doing a DJing showcase. He got through and I didn't. They told me to go in the back and sit down. Then they called Craze back, looked at his paperwork, and told him it wasn't good any more. They kept us there for a couple of hours and were messing with us, and then took us to the airport jail. We were just sitting there in this one tiny room for twenty-eight hours. Eventually police with M-16s walked us to a plane and made us get on—we got deported!"

BEYOND THE BOOTH: THE FRIENDS AND FAMILY CONNECTION

I'd have to slide a milk crate up to the turntables for Theodore to stand on because he was just a little kid and couldn't reach them.

— Grandmaster Flash

Although they're often solitary creatures by necessity, great things can happen when DJs collaborate "I was playing with Mean Gene at the time and found out that his little brother, Theodore, was the best around at needle dropping," says Grandmaster Flash. "I asked Gene if I could teach Theodore my Quick Mix Theory and he said, 'No, I don't want that kid in my room messing with my records.' People were kind of scared of Gene, because he got in a lot of fights: that's why we called him Mean. So I'd teach Theodore when he wasn't around. Gene was really angry when he found out what we'd been doing, but he got over it. I'd have to slide a milk crate up to the turntables for Theodore to stand on because he was just a little kid and couldn't reach them. I loved being able to share my science, which was difficult because a lot of people ridiculed my mixing and called me 'record destroyer,' and a lot of other names you can't print, at the time, as touching vinyl while playing was taboo."

Danny Rampling's *Love Groove Dance Party* show on BBC Radio 1 was famed for including the hottest exclusive tracks and most renowned DJs. "I made a huge effort to go and meet people," Rampling says. "In fifteen years of broadcasting my shows were a reflection of the radio programs that had impacted me. The DJs I looked up to had all these exclusive tracks. I made friends with a lot of folks in the U.S. and Europe and I'd just fly to meet them and source music that way. That gave my Radio 1 show an authenticity and warmth, more than just a playlist. You get people excited about a track, and they want it but can't get it. It created demand. That music was a mark of respect from artists and producers for the friendships I'd forged with them over my whole career."

For other DJs, the relationships forged in clubs and on the road extend to include members of their families. Says Jazzy Jeff of his days with DJ Jazzy Jeff and the Fresh Prince:

"Me and Will [Smith] went with Run-D.M.C. on their *Raising Hell* tour as the warmup act. I took my son Cory, who was eleven months old at the time, with us. One day we were going back to the hotel room and I was carrying him because he couldn't walk. I ran into Jam Master Jay in the hall and he was really cool with Cory. He said, 'Hey, I'm going to take your boy for a walk, we'll be back soon, alright?' I told him 'sure' and went to my room. About an hour later, Jay knocked on the door and told me to come into the hall because he had something to show me. I went out there and Cory was walking up and down. I always remind him, 'Jam Master Jay from Run-D.M.C. taught you how to walk!' "

ACKNOWLEDGMENTS

A VERY SPECIAL THANKS TO ALL THE DJS WHO HAVE CONTRIBUTED TO THIS BOOK:

Paul Oakenfold

Annie Nightingale

BT

DJ Jazzy Jeff

Brandon Fluharty

Grandmaster Caz

Grand Wizard Theodore

Grandmaster Flash

Mark Brown

Richie Hawtin

Sasha

DJ AM

DJ Hapa

John Digweed

Matt Black

Darryl "D.M.C." McDaniels

DJ Z-Trip

DJ Yoda

Pete Tong

Danny Rampling

Tom Middleton

DJ Nu-Mark

Q-Bert

Jay Jung

Junior Sanchez

Josh Wink

DJ A-Trak

DJ Craze

DJ Skribble

Harry "Choo Choo" Romero

Nick Warren

DJ Immortal

Stéphane Pompougnac

Rob Swift

James Zabiela

Nic Fanciulli

Lars Sandberg (Funk D'Void)

Stretch Armstrong

DJ Vice

DJ Daddy Dog

Jahi Sundance

Jesse Felluss

Zander Chemers

Steve Lawler

Tony McGuinness

DJ Excess

DJ Noumenon

Scratch DJ Academy faculty

Tony Humphries

Klever

Oscar G

Gildas Loaëc

ROB PRINCIPE WOULD LIKE TO THANK THE FOLLOWING PEOPLE:

Phil and Luke for their tireless work and great talents. Marc Gerald at the Agency Group and everyone at St. Martin's Press for seeing and giving us this amazing opportunity. Mom, Dad, Mike, Jamie, Nikki, and Ray for their unending and unwavering support.

LUKE CRISELL WOULD LIKE TO THANK THE FOLLOWING PEOPLE:

Phil, for being the best co-author I could imagine and, more importantly, a great friend. Kate, for her patience, support, and love. Jon Manley, for getting me into playing records in the first place. My family, for putting up with me playing records so loudly, and for so long. Rob Principe, for the opportunity. All the DJs we spoke to for sharing their knowledge and enthusiasm. Andrea Fella, Mickey Pangilinan, Mallory Rice, Diane Vadino, Christine Colbert, and Mrs. Errington.

PHIL WHITE WOULD LIKE TO THANK THE FOLLOWING PEOPLE:

Nicole and Johnny for their love. Luke for the late-night writing sessions and friendship. Rob Principe for the opportunity. Barrie (still my best man), Meg, Ian, Debbie, Jacqui, and the Stephens family for their support. Jon Manley and Jono Lloyd for sharing the love of music. Tyler Blake for the mentoring. Tim Keel for the guidance. Brett Chalmers, Tom Seibold, and Henry Worcester for the coffee-fueled discussions. David Moldawer and Yaniv Soha, for the expertise. All the DJs for their interviews and artistry, and most of all the Lord for the blessing of this project.

APPENDIX:
TOP TENS (AND A FEW TOP THREES)

GRAND WIZARD THEODORE'S TOP 10 RECORDS OF ALL TIME

1. James Brown "Give it Up, Turn it Loose"
2. The Incredible Bongo Band "Bongo Rock"
3. John Davis "I Can't Stop"
4. Earth, Wind and Fire "Brazilian Rhyme"
5. James Brown "Sex Machine"
6. Herman Kelly "Lets Dance to the Drummer's Beat"
7. Bob James "Nautilus"
8. Discotech "Scratching"
9. The Incredible Bongo Band "Apache"
10. James Brown "Funky President"

A-TRAK'S TOP 10 TIPS FOR WINNING
THE DMC WORLD MIXING CHAMPIONSHIPS

1. Bring something new to the table.
2. Practice, practice, practice. Anticipate every possible way that something could go wrong.
3. Study your competition.
4. Have something catchy in your set that people will be talking about.
5. Start with a bang.
6. End with your most creative segment. That's what the judges will remember.
7. Cover every base and be well-rounded.
8. Use records that sound good over a big sound system.
9. Avoid monotone sets. Build strong dynamics in your set's structure.
10. Film yourself practicing. Be aware of how you look when you perform.

A-TRAK'S TOP 10 BATTLE RECORDS

1. Turntablist "Superduck Breaks"
2. Q-Bert "Dirtstyle Deluxe Shampoo Edition"
3. D-Styles "Sqratch Fetishes of the 3rd Kind"
4. DJ Swamp "Skip-proof" series
5. A-Trak "Monkeyboy Breaks"
6. Ricci Rucker "Utility Phonograph Record"
7. Mr Dibbs "Unearthed Vol. 3"
8. Q-Bert "Toasted Marshmellow Feet Breaks"
9. DJ Craze "Bully Breaks 2"
10. Tittworth & DJ Ayres "T&A Breaks"

DJ CRAZE'S TOP 10 PLACES TO LOOK FOR MUSIC

1. iTunes
2. Beatport
3. Digiwaxx
4. Discobelle
5. Palms Out Sounds
6. Mad Decent/Blog
7. Missingtoof
8. The Sexy Result
9. OnSmash
10. Last but not least—your local record store—if you've still got one

DJ CRAZE'S TOP 10 FAVORITE MIAMI BASS PRODUCERS

1. Magic Mike
2. Beat Master Clay D
3. Jealous J & Jock D
4. Danny D
5. Amos Larkin
6. Mr. Mixx
7. DJ Laz
8. Dynamixx 2
9. Disco Rick
10. DJ Uncle Al

DJ CRAZE'S TOP 10 TIPS FOR PUTTING TOGETHER A WINNING DMC ROUTINE

1. Watch all the DMC videos.
2. Learn as many styles as you can from watching those videos.
3. Pick records that people like so you can get them on your side just with your selection.
4. Try to come up with something original.
5. Do some research on your opponents (what they're good at and what they're lacking).
6. Practice the whole year and try to come up with as many routines as you can.
7. Pick your five strongest routines that you've practiced the whole year.
8. Practice those routines—and keep practicing till you can't practice anymore.
9. Practice messing up and recovering.
10. PRAY that the day of the battle everything comes out all right!

ROB SWIFT'S TOP 10 DJ BATTLES OF ALL TIME

1. X-Men (former name of X-Ecutioner) vs. Invisibl Skratch Piklz. International Turntablist Federation. 1996. (Winner: There was no winner declared. We left it up to the audience to decide for themselves.)
2. Aladdin vs. Miz. New Music Seminar Battle for World Supremacy. 1989. (Winner: DJ Miz)
3. Steve D vs. Francesco. New Music Seminar Battle for World Supremacy. 1990. (Winner: DJ Steve D)
4. Cash Money vs. Joe Cooley. New Music Seminar Bat-

tle for World Supremacy. 1987. (Winner: DJ Cash Money)

5. Roc Raida vs. Supreme. Clark Kent Battle for World Supremacy. 1991. (Winner: DJ Supreme)

6. Mista Sinista vs. Eightball. Clark Kent Battle for World Supremacy. 1993. (Winner: DJ Eightball)

7. Mix Master Mike vs. Supreme. Clark Kent Battle for World Supremacy. 1992. (Winner: Mix Master Mike)

8. Flamboyant vs. Francesco. New Music Seminar Battle for World Supremacy. 1990. (Winner: Francesco)

9. Babu vs. Total Eclipse. International Turntablist Federation. 1996. (Winner: Total Eclipse)

10. East Coast DMC. 1992. (Winner: 1st Place-Rob Swift, 2nd Place-Roc Raida, 3rd Place-Jonny Cash)

DJ NU-MARK'S TOP 10 FUNK SAMPLES

1. Joann Garrett—"It's No Secret," Cadet Records. Produced by Andre Williams.

2. Skip Easterling—"I'm Your Hoochie Coochie Man," Instant Records. Produced by Huey Smith and Tex Liuzza.

3. Soul Rhythm Band—"Mamma's Little Baby," Pelikin Record Company. Produced by Artie Fields.

4. Linda Mackey—"Gotta Find My Man," VJ International Records. Produced by Gabriel Flemmings.

5. Deniece Chandler & Lee Sain—"Hey Baby," Toddlin' Town Records. Produced by C. Johnson & Vineyard.

6. The Battered Ornaments—"Late into the Night," Harvest Records. Produced by Andrew King.

7. Film Vertonungs Platte—"Get Up," Golden Ring Records. Produced by Klaus Weiss. 1977.

8. The Romeos—"Precious Memories," Revue Records. Produced by N. Montague.
9. Bill Moss—"Keep on Using Me Jesus," Bilesse Recordings. Produced by Bill Moss.
10. Jimmy Takeuch—"Dock of the Bay," SRM Records. Produced by S. Cropper.

OSCAR G'S TOP 10 EARLY HOUSE LABELS

1. Traxx
2. Strictly Rhythm
3. Nu Groove
4. DJ International
5. Nervous
6. Tribal America
7. Freeze
8. Irma
9. Junior Boys Own
10. FFRR

COSMO BAKER'S (NYC—THE RUB)—TOP 10 SONGS TO END THE NIGHT WITH (AKA "FINISHING OFF STRONG")

1. M.F.S.B.—"Love Is The Message"
2. Eddie Kendricks—"Date With The Rain" Extended Disco Version
3. Womack & Womack—"Baby I'm Scared of You"
4. LTD—"Love To The World" Extended Edit
5. John Paul Young—"Love Is in the Air"
6. Billy Paul—"East"

7. The Chi-Lites — "My First Mistake"
8. Billy Stewart — "Summertime"
9. Marvin Gaye — "Got to Give it Up"
10. Roy Ayres — "Everybody Loves the Sunshine"

COSMO BAKER'S (NYC—THE RUB) TOP 3 RULES FOR OPENING DJS

1. Play your position! Understand that you are setting up the volley for the main event so make sure that you don't go too hard too early. You'll only sour the vibe if you try to play like you're the headliner when it's not your job.
2. Keep the people engaged in a gradual way that builds. Understand the natural arc of the night and make sure your set builds accordingly. Get the people's attention and work with it in a smooth way that slowly increases their excitement and anticipation, which is going to build the dancefloor and the party.
3. Be creative! The opening slot is a great opportunity to try out new songs and ideas, and in trying those ideas out in a live setting, it might give you an opportunity to get noticed and booked to be a headliner next time.

DJ GEOMETRIX'S (WASHINGTON, D.C.—TROOPERZ CREW) TOP 10 SONGS THAT WILL GET A REACTION 10 YEARS FROM NOW

1. Juvenile — "Back that Azz Up"
2. Lil Jon & East Side Boyz — "Get Low"
3. Ying Yang Twins — "Salt Shaker"
4. 50 Cent — "In Da Club"

5. Usher—"Yeah"
6. Mystikal—"Shake Ya Ass"
7. Nelly—"Hot In Herre"
8. 2Pac—"California Love"
9. House of Pain—"Jump Around"
10. Rob Base and DJ Easy Rock—"It Takes Two"

DJ MAJOR TAYLOR'S (CHICAGO) TOP 10 TRACKS TO END THE NIGHT WITH

1. Toto—"Africa"
2. R. Kelly—"Step in the Name of Love"
3. Ray Charles and Betty Carter—"It's Cold Outside"
4. The Verve—"Bitter Sweet Symphony"
5. Miles Davis—"All Blues"
6. Weezer—"Say it Ain't So"
7. Gerry Rafferty—"Baker Street"
8. Earth Wind and Fire—"Reasons"
9. Mtume—"Juicy Fruit"
10. Marvin Gaye—"Sexual Healing"

DJ MAJOR TAYLOR'S (CHICAGO) TOP 10 MOST REQUESTED

1. Michael Jackson—"Billie Jean"
2. Prince—"Kiss"
3. Cajmere—"The Percolator"
4. Salt & Pepper—"Push It"
5. Journey—"Don't Stop Believing"
6. Biggie Smalls—"Juicy"
7. Michael Jackson—"PYT"

8. Anything by Jay-Z
9. Anything by A Tribe Called Quest
10. I'm going to leave this last slot open for whatever pop song is huge in the last two-month period

DJ ANI QUINN'S (NYC) TOP 11 QUESTIONS DJS DON'T WANT TO HEAR WHILE DJING

1. "Can you play something good?"
2. "If you play such and such, I promise everyone's going to start dancing!"
3. "If you play such and such, my friends and I will start dancing and we'll really get the party started!"
4. "Can you make an announcement? I can't find my friend (keys, cellphone, purse, jacket, hat, etc.)."
5. "I know you just played such and such, but could you play it again for me?"
6. "I missed it. I was in the bathroom."
7. "You said you'd play such and such. Can you play it now? My friends and I are leaving."
8. "It's my birthday! Can you play 50 Cent's, 'It's Your Birthday?'" (The name of the song is "In Da Club!" At least get that right.)
9. "Can you play something faster?"
10. "Is this what you're playing all night?"
11. "Can I leave my coat with you?"

DJ GRAFFITI'S (ANN ARBOR, MICHIGAN) TOP 10 RECORDS TO GET YOUR DANCEFLOOR BACK (AKA WHEN IN DOUBT, DROP CLASSICS!)

1. Michael Jackson—"Billie Jean"
2. Al Green—"Let's Stay Together"
3. Prince—"Kiss"
4. Eurhythmics—"Sweet Dreams"
5. Notorious B.I.G.—"Juicy"
6. Pete Rock & CL Smooth—"Troy"
7. The Gap Band—"Outstanding"
8. Ice Cube—"Check Yo Self"
9. Rakim—"I Ain't No Joke"
10. King Floyd—"Groove Me"

DJ GRAFFITI'S (DETROIT) TOP 3 DJ RULES

1. No bumping the DJ table/booth!
2. Stop sending your friends up to request the same song you just asked for.
3. Touch the turntable and you might lose your hand.

DJ EXCEL'S (PHILADELPHIA—SKRATCH MAKANIKZ) TOP 10 "OH CRAP, I JUST CLEARED THE DANCE FLOOR, HELP ME GET THEM BACK" SONGS

1. Bell Biv Devoe—"Poison"
2. Rob Base & DJ EZ Rock—"It Takes 2"
3. Michael Jackson—"Wanna Be Startin' Somethin'"
4. Daft Punk—"One More Time"
5. Sean Paul—"Temperature"

6. Stardust—"Music Sounds Better"
7. AC/DC—"All Night Long"
8. Beyonce—"Crazy in Love"
9. 50 Cent—"I Get Money"
10. Enur f. Natasja—"Calabria"

DJ EXCEL'S (PHILADELPHIA—SKRATCH MAKANIKZ) TOP 10 SONGS DJS WILL RESPECT YOU FOR PLAYING

1. Any Wu Tang Clan song
2. Mobb Deep—"Shook Ones"
3. Any James Brown/Fres Wesley
4. Any Original Samples
5. Gangstarr—"You Know My Steez"
6. Slum Village—"Players"
7. Black Star—"Respiration"
8. D'Angelo—"Spanish Joint"
9. AC/DC—"TNT"
10. Nirvana—"Lithium/Come As You Are"

DJ EXCEL'S (PHILADELPHIA—SKRATCH MAKANIKZ) TOP 10 SONGS TO END THE NIGHT WITH

1. Semisonic—"Closing Time"
2. Lynard Skynard—"Free Bird"
3. Red Hot Chili Peppers—"Under the Bridge"
4. Mad Cobra—"Flex"
5. Usher—"Lovers & Friends"
6. Tweet—"Oops"
7. Kanye West—"I Wonder"
8. Guns n' Roses—"Knockin' on Heaven's Door"

9.   Prince—"Purple Rain"

10.   Aaliyah—"Four Page Letter" and "One in a Million"

DJ EXCEL'S (PHILADELPHIA—SKRATCH MAKANIKZ) TOP 10 MOST REQUESTED SONGS OF MY CAREER

1.   50 Cent—"In Da Club"

2.   Sean Paul—"Temperature"

3.   Usher—"Love in the Club"

4.   Britney Spears—"Gimme More"

5.   Ludacris—"Move Bitch"

6.   Jay-Z—"I Just Wanna Love U"

7.   Justin Timberlake—"Sexy Back"

8.   Beyonce—"Get Me Bodied"

9.   LL Cool J—"Doin' It"

10.   Lost Boys—"Renee"

DJ RASTA ROOT'S (ATLANTA—SMOKIN' NEEDLES) TOP 10 CLUB RECORDS

1.   Pharoah Monch—"Simon Says"

2.   MOP—"Ante Up"

3.   Red & Meth—"Rockwilda"

4.   Kanye West ft. T-Pain—"Good Life"

5.   Mobb Deep—"Quiet Storm"

6.   Frankie Beverly ft. Maze—"Before I Let Go"

7.   Audio 2/50 Cent—"Top Billin'/I Get Money"

8.   Goapele—"Closer"

9.   Nas—"Made You Look"

10.   Chubb Rock—"Treat 'Em Right"

DJ EXCESS'S TOP 10 CLUB TRACKS

1. Eric B. & Rakim—"Paid in Full"
2. The Pharcyde—"Runnin'"
3. A Tribe Called Quest—"Electric Relaxation"
4. Black Sheep—"The Choice Is Yours (Remix)"
5. De La Soul—"Buddy"
6. Busta Rhymes—"What it Is"
7. 50 Cent—"Just a Lil' Bit"
8. Dr. Dre ft. Snoop Dogg—"The Next Episode"
9. Jay-Z—"Public Service Announcement"
10. The Notorious B.I.G.—"Hypnotize"

GLOSSARY

ACAPPELLA—A track that just contains vocals. DJs often use these to play over records that have no vocals. Many labels release acappellas of their most popular songs for this purpose.

BACKSPIN—Spinning a record back to a previous point so a certain section can be replayed.

BALEARIC HOUSE—The brand of house music Danny Rampling, Paul Oakenfold, and other British DJs discovered in Ibiza in 1987, which is recognizable by its laid back grooves and prominent vocals.

BATTLE—A competition between DJs and/or MCs.

B-BOY/B-GIRL—Male or female break dancer.

BEAT MIXING/BEAT MATCHING—Just like it sounds—matching the exact beat and tempo of an outgoing track with that of the incoming track, altering the pitch control if necessary. Pioneered by Francis Grasso in 1979.

BEAT JUGGLING—Combining beats from two records to create a new rhythm. Very difficult to do and sounds awful if done wrong. Pioneered by Steve Dee.

BELT-DRIVE TURNTABLE—A deck with a motor-driven belt that spins the platter. Over time the belt can stretch, leading to inconsistent rpm.

BLENDING—When a DJ mixes two tracks by combining parts of each that don't contain beats.

BLOCK PARTY—As the name suggests, a party where an entire city block is set aside for DJs, MCs, graffiti artists, and b-boys to do their thing.

BODY TRICKS—Using parts of your body other than your hands to perform scratching, mixing, or beat juggling and other movements that add a visual element to a DJ's performance but do not involve the turntables.

BREAK BEATS—The part of the song where the vocals fade out and the instrumentation reaches its climax. Kool Herc gave hip hop its groove by isolating the breaks.

BUZZ CHARTS—A DJ's list of their current hot tracks.

CANS—Slang name for headphones.

CARTRIDGE—Part of the tone arm that houses the stylus.

CLOCK THEORY—Grandmaster Flash's technique of backspinning the record to a part you wanted to mix or cut using a label or marker to indicate the targeted spot.

CREWS—Groups of DJs, MCs, graffiti artists, b-boys, and b-girls.

CROSSFADER—Horizontal switch that allows DJs to switch sound output between the turntables.

CUE—Spinning the inactive record and getting it ready to be mixed into the record that is already playing.

CUE POINTS—Visual markers placed on a record to show the DJ where he should bring the track into the mix, either by dropping the needle onto it or using the crossfader.

CUTTING—Quickly moving between the track playing on the first turntable and that on the second turntable by using the crossfader.

DECKS—Another name for turntables.

DETROIT TECHNO—Musical style created in the Motor City that is characterized by a rapid tempo, sparse instrumentation, and heavy beats.

DIRECT-DRIVE TURNTABLE—A deck that operates by electromagnets that spin the platter. This type of turntable delivers consistent power and rpm that do not degrade over time like the earlier belt-drive turntable.

DROPPING ON THE ONE—The act of cueing up the "1" beat of the incoming record and releasing it on top of the "1" beat of the outgoing record.

EQING—Altering the bass, treble, or mid-range frequencies to emphasize a certain part of a track or mix.

FADER—Sliding or rotating control on a mixer that enables you to fade sound in or out.

FILLER—A track used after a big record to bring the crowd's energy level back down a little before the DJ plays their next song.

HARMONIES—Combinations of two or more melodies.

JOINT—Another name for a song.

LOOP—Most modern electronic dance music consists of loops, which are parts of a song that can be repeated over and over. Typically a loop will consist of 16 beats although loops of 4, 8, 16, and 32 beats can also be found.

MASH-UP—Pioneered by Z-Trip, this is a mix that involves taking songs from varied musical genres.

MC—Melle Mel used the term "Master of Ceremonies" to refer to someone who uses the microphone to rhyme over a DJ's beats. Nobody wanted to use the full phrase, so the abbreviation MC became the common usage. MCs are the predecessors of today's rappers.

MELODIES—Rhythmically ordered sequences of distinct sounds.

MIXER—A machine that combines multiple inputs and outputs to process sound to and from the turntables, headphones, speakers, and any other audio equipment. The mixer allows the DJ to listen to the input and output channels via headphones and to control the volume levels, frequencies (e.g. bass, treble, and mid-range), and other elements of each record being played.

MIXING—How you transition from one song to another. You need to match the tempo and the beats (beat matching) to mix two tracks successfully and a common way to introduce a second track is to drop on the one.

MIXTAPE—A recorded version of a DJ's set (whether it's from a bedroom or a festival). The mixtape is used as a promotional tool by DJs, being the equivalent of an actor's head shot.

NEEDLE DROP—Instead of cueing up the record he's mixing, the DJ drops the needle onto the starting point of the record. Grand Wizard Theodore deserves the credit for this one, too.

ONES AND TWOS—Turntables so-called because of Technics' ground-breaking 1210 model.

PITCH—Highness or lowness of sound, determined by wave frequency.

Q & A—One DJ scratches a pattern and another DJ responds to their cuts with another pattern. This method was developed by Q-Bert and Mix Master Mike.

QUICK MIX THEORY—Grandmaster Flash's method of quickly blending one break into another.

RHYTHM—Sequence of sounds organized to create a beat.

RPM—Revolutions per minute. This is how fast the record spins on the platter.

SAMPLING—Recording a snippet of a song so that you can repeat it as many times as you like during a mix.

SCRATCHING—Invented by Grand Wizard Theodore, accidentally. The repetitious sound of moving the record back and forth greatly influenced the onset and development of hip hop culture, and the music world has never been the same.

SLIP CUEING—Cueing up a record and holding it while the turntable spins below until releasing it at the perfect moment to mix into the record on the other deck. Francis Grasso gets the credit for this one, too.

SELECTOR OR SELECTA—Slang for DJ, commonly used in Jamaica.

SLIPMAT—A felt disc that goes between the platter and record to make the record slip, enabling the DJ to manipulate the vinyl.

STORMER—A well-known or classic track that gets everyone dancing.

STYLUS—Needle that is in contact with the record.

SUPERCLUB—A large club that's involved in other business activities such as hosting events in other countries, running a record label and/or radio station, publishing a magazine, and selling merchandise. The term was coined by U.K. publication *Mixmag*.

TEMPO—The speed of a piece of music.

TRAIN WRECK/AMTRAK—A horrible mix that leaves the crowd in a state of confusion on the dancefloor. A train wreck is a term used to explain when two tracks that are playing at the same time have their beats out of phrase and out of time. Also known as beat clashing.

TRICK MIXING—When playing the same track on each turntable, the DJ performs scratching, looping, and doubling-up of drumbeats to give the track new elements and appeal.

TURNTABLISM—Using a turntable as an instrument by manipulating records to create new percussive elements and sounds.

SCRATCHING MINI GLOSSARY

Since Grand Wizard Theodore invented scratching more than thirty years ago, and Afrika Bambaataa and Grandmaster Flash took it to a new level in the early '80s, countless variations have evolved. Here, we break down what you need to know:

BABY SCRATCH—The classic scratch, performed by pushing and pulling the record over the tip (the beginning) of the sample.

BACKWARDS SCRATCH—Pulling the record backwards over a sample and then closing the fader while pushing the record forward to the end of the sample.

CHIRP SCRATCH—First done by Jazzy Jeff, this makes the record sound like a bird's chirping. It's performed by fading the sound out with the crossfader as you push the record forward and fading the sound back in with the crossfader as you pull the record back.

DRAG SCRATCH—The drag scratch is the process of slowly pushing and slowly pulling the record over a sample.

FLARE SCRATCH—The flare scratch begins with the sound you are cutting on, as you move the crossfader back and forth to cut the sound in half. The movement creates a clicking sound in the process. DJ Flare pioneered the sound in 1991, but it was later perfected by Q-Bert.

FORWARD SCRATCH—Opposite of the backwards scratch (you'd never have known that without our help, would you?)

RELEASE SCRATCH—Releasing the record at the tip of a sample, allowing it to play, and then catching the record at the end of the sample and pulling it back to the beginning.

SCRIBBLE SCRATCH—A scribble is performed by pulling and pushing the record very quickly over the tip of a sample.

STAB SCRATCH—Do this by quickly pushing the record over the tip of a sample, and then closing the fader while pulling the record backwards to the start of the sample.

TRANSFORM SCRATCH—The opposite of the flare scratch, the transform scratch begins with the sound you are cutting off. As you move the crossfader back and forth quickly to hear the sound, you will create a tremolo effect. The technique was invented by DJ Spinbad and expaneded upon by Jazzy Jeff.

INDEX